LIBRARY YOUTH OUTREACH

26 Ways to Connect with Children, Young Adults and Their Families

Edited by Kerol Harrod *and* Carol Smallwood

Foreword by Lesley S.J. Farmer

McFarland & Company, Inc., Publishers
Jefferson, North Carolina

SELECTED RECENT MCFARLAND WORKS FROM CAROL SMALLWOOD AND COEDITORS

Job Stress and the Librarian: Coping Strategies from the Professionals, edited by Carol Smallwood and Linda Burkey (2013). *Continuing Education for Librarians: Essays on Career Improvement Through Classes, Workshops, Conferences and More*, edited by Carol Smallwood, Kerol Harrod and Vera Gubnitskaia (2013). *Marketing Your Library: Tips and Tools That Work*, edited by Carol Smallwood, Vera Gubnitskaia and Kerol Harrod (2012). *Mentoring in Librarianship: Essays on Working with Adults and Students to Further the Profession*, edited by Carol Smallwood and Rebecca Tolley-Stokes (2012). *Women on Poetry: Writing, Revising, Publishing and Teaching*, edited by Carol Smallwood, Colleen S. Harris and Cynthia Brackett-Vincent (2012). *Thinking Outside the Book: Essays for Innovative Librarians*, edited by Carol Smallwood (2008). *Internet Sources on Each U.S. State: Selected Sites for Classroom and Library*, compiled by Carol Smallwood, Brian P. Hudson, Ann Marlow Riedling and Jennifer K. Rotole (2005).

LIBRARY OF CONGRESS CATALOGUING-IN-PUBLICATION DATA

Library youth outreach : 26 ways to connect with children, young adults and their families / edited by Kerol Harrod and Carol Smallwood ; foreword by Lesley S.J. Farmer.
p. cm.
Includes bibliographical references and index.

ISBN 978-0-7864-7345-8 (softcover : acid free paper) ∞
ISBN 978-1-4766-1420-5 (ebook)

1. Library outreach programs—United States. 2. Libraries and teenagers—United States. 3. Libraries and families—United States. 4. Libraries and community—United States. 5. Libraries and minorities—United States. 6. Children's libraries—Activity programs—United States. 7. Young adults' libraries—Activity programs—United States. 8. School libraries—Activity programs—United States. 9. Library cooperation—United States. I. Harrod, Kerol, 1972– editor of compilation. II. Smallwood, Carol, 1939– editor of compilation.
Z711.7.L55 2014 021.2—dc23 2013046141

BRITISH LIBRARY CATALOGUING DATA ARE AVAILABLE

Front cover image (Collection Mix/Thinkstock)

Manufactured in the United States of America

McFarland & Company, Inc., Publishers
Box 611, Jefferson, North Carolina 28640
www.mcfarlandpub.com

To Albert and Dorothy Harrod—K.H.

To the contributors—C.S.

Table of Contents

Foreword by Lesley S.J. Farmer

This book might have been titled *Get Real: How Real Librarians Do Real Outreach Programs for Real Communities*. The twenty-six essays in this very practical book provide experience-based insights into successful outreach efforts that touch the lives of communities' youth. The reader will see that success does not require lots of money or a big system, but rather dedicated and creative professionals who know and embrace their communities. All of the authors identified a community need and leveraged his or her library's expertise and resources to plan and provide engaging activities that empower young people. When reading the book, the reader is likely to say, "I want to do that—and I *can*!" Who wouldn't want to put on a show, brighten the eyes of a child with cancer, Skype a story hour, hold a tardeada (afternoon dance/party), or have a library photo booth?

Most of the authors are public librarians, although a few are school librarians, academic librarians, and university faculty. Therefore, most of the projects have a public library perspective, although collaboration with schools is frequently featured. The authors themselves represent fresh faces to the profession as well as seasoned librarians. Large and small systems, in both rural and urban settings, are represented.

The book is divided into six sections, although the essays could have been parsed out in other ways, depending on the reader's needs. Individual essays provide breadth (e.g., Adams and Naidoo), depth (e.g., Nethers and Morehart), or a combination. All are inspiring.

Part 1, "Community Outreach," highlights the importance of getting to know the community and creatively leveraging those contacts. The authors emphasize the point that residents may not visit the library or know about its resources and services, so the library has to proactively seek existing venues where people congregate, including the laundromat (Adams), as well as identify underserved populations such as hospitalized children (Powe). McIntyre and Ramsey focus on ways to work with outreach partners in small and rural libraries. Likewise, Houston explains how to get local sponsors to support fun library contests for youth. Similarly, McDuffie points out the opportunity for the library to draw the community together to share local groups' services.

Part 2, "Library Partnerships," offers two approaches: complementary librarian duos who present at local schools (Walsh and Lyttle), and public/school collaboration that actively supports the curriculum through coordinated collection development and services (Miller).

A variety of youth populations, who may be underserved, are the focus of Part 3, "Reaching Patrons and Building Bridges." These authors give very compelling reasons for outreach and point out that librarians do not have to be experienced with these groups, but rather respectful of them and open to learning and sharing. Terrile explains how children in particular experience homelessness and how libraries can provide important literacy activities and resources. Zettervall and Mars illustrate how outreach programs and collections can impact the reading habits of incarcerated teens. Nethers

1

details the use of teen focus groups to make sure that libraries remain relevant to them, wisely differentiating younger and older teens. Kaufman points out the need to understand the cultural norms of Latinos and to build on family strengths in providing relevant programs. Naidoo focuses on the experiences of LGBTQ youth and offers a rich variety of resources and services. Teen parents are often overlooked, but not by Sanchez and González; they provide great low-cost ideas that enable these teens to help their own children, including gel boards (these are definitely cool!).

Nichols Hess begins Part 4, "Technology," with ideas on how to update the library website to make it more youth-relevant, and then explains how to leverage a wide range of technologies that actively engage and involve students. Creel goes into depth about e-book creation and contests for students.

Part 5 is "Preschool and Elementary Outreach." Richardson provides valuable lessons on negotiating and coordinating with community services. Hanneman explains how to plan and carry out community-based STEM programs, identifying valuable community venues. Wick details several types of resource-rich activities for after-school enrichment programs. "Let's put on a show!" is the spirit of Waxman and Hansen, whose library staff script and act out skits each year to encourage summer reading. Morehart cleverly builds a repeat audience and big "payoff" in her detailed storyhour program that leads to a special overnight event. Carolan leverages the library's longstanding cultural programs, introducing a wide variety of creative art and music activities to children, all the way down to three-year-olds.

In Part 6, "Middle School and Teen Outreach," Blankenship emphasizes the need for concrete incentives to entice and reward middle schoolers, and notes how these preteens gain friendships as well as reading enjoyment. Woznick suggests a bounty of ideas for contests and after-school activities for middle school audiences. Can libraries do lunchtime outreach programs? Just ask Durand, Harwood, and Wilk, who also evaluated those efforts to ensure success. Nelson and Hoke explain how the Pikes Peak Library District systematically offers booktalks and informal education such as resource classes. Colvin concludes the book by detailing how to recruit, train, and optimize teen volunteers.

Across the essays, several messages are clear. It's all about connections and creating a sense of community. Get to know that community, and build on its members' strengths. Plan thoroughly, and clear efforts with decision-makers first. Resourcefulness can overcome financial constraints. Face-to-face trumps technology, but technology can expand the library's reach. Encourage active youth participation and creativity. Hanneman summarizes outreach planning well: "Make sure your offer is well 'packaged' and ready to sell when you dial the number or type in the e-mail address. Your skills are important, and children will prosper from being exposed to your knowledge. If you don't communicate this effectively, you'll never get the opportunity to share." Powe's work in hospital storytelling exemplifies the spirit of this book: "When we go out beyond the physical library branch, the community recognizes that the library truly does care. By sending readers out to medical institutions, the library carves out a niche, a space for informal learning and literacy."

The library world is very lucky to have such experienced and resourceful professionals who care deeply about youth, and who know how to engage and empower them effectively. The library world is also lucky to have this book, which has gathered together realistic outreach ideas that librarians can replicate in light of their own communities' needs. The reader will be inspired by these essays—and inspired to reach out and empower local youth.

Lesley S.J. Farmer coordinates the librarianship program at California State University Long Beach. She earned her MLS at the University of North Carolina and her doctorate at Temple. She has worked in school, public, special, and academic libraries, and her research interests include information literacy, assessment, collaboration, and educational technology.

Preface

Is outreach essential for the survival of the library? What does library outreach look like? What's working now? These were just a few of the questions we sought to answer with this collection. With tightened library budgets becoming the norm, librarians run the risk of cutting back so much that they isolate themselves from their patrons and their communities. This doesn't have to happen. It's true that outreach can be seen as part of the library's marketing and branding strategy, but it's more than that. It's a way of connecting with the community that invites it to reciprocate by connecting with the library. Some of the people you need to reach already visit your library, but most don't, and they need to be introduced or re-introduced to the library.

We were amazed with the range of subjects and experiences we received for this collection, reflecting the rich diversity of approaches to outreach. Each of the 26 essays is between 3,000 and 3,500 words, written by one, two, or three authors. Public, academic, and school librarians, as well as LIS faculty, contributed. The book is divided into six parts: Community Outreach; Library Partnerships; Reaching Patrons and Building Bridges; Technology; Preschool and Elementary Outreach; and Middle School and Teen Outreach. Many of the essays have themes that extend beyond the parts they populate, blending together to form a set of outreach principles that can be applied to different types and sizes of libraries. Lesley S.J. Farmer, renowned for her work in the area of school libraries, greatly honored us by writing the foreword.

Outreach may not come naturally to everyone, but the good news is that this book provides a wide variety of ways to get started. Outreach methods detailed here range from simple actions to detailed processes, providing helpful information for those new to outreach and those with years of experience. It is our hope that reading about the successes and challenges herein will inspire and direct you in your own outreach endeavors.—The Editors

Creative Community Connections

GLORIA ADAMS

Why Reach Out?

Every library belongs to a community; the people of that community are who the library serves. But the community also serves the library, both financially and physically. Support through levies, donations, volunteer hours, materials checkout, and program attendance are the basis for the library's existence. Without community involvement, the library would disappear.

Our job, then, should be to nurture the people of that community so that they know who we are and what we have to offer. The focus of children's programs should be to encourage a love of the library and learning, promote early literacy, and enrich lives through exposure to the arts, other cultures, and hands-on experiences. But what about those who don't regularly attend programs or even read? What if they don't own a computer or don't get a local newspaper? Why should they vote for library levies if they never use the library? How do we reach them? By moving beyond the library confines and stepping out into the community.

Where to Start?

Begin by making a list of every organization and business in the community that your library serves. Your list of organizations might include some of the following: historical societies, garden clubs, environmental clubs, sports groups, quilt or craft clubs, knitting/crocheting/sewing clubs, musical clubs, drama clubs, newcomers groups, Girl and Boy Scouts, homeschoolers, church groups, service organizations, mothers' clubs, art clubs, culinary clubs, dance groups, investment groups, cultural groups, or any specialty groups specific to your community.

Businesses might include the following types of establishments: pizza shops, restaurants, bicycle shops, bakeries, and hair/nail salons. Also take into account local grocery, sports equipment, garden, clothing, toy, music, ice cream, book, and jewelry stores.

Don't leave out your local parks or a national park if there is one close by. Doctors' offices, veterinary clinics, and emergency rooms can also be places where the library can partner up for programs or services. Is there a food bank in your city? Think of ways the library could be involved. What about attorneys, political figures, police, and firefighters?

Join a Listserv

If you haven't already done so, join a listserv of other librarians who work in public libraries. Ask for ideas they have implemented at their libraries for outreach services. Don't just ask what they have done, but also ask if any of them have implemented ideas similar to yours. You may even learn to avoid some of the pitfalls they encountered or discover an enhancement or a new twist on your idea that will make it work better. And don't forget to return the favor down the road; share your outreach experiences and ideas with others. One good listserv used by many librarians is PUBYAC; access it at www.pubyac.org. Most state libraries offer a listserv on their website. Ohio offers one for youth services at http://library.ohio.gov/youthservices/youth_services_listserv.

Serve on a Community Committee, or Two, or Three

Serving on a committee within your community can be a very gratifying experience. It also makes a very consistent connection because you will be meeting monthly or biweekly with the same people. You not only get to know some of your community members, but it is often a springboard for outreach programming ideas. Find out what committees need members in your community and offer to serve on one or more, if time permits. It can often open doors that would otherwise be closed if you were not a member of the committee.

Attend Workshops

Every year, organizations such as ALA, the state library, and local library consortiums offer workshops for librarians on program ideas. Take advantage of any that are offered and learn what has worked for other outreach librarians. Get contact information from those who interest you in case you implement one of their programs; you may have a few more questions to ask them.

Design Some Programs

Now it's time to take a look at each of the organizations and businesses and begin designing some program/partnership ideas for each one.

Before you contact any of the organizations with your ideas, answer the following questions:

1. How will this benefit the library?
2. How can results be measured?
3. How will this engage and enrich children?
4. What will be the time commitment?
5. How many library staff will be needed?
6. What will it cost?

The possibilities will only be limited by the above factors, willingness of participating groups, and whether or not your supervisors, administration, and library board will support it. Present it in writing to have more impact.

Outline of a Successful Project

At a workshop I attended, another librarian presented the idea of establishing a small library at a local laundromat. I thought it sounded exciting. However, when I mentioned it to my director, he blanched, thinking that it would cost the library hundreds of dollars in lost materials if people walked off with the books. But after he read my proposal, he gladly gave the go-ahead.

I began by answering the six questions I posed earlier:

1. How will the laundromat library benefit our library?
   - We will establish a permanent visible presence at an off-site location.
   - We will reach persons who possibly never visit the library.
   - We will include flyers to advertise programs.
   - We will establish a good relationship with the owner of the laundromat.
   - We will provide a service by selecting books that can be read while people are waiting for their laundry to finish.
2. How can results be measured?
   - We will keep track of the number of books that need to be replaced.
   - We will solicit comments from the patrons through the attendants who staff the laundromat every day.
   - We will solicit feedback from the owner.
3. How will this engage and enrich children?
   - A portion of the books delivered to the laundromat library will be children's books that focus on early literacy and good quality writing/high interest level.
   - It opens up an opportunity for parents/caregivers to read to their children.
   - It may reach children whose parents do not normally bring them to the library.
   - Upcoming children's programs can be advertised with flyers at the laundromat.
4. What will be the time commitment?
   - We will visit once per month to deliver books.
   - We will add library-generated stickers on the back of all books to advertise the library.
   - We will allow time for a staff member to go through the donated books to choose some to take to the laundromat.
5. How many staff will be needed?
   - Only one staff member will be needed.
6. What will it cost?
   - We will use book donations from the Friends of the Library book sale with permission from the head of the book sale committee. Cost will be $0.
   - We will purchase a small shelf unit to hang on the laundromat wall for $50. The laundromat will foot half the bill, so net cost will be $25.

The laundromat library has been up and running for about five years and is still going strong. It has been written up in the local newspaper and feedback from laundromat patrons continues to be positive.

Get Ideas for Outreach Programs

Begin with the organizations.

• Historical societies are valuable resources that exist in almost every community. They typically are run by a small group of dedicated volunteers who care about preserving the history of the community. If the society runs a yearly festival, ask if the library could participate. Offer to bring and demonstrate games that children played a hundred years ago; bring books about local history and dress up in period costumes. Research (with the help of the society members) some of the founders or famous people in your community's history and present a reader's theater for children at the festival. Do storytelling or cooking demonstrations of food from a previous century. Get to know the members and keep in touch; you may be interested enough to join!

• Garden clubs abound with expertise; ask if one or more of their members would offer to co-run a program on gardening at the library. Form a kids' garden club and see if you can get permission to grow flowers or vegetables on the library grounds or in containers. Ask for help from the garden club members. Host a children's flower-growing contest with garden club members as judges. Incorporate stories such as Demi's *The Empty Pot* or picture books like Lois Ehlert's *Growing Vegetable Soup* and/or *Planting a Rainbow*.

• Environmental clubs raise awareness of environmental concerns in the community. Invite members of these groups to come and speak, do some hands-on "recycled" crafts, or talk about ways kids can help protect the environment.

• Sports groups can show off their skills with a demonstration or hands-on teaching for a library program. Set out sports books and refreshments. Conduct a "sports in history" day with help from the club members.

• Quilt, craft, knitting, crocheting, and sewing groups usually love to share their skills with children. Host a "Learn to (fill in appropriate skill) Day" at the library. Involve the groups in designing a quilt for your library's bicentennial celebration, or engage their help making clothing for a special reader's theater presentation.

• Musical clubs and drama clubs love to perform; host an evening for members to show off their talents and do some hands-on instruction. Collaborate on writing a literature-based musical play, host a "How to be an Actor or Singer" program, or learn how to do theater makeup.

• Newcomers' groups can be found in most cities. Ask if you can provide a book bag and library flyer for each packet given out to new homeowners in the community. Include a children's book if you can secure the funding.

• Girl and Boy Scout groups need to earn badges for many things. Offer library tours and other programs that will help children earn their badges.

• Homeschoolers often depend on the library for resources and workspace. Ask them if you can do any programs for them at the library that will enhance their curriculum. Offer to go to where they meet and present programs there.

• Mothers' clubs are a great place to reach out. Offer to put on a puppet show just for their group or do storytelling and face painting with them.

• Art clubs can provide a great deal of options, such as painting classes, drawing classes, sculpting classes, etc. Ask for their expertise and help with your programs. Run some contests and use the club members as judges. Start a Caldecott Club and practice different artwork from the books that have won this award.

• Culinary clubs are always favorites! Have members in for a series of "How to Cook" classes. Host a bake-off with help from the members. Read books or tell stories about food and cooking.

- Dance companies always want advertising; what better way than to offer to do a program with you at the library? Ask them to do some interactive instruction or bring a performer from their upcoming dance recital. Enlist their help to judge a library dance contest.

- Investment groups can prove to be a rich resource; everyone is interested in how to make money, including children. Collaborate on a fun learning experience using this group's expertise.

- Cultural and ethnic groups offer a way to learn about another culture. Ask if someone will come to the library and talk about his or her country. Have food and clothing samples, do crafts, and play games particular to these countries or cultures. Explore music or dance programs from around the world.

Use Business Connections

Review the list you made of all the businesses in your community. Some are probably big franchises, while others are locally owned. Both can be great resources for community connections. Remind them that any programs they do for the library or in collaboration with the library will generate advertising for their business. Here are some ideas for reaching out to businesses in your area:

- Ice cream shops will often provide contest prizes for special events at your library. Host a "How to Make Ice Cream" program. Read some fun stories that feature ice cream and include some nonfiction about how ice cream is made.

- Local grocery stores, pizza shops, and restaurants can provide food for programs, speakers for a cooking program, or collaboration for a food bake-off or contest.

- Jewelry stores are a good source for programs on how jewelry is made, how to accessorize with jewelry, or the history of jewelry. They might also be willing to donate prizes for contests or summer reading programs.

- Bicycle stores might offer to bring bikes to the library for a hands-on "Repair Your Own Bike" program. Ask for collaboration with the local police on bicycle safety.

- Bakeries: who can resist them? A collaborative bake-off or a cupcake decorating demonstration make for fun programs. Find a local food bank that might be interested and have the bakery help the children make bread to donate to the food bank.

- Sports equipment stores might offer speaking programs or co-sponsor a charity race or sports event. Ask them to bring all different kinds of equipment to let kids "try out" some sports to see which ones they might like.

- Garden stores are a great resource for finding speakers, getting help with starting a garden club, and they may even be willing to donate plants and containers. How about a "Bugs in the Garden" night?

- Hair and nail salons might be willing to help host a makeover day, hair styling, or fancy nail design programs. This would tie in well with a "Fancy Nancy" program or another favorite book character.

- Clothing stores offer opportunities, such as hosting a fashion show, either at the library or the clothing store. See if the owner will speak about fashion, clothes buying, and the latest clothing fads for kids and teens.

• Toy stores are a great place for prize donations, but go beyond the obvious. Could you do a program at their store about the history of toys or toy characters featured in books, such as *Winnie-the-Pooh* and *The Velveteen Rabbit*? Perhaps they could offer a program on how toys are made. Pique their interest by pointing out the positive public relations these programs would afford their business.

• Music stores might be willing to bring a sample of instruments for children to "practice" to see what instrument they want to learn how to play. Craft a program around a specific instrument, such as the drums, and ask the owners to bring drums for the kids to play, tell drum stories, etc. Find out if any of their employees plays in a band, and then ask if they would perform for you.

• Bookstores are the perfect venue for collaboration in a field you both love. Offer to be a guest storyteller, host a reader's theater night, or just present booktalks featuring the store's newest offerings.

• And don't forget to check out your local laundromat if there is one close by!

Visit Parks and Local Festivals

Local parks are a great place to look for community collaborations. They host a wide range of programs themselves and might be interested in including the library in some of these programs. They regularly generate brochures that advertise programs; look them over and see where the library could contribute. Are they planning summer camps? Offer to go out to the various sites to tell stories, read, or do face painting for them. The parks are steeped in local history; have someone from the library come out and talk about what kids did at the parks a hundred years ago.

Local festivals pop up every year; the library should always try to be a participant. Host a table, hand out brochures, have a fun prize drawing, do face painting, bring a costumed character, or do storytelling or readings at special times. Ask the coordinators of the festivals if there is anything they need help with, and don't hesitate to pitch in!

Contact Health Organizations

Health organizations are part of every community and many people pass through their doors daily. Provide books for waiting rooms, or go a little farther and try to set up some collaborative projects together. Ask local doctors to come and talk about healthy eating, fun ways to stay healthy, or why you shouldn't be afraid of the doctor or dentist. Have a local veterinarian bring some small animals to the library and talk about pet care.

Don't Forget the Schools

Collaborating with the local public and private schools is an important community connection. They are, after all, in the same business as libraries: educating and inspiring children. Begin with the school librarians and brainstorm ways to implement effective communication. Do they know you offer teacher loans, teacher kits, books in boxes, storytelling visits, booktalks, or other curriculum-related programs? Ask if you can visit during teacher meetings to let them know what is available for teachers and students at the library. Find out what programs or materials they would like you to add to what you already provide. Host a teacher luncheon for teachers and principals annually.

Outreach to local daycares and preschools is often a large undertaking, but will prove to be well worth the time. Make monthly visits to do storytimes for them or host a one-time evening at the library with stories, crafts, food, and fun just for their individual preschool or daycare.

Get Permission

None of your ideas will ever come to fruition without permission from supervisors, the director, and the board. In order to convince them, you need to be prepared. Answer the six questions under "Design Some Programs" and submit them to the people from whom you need permission. This format worked very well for our laundromat library project and should prove effective for most programs.

Contact the Organizations

After you have prepared your ideas and obtained permission to implement them, it's time to contact the organizations. This will take some research, but you can usually find the name of the contact person in the advertisements for the various organizations, often in the local paper or directory, or online. An initial phone call or e-mail is best with a follow-up in person if the organization is interested in your idea. Since you are usually not asking them to put up any money and you are offering your time for free, most groups are more than willing to talk with you.

Implement

You have prepared everything well; now it's time for the implementation. Since even with extremely detailed planning things can still go wrong, I recommend that you always have a Plan B. And maybe plans C, D, and E! Try to anticipate any problems you might have. If you are working with volunteers, remember that they are volunteers and not library employees. Their priorities are different from yours, and they may not always be able to come through with what they promised. Make sure that a backup plan is in place just in case Plan A falls apart.

It is important to maintain communication with all parties involved. Does the speaker have the correct date and time? Set up phone numbers, e-mails, and back-up phone numbers and stay in touch, especially as you get closer to the program. Does your contact person have YOUR phone number and e-mail? Try to make sure all your bases are covered, and then check them one more time.

Community connections provide great public relations for the library and are effective in reaching non-library users, but they also open up a whole world of possibilities for programming, offering services, and forming new and often lasting relationships with people in the community. The opportunities for enhancing children's lives abound in the outreach arena. The only thing stopping you is your imagination. So get creative and reach out!

Hospital Storytelling Outreach

André R. Powe

"I explained to a non-reading seven-year-old that his job was to make up a story for the pictures in *Frog and Toad* and tell it to his mom. She agreed."
"I showed a very young Urdu-speaking mom how to use *What Color Is It* with her infant."
"While a child was reading *Wild Baby Animals*, the mom was able to talk to the nurse."
"The only high school student I saw today recognized me from the Oncology Center; he said he was hoping for a new book to read."—Recent Hospital Storytelling Reports (HSR)

Hospital storytelling is a Brooklyn Public Library (BPL) family literacy program that conducts outreach to medical facilities in Brooklyn. Trained readers are dispatched to give out free books for children and to read stories aloud.

The hospital storytelling program has two components. The first, a volunteer group called "reading troubadours," commits to working once a month for a year, or twice monthly for six months, going to storefront, neighborhood, or primary care pediatric well-child clinics. The second, our "hospital storytellers," are paid contractors who, once per month on an ongoing basis, visit sites such as hospital inpatient wards, hematology/oncology clinics, and pediatric congregate care facilities. All readers thus serve children receiving care at medical facilities in Brooklyn as a part of a literacy intervention strategy. Along with reading aloud, role modeling for parents and caregivers, and helping children to select a free book to keep, readers counsel families on the importance of books and literacy and provide information on programs and services offered at the 60 local branches of the BPL. The hospital storytelling program started in 1999 with two sites, and by 2001, there were six locations. Today the program serves 3,000 to 5,000 children annually. Currently there are 28 sites with 32 visits conducted monthly by 11 contractors and volunteers. Hospital storytelling is part of the Child's Place for Children with Special Needs, a BPL department providing both branch-based and outreach library services to children with special needs and their families. More than raising the spirits of children and caregivers, hospital storytelling is a tool used by BPL to reach the hardest-to-reach consumers in Brooklyn's diverse population of 2.7 million inhabitants.

Recruitment and Training

There is a three-step process of recruitment and training. When the hospital storytelling program began in 1999, readers were contracted as per diem employees. After the program's pilot funding ended, a volunteer component was developed.

For reading troubadours, the process begins with BPL's Office of Volunteer Resources. Potential volunteers submit a volunteer application form along with a schedule of their availability and preferred geographic areas of deployment.

Recruitment for hospital storytellers begins with recommendations, referrals, and résumés that are submitted for consideration. The type of site decides whether the individual servicing the site is a volunteer or a contractor. Over the years, there have been times when contractors have been sent to a site where they are paid while also continuing to visit a site where they had long been volunteering. There is therefore no competition between the two arms of the hospital storytelling program. In fact, our longest-serving reading troubadour and hospital storyteller both have tenures exceeding five years.

The second step in the recruitment and training process for both troubadours and storytellers is attendance at a required two-hour workshop. Topics include issues of dealing with children in medical settings such as confidentiality, safety considerations, and infection control. Also discussed is the importance of reading aloud, along with the six skills needed for children to read: print motivation, print awareness, vocabulary, phonological awareness, letter knowledge, and narrative skills. In addition, we present a broad framework for communicating within a diverse cultural landscape, reflecting on the fact that we all see the world through different lenses. While we do not censor material per se, we recognize the need for cultural sensitivity in materials acquisition and service delivery. We are aware of our positions of power interacting with children and families in crisis, and ostensibly this affects how and what we offer children to read. As such, we also cover issues of race, gender, and social representations.

Readers, at the start of workshop trainings, will often anxiously ask how they can supply the needs of a clinic full of children. There is often surprise at the limited but effective hospital storytelling "suitcase collection" used for the visit. All materials must fit into a rolling suitcase, enabling the reader to travel to the site by bus or subway. Guidance is provided to determine how many books to bring, what types of subject matter to use, and what age ranges to target.

Readers are additionally shown how to complete the Hospital Storytelling Reports (HSR), which chronicle sites visited, statistical information on age ranges, numbers of children served and books distributed, and are quoted throughout this essay. Space on the report allows readers to make comments and observations on individual sessions. At the end of the training workshop, signed permission forms are obtained so all applicants will have a background check performed, as is standard library procedure.

The third and final step in the recruitment and training process takes place onsite at the location where the reader is assigned. At this visit, joining the reader are representatives from BPL's Child's Place for Children with Special Needs, the Office of Volunteer Resources, and a staff member from the medical institution. This ensures that, at the start of their commitment, readers have an opportunity to ask questions and have concerns addressed from all the invested stakeholders. We consider the culture of the community and the services provided by the clinic. The physical layout of the waiting room is studied to determine the best place to form a group to read and minimize environmental distractions. Readers complete their first session under observation and with support.

Sites, Staff, and Partners

There are three types of medical facilities that hospital storytelling serves. Reading troubadours visit the first type of facility, which includes well-child clinics, community clinics, and pediatric hospital clinics operating either within a main hospital facility or off-site. These are all places where children go for general pediatric care, checkups, etc. Hospital storytellers visit the second type of facility, concentrating on the more seriously or chronically ill patients. These children are in pediatric inpatient hospital wards, hematology/oncology clinics (for children with cancer, sickle cell, or receiving kidney dialysis treatment), pediatric ophthalmology clinics, and AIDS clinics. The third category of site includes residential facilities for children who may be autistic, have other disabilities, or require ongoing medical care. These sites are serviced by hospital storytellers and are in hospitals or group homes.

Over the years, we have had an assortment of readers in the program. These individuals hail from all over New York City with a wide variety of cultural and educational backgrounds. There have been retired teachers, retired librarians, social workers, stay-at-home mothers, emergency medical service workers, high school students, and college students. The program endures because of the enthusiasm and dedication of all participants. Hospital storytelling is grant-funded, except BPL pays the salary of the coordinator, the only library staff member assigned to the program. At times, there are volunteers to help out in the office with paperwork and shipments of books and supplies.

There are several organizations that we have partnered with over the years. Reach Out and Read (ROR) is a program of the American Medical Association. Doctors write a prescription for a book, and patients from six months to five years of age visiting the doctor receive a free book. ROR operates in many of the sites that we visit. "The hypothesis underlying ROR is that pediatricians can intervene to improve the home literacy environment of poor children, and thereby alter preschool language development, as well as later reading ability and school motivation and performance" (Mendelsohn et al. 2001). The two programs complement each other. While ROR gives only the patient a book, hospital storytelling will also give a book to any of the children accompanying the patient, as long as they fall within the targeted age group. The cited study showed that clinic-based literacy intervention has a positive effect on the language development of preschool children, and calls for the integration of ROR into routine healthcare, thus providing an opportunity for libraries to collaborate with pediatricians nationwide in promoting early literacy.

New York City children in hospital wards receive instruction from teachers who are part of the Schools in Hospitals Program/P403. These New York City Department of Education teachers are important partners, and they are always happy to let us know about the needs of particular children with regard to cognitive abilities and reading levels.

The Mission

On location at the medical facility, every child present gets a book, and each child is encouraged to pick his or her own book. Gift books are provided for children up to and including age 20. A volunteer said, "Today's session went great. Every patient took a book and I read to an infant. Two patients, 18 and 20 years old, took two books each. It's great to see a smile on a patient's face when books arrive" (HSR). In high schools, there are still some 12th-grade students who have reached age 20, and in the community of children with disabilities, this is often the case. We have the unique pleasure therefore of giving books to the whole family when we meet teen parents with their children in a clinic. The program operates to encourage family literacy and provides the atmosphere and the support to this end. When we run across parents who do not read English, we suggest they use picture books and make up their own story to accompany the illustrations. Just because people cannot read does not mean they cannot learn, or that they cannot be empowered to support their children's literacy development. Sometimes what is said or spoken can be a more effective tool in learning than what is read or written. There are many cultures where knowledge has been passed down orally generation by generation. At the heart of these procedures, therefore, are the social aspects of literacy and learning. For those parents unable to regularly visit the library to obtain books, we suggest they use whatever they have on hand: the newspaper, the cereal box, or even the Bible, making sure to discuss afterwards with their children what was read. Essentially, this builds a foundation of literacy and learning, of problem solving and engagement. Reading aloud and discussion makes learning more evolved, more participatory, and a less singular and isolating event.

When we read aloud to the children in the clinics, adults are often just as eager to listen, learn, and lend support. "Medical staff is very supportive of this program and helps with pushing reading and interpreting as needed" (HSR). A volunteer in an inpatient ward said of a visit, "Today's session went wonderful. The patients were glad to receive books. One of the patients I read to was really fun and precocious and spoke about the show *SpongeBob*. His name was Eric, and he really loved my presence. He actually did not want me to leave and asked, 'When are we meeting again?'"(HSR). People appreciate the need for a program where children are read to upon request.

Another volunteer reported, "I offered a book to a man and his son (18–24 months). He said, 'Isn't he too young for books?' I said, 'Not at all,' and gave him *Cat's Colors*, explaining that it was very simple and that kids enjoy identifying the bright colors. He took the book and started reading and identifying colors and animals in his own language (I'm not sure what language he spoke)" (HSR). This also shows the response by parents to the program, and the program's encouragement that literacy can occur in English as well as the child's native language.

Contradictions and Communicating Value

Hospital storytelling is a program that seems in opposition to what the conventional library is supposed to be. People are sometimes as confused as they are delighted when we appear. Patrons are accustomed to borrowing books from a library. When we give them a book to take home to start their own home library, they are surprised. Resistance to the program, if any, comes from people initially believing the books are for sale. Patients and parents appreciate the library visit and gift book at a time in their lives when they may feel most vulnerable. They are not used to having someone from the library read the book aloud to them or their family, especially seated at a hospital bedside.

People generally visit a library, a building, to borrow books and are not accustomed to having the library deliver books to them during a visit to the doctor. After all these years, it is no longer a shock when someone asks which branch location they should return the book to when they have finished reading it. For this reason, when we receive a shipment of books, we place a sticker in the book stating that the book "is a gift from BPL, and belongs to ... [*insert child's name*]." We encourage the children to write their names in the blank space provided on the sticker to acknowledge their selection and ownership of the book. This also adds a level of security for BPL's and the funder's property, since the books cannot be confused with other literacy initiatives or book drives.

An early intervention clinic sees many preschoolers, while an oncology or general pediatric clinic's patients will often include older children. We have worked with a pediatric specialty clinic that only sees patients on the first Thursday afternoon of every month. The day and time the reader visits the facility may or may not change every month. Clinics have individual schedules, with different specialists seeing patients on any given day. Bank, school, public, and secular holidays all impact patient attendance at a health facility. As a result, the reader becomes knowledgeable about dealing with the population at the clinic at the time and day they visit. Because each site offers a unique cultural setting, outreach is most effective when localized or practiced at the grass roots. For this reason, guidelines are given, but site/location practices are specific; information obtained by the end of the initial visit provides all the relevant parameters of distributing material.

In an era of growing technological advances where e-books are becoming all the rage, hospital storytelling outreach shows the importance of reading with books as a long-accepted and still-relevant option. It communicates the relevance and value of the library's actions to patrons who may not ever have visited a branch. It shows the library engaged in its own local community, in a participatory, proactive, positive, and meaningful way. It shows parents that it is important to read to their children, and it shows children the value and importance that adults place on their reading.

When we go out beyond the physical library branch, the community recognizes that the library truly does care. By sending readers out to medical institutions, the library carves out a niche, a space for informal learning and literacy. Everyone present in a room while a story is read aloud has the ability to listen and learn, adults as well as children, medical staff and parents. Just as everyone has different levels of education, there may also be a range of fluency in the English language. Yet everyone present in this participatory transaction benefits. Reading aloud thus becomes an encompassing engagement, allowing communication, learning, and literacy to occur on multiple levels. Oral literacy is promoted; group learning is promoted. The connection between literacy, knowledge, and healing in the provision of palliative care by the library as an institution is promoted. Social bonds are established and reaffirmed, between parent and child, physician and patient, library and community.

Monitoring and Evaluation

At the end of each session, readers are asked to file a completed report of service. These HSRs provide an opportunity for readers to share anecdotes as to how the service was received and to report any changes in the demographics of the site. One commented, "I read *Clifford* to a screaming three-year-old, and she quieted down and the nurses could take her vitals" (HSR). While these individual reports do not give extensive data about the ways in which we have affected lifetime literary habits, they give us a good idea of how hospital storytelling outreach makes a difference to those it encounters. In other words, the anecdotes show that it is not the quantity of people served, but the quality of the service we deliver. As one volunteer stated, "Children who came out of the examining room upset usually calm down when they hear a story read. This is especially true of older children, and it doesn't matter whether the book is 'too young' for them. I think they actually take comfort in having a grownup reading aloud" (HSR).

Hospital Storytelling Within Library and Education Debates

The astounding rise of information and communication technologies often places children in hyperactive social and cyber environments. Reading aloud is a way of training young minds to focus, thereby increasing their ability to digest more complex data as they advance in school. Just as we read to the children in the clinics, the children will often oblige by reading aloud to us. A child's listening and reading vocabulary does not increase at the same rate, but the aim is that eventually effective reading, writing, speaking, and listening skills are all attained in full measure. Reading aloud enhances overall comprehension and expression.

Hospital storytelling is well-placed and advances many different educational objectives. Through hospital storytelling outreach, the library provides informal but intentional education, working with community partners (e.g., ROR and P403 schools) to achieve that end. Regarding the promotion of emergent literacy as it applies to Born to Read practices, we have always read and given books to infants and pregnant mothers. In terms of No Child Left Behind, hospital storytelling reaches out to the hardest-to-reach children. Due to chronic illness, some children may not be able to attend school regularly. These children connect to the library, sometimes solely through hospital storytelling outreach.

Outreach is often the social conscience of a library. Outreach activities are targeted communication strategies, as the library tailors the information and resources it possesses to deliver specific messages. Outreach turns information into knowledge at the point of delivery, even if by only reading a book aloud. Readers have told me, after leaving the program, that it was a life-changing experience, and we shared stories of celebration, service, and gratitude.

A volunteer spoke to this point: "The child I read to enjoyed the two books read to him. It was delightful to see all the kids come up to me asking for a book. This reminded me that children still love their books or have a great love for books considering this age of technology. Their parents/guardians thanked me for coming" (HSR). Hospital storytelling outreach is the story of the library making a difference, partnering, connecting with community, learning, and communicating the value of the work it does.

Works Cited

Mendelsohn, Alan L., Leora N. Mogilner, Bernard P. Dreyer, Joel A. Forman, Stacey C. Weinstein, Monica Broderick, Karyn J. Cheng, Tamara Magloire, Taska Moore, and Camille Napier. 2001. "The Impact of a Clinic-Based Literacy Intervention on Language Development in Inner-City Preschool Children." *Pediatrics* 107 (1): 130–134. doi: 10.1542/PEDS.107.1.130.

Rooted in the Community
Small and Rural Library Outreach

MICHELLE A. MCINTYRE
and MELANIE L. RAMSEY

Small and rural public libraries often struggle with developing an effective, quality youth outreach program. They recognize the critical role outreach serves in their communities, but operate on tight budgets with limited service hours and small staffs. This essay discusses the youth outreach activities at the Hollidaysburg Area Public Library (HAPL) and the Roaring Spring Community Library (RSCL). RSCL was established in 1959 and serves a rural population in Pennsylvania of approximately 7,000 residents. The area covers one borough and two surrounding townships. RSCL has one full-time director and two part-time employees. HAPL was founded in 1943 and is located in the county seat of Blair in Pennsylvania. The urban cluster library serves three boroughs and four townships with an overall service population of 14,000. The library has three full-time and several part-time employees. Both libraries have successfully implemented youth outreach programs.

An outreach plan begins with an understanding of your library's current situation. Start with reviews of the strategic or long-range plan, as well as goals and objectives. The plan must begin with a profile of your library and the community it serves. You should also consider your current staffing situation, hours available for outreach, and budgetary resources. Compile a list of all youth programs and analyze each program to determine if it still has value to your library and community. Some programs will be retired, while others may simply need updating. Remain realistic while also striving to make the most of all possibilities. The library's outreach plan should complement your community's values and needs as reflected in your mission and vision statement.

Outreach services can take a considerable amount of monetary resources. It may be easier than you think to locate funding to offset costs. In some instances, grants such as those that include a category for service to an underserved population can be utilized to help defray the costs of planning and implementing these services. If your outreach takes place in a public forum, such as a festival, many times businesses are willing to provide monetary support in exchange for the ability to have their name on advertising or hang a banner showing their support. RSCL has entered into several partnerships where funding for programs has been provided by newspaper publishers, banks, and insurance companies. With a little bit of work and a well-executed outreach plan, funds can be secured to offer services.

Volunteers can help implement a successful outreach program in a library with limited staff. However, you will need to invest time in training a volunteer to provide offsite services. All volunteers should possess current criminal and child abuse clearances. Photographic identification should be provided by the library and worn by volunteers during visits. It is the responsibility of the library to prepare volunteers for the best outreach experience possible.

Potential volunteers include:

- Teachers (retired or on summer break)
- Students on internship
- Local officials or business leaders
- Library board members

The nature of a rural library's service area often creates a travel problem. If you are relying on one staff person or a handful of volunteers, scheduling outreach visits can be tricky. Attempt to schedule several outreach visits on the same day or during the same week. A few simple strategies can assist when preparing for visits. The following is a list of considerations to take into account prior to making a visit:

- What are the number of youth and ages?
- Does the site provide staple supplies (crayons, glue, paper)?
- Does the site celebrate holidays?
- Offer the same program to same age group in different locales.
- Carry extra copies of clearances.

Track the number of youth served during each visit. Accurate record keeping will help the library analyze the success of each program and validate the need for continued programming. Funders often ask for outcome-based assessments of programs. These statistics demonstrate how their dollars were used to enhance services in their community.

Basic Outreach

A successful program can be implemented by rethinking traditional library outreach services. Outreach can be as simple as placing a deposit collection of books. Carefully select deposit book collections, keeping the site and age group in mind. It is important to offer deposit collections to public, private, and faith-based organizations. There is a potential for a loss of books, so factor that into your associated costs.

RSCL has supported deposit collections in Head Start and Intermediate Unit sites for more than ten years. Collections loaned frequently support educational lessons and themes. The library provides a balanced collection of both fiction and nonfiction titles. We also permit the borrowing of big books, learning kits, and puppets to each classroom. The program has been very successful and continues to grow each year.

Recently RSCL started a deposit collection program with the middle school and high school libraries. There was a slight difference with this collection. It was not as easy as just checking out fifty books to each library classroom. A deposit collection agreement was requested by the school administration. The library was asked to create the agreement and present it to the school board for approval. Ultimately the agreement was approved, and students now have additional collections of materials available for their enjoyment and learning.

The deposit collection agreement included the following:

- Library card on file for the site
- Name of person responsible for the collection
- Promotion of public library services and programs
- Discussion of how lost or damaged books would be handled

Possible deposit book collection sites include:

- Daycares and preschools
- Head Start, Intermediate Unit, and life skills classrooms
- After-school programs
- Juvenile detention facilities
- Hospitals
- YMCAs
- Parks and museums
- Group homes
- Laundromats

In addition to the book deposit collection program, RSCL also has a book distribution program. The library has entered a three-way partnership with Nason Hospital and the Blair County Reading Council to provide every baby born at the hospital with a new book. The state organization provides grant funding to the Reading Council for the purchase of books; council and library members select the titles; the library creates packets with reading tips; and the hospital distributes the packets. The project "Do It While in Diapers" has provided over 500 books to new babies and their families since the inception of this partnership.

First Book-Blair County, a local advisory board of First Book National, also partnered with RSCL to provide books to low-income children. The library applied for a First Book grant, noting how the books would be used and to which group the books would be distributed. Groups receiving the books must agree to distribute the titles and not create a classroom library. Each child receives at least four books per grant cycle.

Partnerships

Community involvement is directly related to the success of any library program. Partnerships can be found in unexpected places: chamber memberships, area businesses, other local nonprofits, and by traditional networking. You cannot afford to stand in a corner at a community gathering, interacting only with people you know. Collaboration is an important feature of any outreach program.

Develop a database of current and potential partners with contact information. Meet and discuss possible program ideas with the partner. It is important to determine how each partner can collaborate to enhance services to the community. Be clear and direct in communicating your needs and goals to a prospective outreach partner.

Individual partners represent a unique educational perspective on some aspect of the community. Some specific individual partners to consider include:

- Pageant winner
- Scuba diver

- Helicopter pilot
- Craftsperson
- Spoon player
- Didgeridoo player
- Goat enthusiast
- Belly dancer
- Ghost hunter
- K-9 officer
- Honey bee queen
- Dairy princess
- Meteorologist

Schools have a vested interest in partnering with a library for educational reasons. The local junior high school drama club, HAPL, and a local chain bookstore combined in a three-way partnership. The drama club performed a scene from their play (*Alice in Wonderland*), the library provided a children's librarian who gave a story reading from the book the play was based on, and the bookstore experienced increased traffic while supporting two community nonprofits. Also within the same school district, the LEGO league is required to share informational programming within the community. They are a crowd-pleaser because their presentation includes moving robots and competitions.

The local middle school reading competition offers RSCL an opportunity to provide outreach. Books, volunteers, and judges are supplied by the library. In return, the school provides volunteers for summer reading and community events.

Identify organizations with an educational element and form a partnership. A successful example in our libraries is the Cushion Concerts presented by the Altoona Symphony, which provides all the staff for this program (musicians and narrators). HAPL has a further partnership with our local Family Resource Center to provide related crafts. All three organizations reap the benefits of holding a well-attended event with clear educational and cultural value, including interactions with people who otherwise may never have been exposed to these community groups.

RSCL partnered with the countywide Women, Infants and Children (WIC) program and the Public Broadcasting Service (PBS) to offer a nutrition-themed storytime. The library developed the Food for Thought program, WIC provided the clients, and PBS provided books to be given away at each site. Elements of the program were then instituted throughout the county. The program was awarded a Pennsylvania Library Association Best Practices in Early Learning Award.

HAPL and the Blair County Conservation District had great success with a program called "What's Hatching @ Your Library." Our conservation district's environmental educator purchased an egg incubator from a local raptor rescue specialist who was downsizing. Eggs incubated at HAPL while the outreach person gave updates to the outreach sites. We also used social media in the form of Facebook videos and pictures to promote the program. In this way, more people learned about the process of egg hatching, and more people made the trip to see the eggs in person at our library. Eventually two more libraries in our district held similar programs. Contact your environmental educator. Each conservation district has its own resources and topics of interest.

Larger organizations are interested in outreach, too. Do not neglect to research opportunities to offer themed programming at your library or in other places. Often there will be an educational division of a larger organization that offers programming opportunities for public libraries. The largest and most widely recognizable example is NASA, which is currently employing their educational division to partner with public libraries across Pennsylvania. HAPL and RSCL staff attended several trainings provided by NASA educators in order to prepare for holding space- and science-based programming at their sites. HAPL has since held programming on Jupiter's layers and on weather stations using NASA educational resources provided during these trainings.

Other potential organizations and individuals to partner with include:

- Educational institutions
- Health food stores
- Scout troops
- Genealogical library
- Tea shops
- Insurance businesses (baby seat safety)
- Firefighters/policemen
- Local helicopter pilots (MEDI VAC)
- Local banks (financial literacy programming)
- Sports organizations
- Elected officials
- Healthcare professionals
- Parent groups/special interest groups
- Bereavement groups
- Master gardeners

Community Events

Utilize established community events to provide outreach to larger audiences. Outreach does not always have to consist of a program or storytime at a single site. Community outreach can take place in the form of attending community events. At community events, both youth and adults can experience what the library has to offer. Community events offer libraries the opportunity to showcase their programs and services to larger numbers of people. These events also have an added bonus of attracting new users. This allows the library to demonstrate its value to the community.

Over the past decade, RSCL has participated in a variety of community events with different levels of involvement. Our involvement has been as minor as providing books to be distributed to attendees and as major as planning all of the children's activities. We have been so successful in our community event outreach services that we are now asked to plan and provide youth programming for a number of community events.

Spring Dam Weekend is a three-day event where community members come together to enjoy a variety of programs, outdoor concerts, and a taste of local cuisine. Noting the lack of children's activities, RSCL offered to assist in planning youth-oriented events. RSCL contacted organizations serving children and requested their assistance in offering three hours of children's activities during the celebration. Over 10 organizations responded to the request for programming. Highlights of the weekend included a miniature golf course offered by Penn State Cooperative Extension, the Heaven Scent Search and Rescue Dogs, the Blair County Conservation District with Gyotaku, and the Altoona Symphony Orchestra with an instrument petting zoo. The event was very successful in highlighting community organizations, serving several hundred children in one weekend. It solidified public perception of the library's status as a cornerstone of the community.

The community tree lighting open house is hosted by RSCL. After the community tree lighting, attendees walk to the library for the evening's activities. The school district, town council, and several churches assist with the event. The library coordinates the visit with Santa, along with activities for the evening's festivities. The school district's education association provides volunteers as well as books to be given to each participating child.

A middle school 10 miles away from HAPL requested a story reader for the school's end-of-year fair. The library's staff person brought books in a variety of interest and reading levels to use during the four-hour event. This outreach service garnered approximately 300 participants over the course of the day and also gave opportunities for networking with local talent and community representatives who did not usually interact with our library. The storyteller had to be careful of her voice for a few days afterwards, but we also got many thank-you letters and have had three partnerships as a result of that one-day event.

HAPL's local community partnership has held a pumpkin festival in the center of town each year for the past seven years. Many community organizations participate, and the library is glad to provide a story hour on the kids' stage, a craft and games table, and information about the library and its services. Minimal resources are needed.

Simply marching as a group in a community parade holding handmade signs is a great outreach method that is easy and inexpensive. The HAPL has a vinyl banner (provided by their Friends group) that has held up well. You can explore other options such as book cart drill teams, costumed characters, and celebrity guests. Participation ensures that the library is perceived as part of your community's celebration, and if you use creative and memorable ideas, people will remember and look forward to seeing the library each year.

Social Media

Be sure to take pictures and post them to your website, blog, or Facebook page, and to connect them to other community groups that have similar sites. Social media is a tool of great value that can be used for your benefit and for the benefit of your community.

Video chat using Skype offers many possibilities for rural library outreach applications. Skype is a free, two-way audiovisual communication (e.g., videoconferencing) system that happens in real time. It requires a webcam, computer, high-speed Internet connection, and a free account with Skype.com. A computer may be connected to a projector for large-screen display or to a television monitor for a smaller group.

Skype may be used to supply a program to an out-of-the-way site or to allow the participation of a resource person or audience member who cannot be there in person. Rural libraries can cover hundreds of miles of territory this way. Program planning can be conducted among different organizations in different geographical areas, saving travel expenses and travel time.

It may also be possible to read or present a storytime since the Skype session is real-time and not recorded for later presentation.

Skype's potential for outreach applications could include the following:

- Book clubs chatting with a book's author in another state as part of their book discussion group
- Special guests, such as musicians, storytellers, puppeteers, dancers, or a show with live animals or large props that would be impossible to transport
- Children from one site reading to another group of children at another site
- Contests held over Skype (Library *Jeopardy!*, spelling contests, trivia contests, and so on)
- Celebrations of library anniversaries or special occasions
- Programs such as Jumpstart's Read for the Record, where a whole community reads the same book on one day
- Poetry readings, creative writing
- Safe distance from scientific experiments with potentially messy, dangerous, smelly, or smoky results

Concluding Thoughts

Outreach programming is an essential component of any successful rural library. The main goal of an outreach program is to bring library services to the youth in the community. A key component of a successful outreach program is marketing. Getting the word out to library users is a challenge in any area. RSCL and HAPL employ a variety of methods to inform the public about their programming. Many communities have public or educational access channels that will post library announcements for little to no cost. Check with your local cable company to gather contact information. Hometown newspapers, locally produced magazines, and organizational newsletters often look for local-interest stories involving youth. These are also great photo opportunities for the library. Do not forget to cross-promote library programming between libraries. Share your library programming schedule with neighboring libraries or those in your system.

Suggested areas for promotion include:

- Facebook
- YouTube video of events or commercial about upcoming program
- Flickr with photos of events
- Tweets about your outreach sites
- Flyers, handouts, and bulletin boards
- Church bulletins
- Calendars on websites

Speak up and promote your programming everywhere. Be shameless about it. Carry flyers, handouts, and business cards with website information. Capitalize on every opportunity to share your library with the public and your peers. Share your programming ideas at library meetings, summer reading workshops, and on statewide listservs and blogs. HAPL and RSCL share their programming ideas at regional, state, and national levels. The authors present at regional workshops, Pennsylvania Library Association Conferences, and have at times presented at national venues such as National Association for the Education of Young Children (NAEYC). Always provide your presentation materials for conference handouts.

Maintaining active outreach programs takes staff time, strategic planning, and critical evaluation. A key component to fulfilling outreach programming is community collaboration. Once you begin building a successful youth outreach program, the library will branch out further and take a firm root in the community. Consequently, your community gets to know its library better. Start small, think big, and dare to reach out to your community. The rewards and opportunities are exciting.

Youth Contests as Outreach

Natalie Houston

Until now, you may not have considered contests as a form of outreach, but contests do reach outside the library walls. Contests are something you tell your friends about, and generating peer-to-peer promotion is invaluable for the library. Below you will find ideas for working with local sponsors, creating entry forms, and inexpensive methods of promoting contests.

Background

The Orange County Library System in Orlando, Florida, hosts several contests each year for kids and teens. We support youth by encouraging creativity and showcasing the children's work for the public. We have developed guidelines that promote positive participation, generate program statistics, produce new library card applications, and reach out to youth who may not have visited one of our libraries. Contest examples covered in this essay include a Mascot Games drawing contest, a teen art contest, and kids' and teen poetry contests.

Creating a Contest

Like library programs, contests need a target audience and an objective. Start by thinking through the checklist below, which will help you see if there is enough support to make a contest successful.

- Who are your target participants?
- What is the intention of the contest? For example, is it to promote an event, book, service, or skill?
- Who are potential partners or supporters in your community? Be specific.
- Who are potential prize donors?
- Who are potential judges?
- What is the timeline?
  a. Contest duration?
  b. How far in advance will you advertise?
  c. Deadline for entries?
  d. Timing of winners announcement and/or event?

- What is your promotional plan, including distribution avenues?
- What are your resource considerations? These may include printing, graphic design, storage or display space, time, and staffing.

Once you have considered these elements, you should see where you need to start and whether or not your concept will reach the target audience and achieve your desired outcome. Then start creating the foundation of your contest, which usually includes an entry form, rules, and guidelines. Many of these will be the same no matter the contest, though slight additions or modifications can be made to customize it for a specific contest.

Entry Forms

Almost all contests require an entry form, which serves to keep track of entrant information, so you can contact them and evaluate their eligibility. We accept submissions at all of our library locations, through the mail, and, if feasible, online. We include the mailing address of our main library, directed to the children's department, on all entry forms.

Recommended Information to Collect on Entry Forms:
- Name
- Mailing address, city, state, zip code
- Primary phone number
- Library card number
- Age
- E-mail (if any)
- Title and description of submission

Online Entry Forms

To increase participation among teens, we began offering online submissions for our contests, whenever fitting. For instance, since most photos are now taken digitally, we created an online entry form for our teen photo contest. We have not allowed online submissions for those under 13 due to the Children's Online Privacy Protection Act of 1998. We utilize Google Docs to create forms, but you could use any free survey website, like SurveyMonkey or Zoomerang, to accept submissions. While we receive the majority of our submissions through the online forms, we continue to offer paper entry forms.

Tips for Online Entry Forms:
- Match the online and print forms as closely as possible.
- Include the URL for online entries on your paper form.
- If possible, create short, direct links to online forms. For our Teen Battle of the Bands, we use www.ocls.info/bands to direct people to information about the competition and entry form (which is only available when we are accepting entries).

Contest Guidelines

Over time, we have developed contest guidelines that encourage positive participation and answer many staff and patron questions before they are asked. Most of the guidelines apply to a variety of different contests. We continually update these guidelines to clarify them and address any questions that are raised.

Phrases You Can Use:
- Works, art, photos, or performances should not contain offensive language, including excessive violence or material considered offensive to any religious or ethnic group, gender, or physically or mentally challenged persons, including any drug or alcohol references. Such material will be disqualified.
- Winners must have a library card in good standing.
- Only official entry forms will be accepted.
- The library is not responsible for lost or damaged work.
- The judges' decisions are final.
- I certify that the poem/art/drawing is my original work and neither whole nor part of this entry has been used in any publication. I further release this entry for publication by the library.

By submission, the artist grants permission for the library to display, photograph, and reproduce the submitted work for publicity purposes. Although we accept and usually display all of the submissions that we receive for a contest, only those submissions by library card holders whose cards are in good standing are eligible to win.

Making Contests Count

Making contests count towards your statistics is an important consideration. There are two ways to derive statistics for participation in a contest: by counting entries and by hosting a complimentary event.

First, count the total number of entries you receive for a contest as the number of participants. Recording participation in a contest allows you to compare the participation from year to year and consider making changes to increase participation. Just as planning a program or attending an outreach event requires staff time, planning contests also requires staff to prepare an entry form, market the contest, select and notify winners, recruit judges, and secure donations. Contests offer more flexibility for staff time and may be considered a "passive program," but counting participation is just as important.

Second, try hosting an event in the library to celebrate the contest. For instance, if you have an art contest, host an art show; invite everyone who enters a piece of art, their families, and the public to view all of the submissions and to hear the announcement of the winners. This way the contest not only generates submissions, but it also encourages people to visit the library in person. Also consider keeping track of contacts you establish as a result of the contest and the value of in-kind donations you receive. I'll give more details about keeping track of sponsorships shortly.

Increasing Participation

Once you have developed a contest, why not try to get as much participation as possible? There are several ways to accomplish this. For instance, you could try hosting it at another time of year, advertising in a different way, or offering an incentive for entering. Check with a knowledgeable community member, such as a teacher or parent, who may be able to give you insight into potential timing conflicts, like other contests, exams, or projects. We noticed that for the second year in a row, the number of entries we received for our Mascot Games drawing contest fell. We sought feedback from our branch staff on how we could improve awareness of the contest. Ultimately, we contacted our sponsoring organization, the Central Florida Sports Commission. We asked them if, in addition to donating a prize package for the winner, they would be willing to also donate a free ticket to a sporting event for each child who submitted an entry. They agreed, and our submissions quadrupled!

Local Sponsorship

Seeking local sponsorships is an opportunity to talk to neighborhood businesses and organizations. You can tell them about the valuable work that the library is doing with area youth and invite them to support it. Local business owners and marketing staff usually live in your community and are more than happy to support youth and the library when given the invitation. Just ask them!

Seeking Sponsors

To begin seeking sponsors, identify businesses that have a mutual interest in serving families, supporting youth, or have a connection to your specific contest. For instance, an art supply store might be willing to sponsor an art contest. Let them know how you found out about them. Are you a frequent customer? Did you notice they recently opened a store on your way home? Did a teen volunteer recommend that you contact them? Ask your coworkers for ideas. Familiarize yourself with what the company offers and make a specific request. If you are planning to award first, second, and third place, ask for three prizes. Let the businesses know how you will recognize their contribution. Make contact any way you can. Call and ask to talk to the person who handles community donations. If you cannot find specific information about how a business handles donation requests, do not hesitate to use "contact us" forms on websites or call a 1-800 number. They may require a formal written request by fax or e-mail.

How to Get Sponsorship for Contests:
- Make a personal connection.
- Talk to the right person.
- Familiarize yourself with what a company offers.
- Ask for what you need.
- Recognize contributions in numerous ways.
- Keep good records.

The final step in building local sponsorships for youth contests is to document the donations received and the contacts that you established. A simple form with the contact information for the donor, businesses, and a specific description of the contribution, kept on file, will be a tremendous help next year. This is also helpful if the responsibility for seeking sponsorships shifts to another staff member. He or she will have all the details in hand to continue the relationship. I also recommend keeping a spreadsheet to document donations over the course of the year. Seeking sponsorships and donations takes time out of your day, but if you have numbers to support the value derived from that time spent, you will be in a better position to request the time in your schedule.

Recognizing Sponsors

Recognizing sponsors shows appreciation to the donor and highlights the community support you are receiving for the contest.

Ways to Recognize Sponsors:
- Include sponsors' logos on entry forms.
- Link sponsors' logos to their websites from your web page. Also include sponsor logos on posters, flyers, and backdrops.
- Send a personalized thank-you note as soon as you receive a donation.
- Send a follow-up note or e-mail with photos of the winners.

Contest Examples

Described below are three of our most popular recurring contests: the Mascot Games drawing contest, our teen art contest, and kids' and teens' poetry contests. For each contest, you will find a description and specific rules and guidelines. Feel free to adapt these examples for use in your own library!

Mascot Games Contest

This is a basic drawing contest with an awesome partner and prize. Since the Mascot Games are held locally during the summer, we promote the contest along with our summer reading program. We partner with the Central Florida Sports Commission, which organizes special sporting events for our city.

Here Are the Details:
Draw and tell us about the most daring mascot you can think of! Each child who enters receives a complimentary ticket to the Celebrity Mascot Games, while supplies last! Pick up an entry form at any library or print one from our website. The most impressive artist receives a Celebrity Mascot Games VIP Prize Package for four, including premium seats, a poster, and a meet-and-greet with the mascots! This is the only event of its kind in the world! The Celebrity Mascot Games features over 30 mascots, including the Orlando Magic's very own Stuff, Knightro from the University of Central Florida, and Albert from the University of Florida. For more information about the games, visit: www.mascotgames.org.

Teen Art Contest

For our annual teen art show, we solicit submissions from area middle and high schools and exhibit all the work we receive at our main library. The contest culminates in an art show where the winners are announced and everyone is invited to an exhibition of the work. We leave the work on display for a month to allow the general public and friends and families of the artists to view it. The challenge with this contest was finding a time of year that would not conflict with a popular art festival (which includes tents of student artwork set up by school art teachers). Another consideration was making accommodations for teachers who would like to deliver and pick up student artwork; we handled this by coordinating the drop-off of artwork and making sure that the teacher's name was added to the entry forms.

Teen Art Contest Guidelines:
- Applicants may submit up to two pieces in any category.
- Sculptures should be no larger than 35" × 35" × 10".
- Hanging devices must be placed on art that is meant to be hung.
- Art must be original, not photocopied or reproduced.

Winners are selected in four categories:
1. Painting
2. Drawing
3. Photography
4. Other (sculpture, jewelry or graphic design)

Poetry Contests

Our teen poetry contest is held in conjunction with National Poetry Month in April. Winners are announced and have the opportunity to perform at the Teen Open Mic Night held at the end of the month. Teens often do not bring an extra copy of the poem they submitted to the contest; keep submitted poems close at hand in case the author would like to read it at the open mic event. Prizes for this contest are usually gift certificates to local coffee shops.

Teen Poetry Contest Submission Guidelines:
- Teens ages 13–18 are eligible to enter.
- Poem may be on any subject and in any form (lyric, limerick, concrete, rap, etc.).
- Each applicant may submit up to two poems.
- Each entry must be submitted online or printed on separate 8.5" × 11" pages.
- Attach the entry form to your poems. Do not put any identifying marks on your poems.
- Keep a copy of your poem. Entries will not be returned.
- Would you like your poem posted to the library's website (yes or no)?
- Would you like to perform your work at the Teen Open Mic Night (yes or no)?

Kids' Poetry Contest

Our Celebrate Your World Kids' Poetry Contest invites kids ages 6–12 to write a poem about anything in the world (or out of this world) and enter to win. Winners are announced and invited to perform at our Día de los Niños/Day of the Children celebration.

Kids' Poetry Contest Rules:
- Up to two entries may be submitted per child.
- Entries must be original poems written by the child.
- Do not sign your name or place any identifying marks on the poem.
- Keep a copy of your poem; entries will not be returned.

These are a few examples of contests we host each year, but contests can take many forms. Select the medium that is best for your audience and chosen objectives. Other ideas may include different types of writing, like poetry, short stories, and various other forms of art, including photography, video, drawing, multimedia, or fashion.

Marketing

Outreach is about connecting with people where they are. Oftentimes for children this is at school, after-school programs, or community centers. We frequently cannot transmit information directly to children, relying instead on the adults in their lives to encourage and share opportunities with them. These adults include teachers, parents, caregivers, and mentors, among others. Reach out to these people who have direct contact with children and invite them to participate. A personal invitation goes a long way. If manageable, call teachers at local schools and invite them to have their students enter your contest.

Advertising Contests

- Posters
- Entry forms that are also flyers
- E-mails
- Social media (Facebook, Twitter)
- Library website and online calendar
- Library newsletter and e-newsletter
- Community newspapers, blogs, and bulletin boards

One of the most useful means of promotion is an e-mail distribution list. If you do not already have one, start slowly and continually add people to it. Think about what organizations in your community have large networks and may be willing to share your information. For instance, we often ask the Early Learning Coalition of Orange County to share information with the childcare providers. Also consider where families in your community visit often, such as a favorite bakery or pizza place, and ask if they would allow you to post flyers; many will. Create a list and map out a route to post information. If you can get volunteers to help with this, even better!

Judges

Whenever possible, we recruit volunteer judges from our city. The challenge is finding a person with expertise in the subject matter who does not have any students participating in the contest. Recently, for our teen art contest, we had a public elementary school art teacher judge. Prior to that, an art instructor from a local art school judged the contest. Since students highly value feedback from the judges, we ask the judges to write a few sentences about why they chose a specific piece as a winner. We then read this feedback to the audience at the art show as we announce the winners. We also ask judges to write a short bio for us recognize them at the art show. When a volunteer judge is unable to participate, we often ask our staff graphic designer or a panel of staff members to vote for their favorites. To make judging as fair as possible, names of students are not included while reviewing entries, although age is often considered for children in our youth contests. The children of library staff and board members are never eligible to win contests, although they may participate by submitting entries.

Showcasing Winners

An important element of any work the library does is capturing it as a story to share with the community. Take photographs of winners of contests, along with their submissions, and post them on your website and through social media. To make this a smoother process, we are now trying to incorporate the language from our photo consent form into all of our entry forms. Here is a sample photo consent wording:

"By signing, I hereby grant permission for applicant to appear in person or in voice video or photographic presentation for radio, television, website or print media reports and/or media campaign(s) resulting from participation in an Orange County Library System event, held [insert date] at a library location. The parent/guardian and child, if under 18, must sign and date."

Whatever your means are of recognizing the winners of your contests, do not forget to share this with your community. Photos and videos from previous years' contests generate interest for the future. If time permits, create a photo gallery of all of the submissions. These photos document the impact of the contest through the smiling faces of the children and their often insightful and interesting creations.

Conclusion

Next time you would like to promote something in your library and/or your community, consider a contest. You have the opportunity to involve numerous individuals, community groups, and local businesses that support the kids and the library. Contests reach beyond the library walls and can encourage all kinds of positive activities for your community's youth. See what works for your library, and remember that your inspiration is limited only by your imagination!

Annual Programs for Youth and Community

Ann McDuffie

Even in tight financial times, libraries can still host successful programs for their young patrons. Though staff hours may be limited, outreach is essential, providing the opportunity to spread the library message and build relationships with children and teens. As a youth services librarian, I've organized activities for preschoolers through young adults at two public libraries. These once-a-year events will delight children and create fond memories for those future library supporters.

With all the events listed here, taking the message outside the library is crucial to success. Use all the advertising resources available at your library: post signs in conspicuous locations; make flyers for patrons to take home; print newsletters; meet with outside groups and let them know what you're doing; and, of course, use your web pages and Facebook. Send press releases to local newspapers and regional magazines. Don't forget good old-fashioned word of mouth; talk up events during storytime or while assisting patrons.

Read Aloud to a Child Week

The most successful way to reach out to potential patrons is to visit them at the source. As a newly hired youth services librarian, I wrote letters of introduction to the school principals and librarians in the area offering to visit their schools and tell students about library services and programs. The public library also has a booth at the annual county Teachers' Benefits Fair where we distribute promotional material and library card applications.

We harvested the fruits of this outreach when schools called us to attend Back-to-School events, Family Reading Night, and other special events. I welcome the opportunity to go out into the community to make contact with the public and spread the word about the library. One particularly rewarding outreach program was Read to Them Aloud at a local elementary school. Read to Them is an initiative that advocates the benefits of reading aloud to children (http://readtothem.org/).

To celebrate Read Aloud week, one of the third-grade teachers requested that a librarian visit the school to read to the entire grade level and talk about the public library. I readily agreed to participate, arriving at the school armed with books to read and talk about, bookmarks, library card applications, and a jumbo-sized laminated library card. Waving the card to the group of 60 students, I started a lively presentation by asking who had a library card and describing all the fun things they could do for *free* at the library. I then read my favorite picture book for that age group, *The Secret Science Project That Almost Ate the School* (2006) by Judy Sierra, about a third grader's science fair project gone haywire. I then talked about the difference between real and make believe, nonfiction and fiction, and displayed several nonfiction books about spiders and bats, the scary and gross factor always getting attention. Finally, I booktalked several new chapter book series and invited the children to come into the library to check them out.

At the end of the presentation, I took questions from the children. They were enthusiastic, asking lots of informed questions such as: Can they access the Internet? How many books can they check out and for how long? Where is the library located? How old do you have to be to volunteer at the library? Our future teen volunteers in the making!

TAG Gardening Project

As advisor to the teen advisory group (TAG) at my branch library, I'm always looking for creative ways to engage teens and bring them into the library. To promote TAG events and encourage membership, I reached out to the local high school and met the librarian who allowed me to post signs and agreed to help spread the news to students. For TAG activities, I've organized game and craft days, parties, outside presenters, and book discussions. But I discovered that more than anything young people want to work and feel needed. Give them a job or volunteer opportunity and they jump at the chance to help.

With that in mind, for Earth Day we decided to turn our April TAG meeting into a gardening project at the library. A member of the Cedar Run Garden Club agreed to direct the teens in planting flowers in large decorative pots by the library's front bench and spruce up the front garden of the Bealeton Branch Library. Using Friends of the Library money, the garden club purchased flowers, including petunias, geraniums, and saw grass.

On a sunny afternoon, six teens and three garden club volunteers, bearing work gloves and shovels, met at the library entrance. After introductions, we described the project to the teen helpers. Since we had two large ceramic pots, the teens were divided into groups with garden club ladies assisting. First, a layer of the old soil was removed and fresh potting soil and fertilizer was added. Then the teens planted a mix of annuals and grasses with the tall grass in the center surrounded by begonias and petunias.

Meanwhile, another group of teens removed daffodil bulbs from the dry ground between the sidewalk and building to be stored and replanted in fall. Then river rock was raked and spread to cover bare soil along the building wall.

The TAG team worked hard and seemed to enjoy this hands-on project. They were excited to know that every time they visit the library in the future, they would see the results of their volunteering. Lots of laughter and camaraderie took place. At one point, it looked as if there wouldn't be room in the pot for one last petunia plant. With quick wit, teenager Joelle raised her fist saying, "No flower left behind!" and the petunia was planted.

Reminders:
- Contact administration early for permission to make landscaping changes.
- Contact your local gardening club for ideas and assistance. In our case, the Cedar Run Club had been donating plantings for several years and was excited to get involved in the teen project.
- Notify grounds crew that a gardening project will take place.
- Submit a program publicity request or create your own attention-grabbing signs, and post the event on the library website and newsletter.
- Mention in the announcement the reminder to bring work gloves and shovels.
- Organize watering duty either through library staff or volunteers to ensure that the flowers thrive and bloom throughout the season.
- Don't forget to take pictures!

Stuffed Animal Fashion Show

This program was originally created by a coworker as one of our special summer events. I changed it up for my branch library, adding stories, songs, and rhymes to the craft, making it a hit for our young fashionistas.

Promote early with signs, highlight on web page, and word of mouth at storytimes. Getting the word out to local elementary schools and daycare centers is a good idea for programs with this age group. The program is geared toward young school-age children, but with parent assistance, even younger siblings can participate. Before the program, put out plenty of fabric scraps and felt pieces to make simple outfits.

We began with storytime, and a stuffed animal program wouldn't be complete without a reading of Don Freeman's famous teddy bear story *Corduroy* (1968). Be sure to point out the lonely bear's green overalls with a missing button in preparation of dressing up stuffed animals. This led to a playing of the song on CD "Me and My Teddy" featuring Bill Shontz (*Teddy Bear's Greatest Hits*, 1997).

For a stretch, we stood and performed the traditional rhyme Teddy Bear, Teddy Bear. Harriet Ziefert's (2006) version has teddy bears dressed in knitted sweaters doing all sorts of activities from touching their "toeses and noses" to "reaching for the sky and waving goodbye." The dancing bears served as a good warm-up for costume designing stuffed animals.

After storytime, the 39 children and adults gathered around two long tables, on the floor, and window sill and began creating. No sewing is required in this sewing project. Swatches of fabric were made into capes, hats, and skirts using safety pins. Ribbons were tied and bows attached. Another simple way to make no-sew clothing is to snip a thin strip along opposite sides of a square of fabric, leaving about an inch connected. Then tie it into doll-size skirts and dresses.

When all the stuffed animals were dressed and ready to walk the catwalk, we paraded the supermodels through the library. Two stations were set up where children could stop, show their creations to a staff member or volunteer, and receive a stamp and sticker.

Materials:
- Fabric and felt
- Safety pins

- Ribbon, lace, and miscellaneous craft material
- Safety scissors

Most important—remind patrons to bring a favorite stuffed friend, but it's a good idea to have one or two available in case some youngsters forget theirs.

Community Carnival

Each year to celebrate the end of the summer reading program, the Central Rappahannock (Virginia) Regional Library staged an ice cream social and neighborhood carnival. One summer, I was assigned to lead the planning and organizing of this much-anticipated event, which drew more than 500 visitors throughout the day.

The program involved the coordination of entertainers, games, community organizations, and, of course, ice cream, so planning began months in advance. An event of this magnitude takes many helping hands, so work was delegated and everyone pitched in to make it a success. Two staff members coordinated teen and tween volunteers to assist with games and activities. Others donated coolers to keep the ice cream cold, ordered supplies, and helped on the day of the event.

To publicize the event, I submitted graphics requests for promotional materials. Poster-sized signs were hung in the library foyer and in the children's area. Half-sheet flyers make convenient handouts that patrons can take home and post on the refrigerator as reminders. Eye-catching announcements and art were posted in the library newsletter and webpage. This event, however, has become such a popular tradition that the library needs only to set the date and give the public a friendly nudge and they come in droves.

Community Contacts

About two months before the occasion, I came up with a list of community organizations that would be willing to provide demonstrations or to staff tables promoting their clubs. Most of the groups had previously participated in the social event, so they were definitely contacted. I suggest that each library brainstorm potential groups in your area; many clubs are happy to present themselves to the public, so don't be shy about asking. Some organizations, such as the fire department, require written requests sent to their public information office, so find out their policies and send letters early.

We invited the local fire department and K-9 unit, the Paws therapy dog team, an equine rescue group, a recycling van, Girl Scouts, Cub Scouts, and the local 4-H Club. I contacted a musician and a magician who gladly agreed to perform for free. We even sent invitations to our county supervisors, giving them the opportunity to mingle with citizens and observe first-hand the popularity of the library. I also notified the manager of a local grocery store about the large ice cream order to ensure that a supply would be available at the time of the event. As the program drew near, I confirmed with each group that planned to participate.

Location, Location, Location

It was important to plan the community carnival layout to provide customers with an enjoyable experience without discouraging regular library patrons. We chose to use a large indoor meeting room with outside access to the library lawn and garden. I sketched a diagram marking where each booth, game, activity, and presenter would be located. The day before, we prepared as much as possible with tables set up in a semicircle along the assembly room walls.

Action!

The sun shone brightly on the morning of the event as I made an early trip to the grocery store to pick up ice cream treats and ice bags in donated coolers. Staff and volunteers arrived at the library to set up.

The tween-age volunteers manned game activity stations:

- Penny Splash – an aquarium filled with water, three glasses, and pennies to toss
- Sponge Toss – a bucket of water and four sponges
- Bubble Station – bubble solution and wands
- Blindfold Sniffing Guessing Game – plastic cups covered with aluminum foil and filled with aromatic items, including cinnamon, mint, syrup, coffee beans, onion, and lemon
- Magnetic Fishing

Older teen volunteers handled face painting and balloon art, both extremely popular activities. To keep the lines moving, we had four face painters and four balloon artists using hand pumps. Teens also helped distribute ice cream cups and managed the popcorn machine.

Community clubs set up their displays at the tables inside. Cub Scouts, Girl Scouts, and the 4-H Club brought registration information and simple crafts to encourage young patrons to visit their booths and sign up. A computer at another table enabled summer reading finishers to register. We also snapped their photographs, which were then downloaded to a template for participants to pick up later. Paws dogs had a spot on the floor to greet youngsters.

Wall-to-wall windows and two glass doors provided a view of the outside activities, and people spilled out onto the lawn. The musician and magician alternated performance hours under a large shady oak tree. Carnival games were set up along the curb of the blocked-off driveway. The fire truck and emergency vehicle were parked in the lot at the end of a sidewalk. And the recycling van was parked on the opposite side of the lot. From 10:00 A.M. to noon, music and happy laughter filled the air to highlight a successful event.

Scavenger Hunt

School-age children love the adventure of a scavenger hunt in the library. "Make a Splash" was based on the 2010 Collaborative Summer Library Program (CSLP), although I tailored the quest to items I could provide and activities familiar to the children. Setting up a scavenger hunt takes plenty of pre-planning but is worth every minute of seeing the children's excitement as they race to accomplish the tasks.

To prepare for the scavenger hunt, I created a list of objects to find, activities to do, and facts to find out. The objects were a variety of die-cut sea shapes such as crabs and fish. These flat images are easy to slip between the pages of books or stack on shelves. Things to do consisted of funny phrases to sing or say, a hidden picture search, and clown fish coloring pages reproduced from the CSLP manual. Things to find out were also drawn from the CSLP manual, but I first verified that the library had books available with the correct answers. Before the program, I hid the die-cut sea shapes around the children's area of the library. I also put out a basket of lollipops because a treat to take home always adds to the fun.

When the children arrived, we sat in story area and I introduced the ocean and sea life topic. I displayed a large conch shell and let the children "listen" to the ocean. To break the ice, I read a few jokes and riddles, then read the picture book *Atlantic* (2002) by Brian Karas. The story explores facts about the ocean told by the Atlantic itself in an entertaining way.

The Atlantic tale segued nicely into an introduction of the "Make a Splash" scavenger hunt. The children—from kindergarten through fifth grade—were divided into teams of two to three and encouraged to work together to complete the scavenger list. Older children were grouped with younger so the bigger kids could help the youngsters read through the list of activities. When they were set free, they scurried about the children's area enthusiastically doing the tasks, and no prizes were necessary.

Christmas Tree Lighting and Santa Visit

Remember days gone by when the whole community gathered to sing carols, share stories, and spread Christmas cheer? This old-fashioned gathering brings friends and neighbors together to share holiday traditions, old and new.

Just as with the community carnival, plenty of volunteers and staff were engaged to help with this event. Several months prior, we booked our volunteer Santa and Mrs. Claus. We also confirmed the participation of the local high school chorus. Previously, a live Christmas tree had been donated by the local business owners' association and planted near the front entrance of the library. Each year, outdoor lights are strung, but the actual lighting is saved for this holiday party. Just after Thanksgiving, artificial trees were set up inside the library, and we began decorating for the festivities.

Publicity requests were submitted to the publications department, which created signs and posted an announcement in the monthly print newsletter and on the website. Most beneficial was a press release sent to the local newspaper that resulted in a news brief in the community news column. The public was invited to sing carols, hear their favorite Christmas stories, and have a jolly good time with the Clauses. Folks were encouraged to bring their own cameras to preserve the memory of Santa's visit.

That evening, nearly a hundred guests gathered in the front courtyard of the library. Branch manager Natalie Wheeler welcomed the families and introduced the high school chorus, which led the audience in Christmas carols. At a designated place in the song list, volunteers passed out jingle bells while Ms. Wheeler explained the plan for Santa's upcoming visit. Then she led the countdown to the spectacular lighting of the Christmas tree.

After the final song, "We Wish You a Merry Christmas," the crowd moved into the library, and each family was given a decorated and numbered card. Guests were directed to the story area where I began to read a Christmas story. Suddenly, who should appear but Saint Nick himself? He greeted the children and then went to his seat in a curtained-off area. Storytime continued while small groups of families were ushered to Santa for photos. Meanwhile, waiting children were occupied with simple crafts that had been set out beforehand. A teen volunteer dressed as an elf helped with the Santa line, Mrs. Claus gave out candy canes, and volunteers and staff monitored the crafts and refreshment tables.

Larger programs like Santa's visit and the community carnival serve as a form of outreach by bringing patrons in who might not otherwise use the library. Smaller programs like the scavenger hunt and the gardening project give regular customers programming opportunities and allow non-users to witness firsthand the many services the library has to offer. Though budgets may be slashed, maintaining affordable programs and outreach is vital if libraries are to remain vibrant centers in their communities.

Team Outreach
Librarians Pairing Up
SHAWN D. WALSH *and*
MELANIE A. LYTTLE

"It's so much more friendly with two."—A.A. Milne

Piglet had it right. It's best to be with Winnie-the-Pooh. Being part of a team is better than being alone. When it comes to doing outreach, you'll reach more kids when there are two people. Whether you're doing library promotion in your community or leading a program off-site, it's so much easier and less stressful if you're out there with a friend. Unfortunately, you can't always be lucky enough to have two people as opposite as Winnie-the-Pooh and Piglet, but finding two individuals with complementary skills to work together can only benefit the library.

At a time when some libraries are eliminating outreach altogether, how can you convince your library administration that it's worth the time, money, and/or staff to send two people to visit children in the community? When you need all the community support you can get, how can you afford not to do all you can to reach potential library supporters?

A Happy Accident

The intention was never for Madison Public Library (MPL) to have two people who went out to schools and other locations in the community to visit children of all ages. However, in the process of training a new employee, it turned out that two people with complementary skills, the trainer and trainee, truly did much better together than either did on their own. Therefore, the Shawn and Melanie team was created.

Melanie trained all her new employees the same way. They learned mostly by doing, but at first they did very little. Melanie was always with them. As time went on, they took on more and more responsibility until Melanie was no longer actively involved. The new employee was now capable of handling everything on his or her own without Melanie watching or helping. Shawn went through this same process when trained by Melanie. Little by little, the supports were removed until Shawn was doing everything on his own.

41

Training proceeded as normal until something out of the ordinary started to occur. Melanie noticed that during the presentations and visits they were making, more kids were paying attention than ever before. In fact, it was significantly more kids than when she had done outreach on her own. What was the difference? The things easiest for Shawn to start doing in presentations were things Melanie never did in the first place! Instead of mimicking Melanie's presentations, Shawn was adding additional content and insights. Conversely, when Shawn tried to do some of the things Melanie did the way she did them, it just didn't quite work right. Each person was bringing complementary skills to the visits, and it was soon obvious the team was producing more interest together than Shawn or Melanie generated individually.

An Example of How Team Outreach Worked for Us

While it is possible to build a rock-solid outreach team without the pair being friends, it definitely doesn't hurt if they are! Shawn and Melanie were friends before Shawn came to work at MPL, and as a result, they were well aware of each other's strengths, weaknesses, likes, and dislikes. Before Shawn came to MPL, he was Melanie's "phone-a-friend" when she needed help with good science fiction books to recommend to children or a good idea for a "boy program" to have at the library. And Shawn knew when he took the job at MPL there was no way he was going to be able to recommend teen romance books with a straight face, and he would not be hosting any tween manicure parties at the library, either!

Summer reading presentations with a partner were very different than going to the schools alone. As Shawn and Melanie discovered a way to flow back and forth with who presented what and who interjected loud side comments, they were able to capture the attention of a wide range of children. The much more "librarian-ish" Melanie was frequently interrupted by the snarky side comments of Shawn, who was determined that all presentations got neither too girly nor too serious! When exuberant Shawn started to get out of hand with all his fabulous boy books and upcoming boy-ish library activities, Melanie shot him some comments that made sure he stayed in his place! This worked particularly well in the middle school and the high school. Those students responded to the range of books and programs being offered at the library for the summer. More importantly, they also saw the obvious joy and friendship that existed between Shawn and Melanie. The middle schoolers could participate in or instigate the continual "disagreements" over any number of things that Shawn and Melanie had during the presentations. The number of fist bumps Shawn got from children at these school visits was amazing. For Melanie, she was already fairly well known at the schools, but even she gained some "playground cred" with her ability to verbally spar with Shawn during presentations. She wasn't as much of the typical female librarian anymore!

Elements of Developing an Outreach Team (or Perhaps Any Team?)

In the case of Shawn and Melanie, they had a team long before they realized it. Knowing you have a good team to do outreach is probably the first step before trying to convince anyone that your team should be allowed to leave the library to do outreach to children. The question is, how do you develop a good team?

• Find your individual passions and strengths. Shawn loves graphic novels and science fiction and fantasy. He listens to heavy metal and plays video games. His training was in computer science and marketing. He identifies more with middle school and high school kids. Melanie loves happy endings, or at least definite endings! If there isn't a romance or a murder in the book, she probably doesn't read it. She is a pop music listener who can't drive her Mario Kart around the track in the correct direction to save her life! Her training was in elementary and early childhood education. She's at home in the preschools and elementary schools.

• Find your commonalities. For Shawn and Melanie, they were both teachers. Shawn spent much of his career instructing adult librarians or library patrons about how to use technology or computers. Melanie taught elementary school and then spent many years doing storytimes. Their common age group was tweens. Melanie was very successful with children up to tween age. Older than middle school, that was hard. Shawn was very successful with adults and teens and tweens. Working with younger elementary kids, it was a stretch. They also both completely agreed that getting children involved in and supporting the library would help libraries survive in the future. Even for as long as Shawn and Melanie have known each other, they are still finding new places where they agree and overlap. Building as many commonalities as possible makes the marked differences between each other easier to handle.

• Respect each other. Though Shawn and Melanie were friends before working together at MPL, being friends isn't as important as respecting each other. There are many things Shawn and Melanie do not agree on, inside and outside the library profession, but they respect each other's opinions and ideas. Agreeing to disagree is key to how Shawn and Melanie operate. You can have a great partnership with someone you respect whether or not you think they are a good person to go hang out with on the weekend.

• Anticipate what the other needs. If Shawn is doing a booktalk, he knows Melanie is there waiting to hand him the next book so he doesn't break his rhythm. If Melanie is leading a program, Shawn has all the materials for the next game they're playing laid out and ready to go. If a presentation is going badly, if kids are misbehaving at an off-site program, the one will always be there to bail out the other. It's not pushy. It's making programs and presentations flow effortlessly because there is one person leading and one person taking care of everything else.

• Trust each other. Shawn and Melanie trust each other implicitly. While this trust is related to the respect they have for each other, it's more than that. And it's more than being convinced that someone will always have whatever you need before you need it. Rather, it is the expectation that if one person is behaving in a way that is counterproductive to the cause, the other can step in and say, "what the heck?" without fear of repercussions or permanently damaging the team. Anyone can get wrapped up in what he or she is doing and lose focus. Knowing that there is always someone who is willing to tell you that you are completely crazy is critical to keeping the team intact.

• Figure out how your personalities fit together. In many ways, Shawn and Melanie are like Pooh and Piglet. Shawn is easy-going and happy. Melanie is more of a planner and worrier. Shawn is the extrovert and Melanie is the introvert. How will these personalities play to the intended audience? The answer to this question is the key to good outreach teamwork.

• Decide what your "characters" are. How are you planning to interact with each other in front of the children? Shawn's energy could power a medium-sized country, while Melanie is focused and quieter. That doesn't mean that Shawn is always in front and Melanie is the background person. The nature of the outreach activity determines who plays what role in the presentation.

• Plan how to reach as wide a range of people as possible. Since the team has complementary skills and talents, use them! This is easier for Shawn and Melanie because their interests are so diverse. For example, Shawn likes to do booktalks with graphic novels, fantasy, and science fiction. Melanie likes romances and mysteries and biographies of pop culture icons. When talking about programs, Shawn does the programs that are messy and loud and Melanie talks about the more mellow offerings.

• Can you both interrupt each other? A little well-timed or well-placed interruption goes a long way in making sure children of any age are paying attention to your presentation. It is a great way to refocus those who are drifting off and no longer following your presentation. It's something that causes them to react with a "what was that?" or "I didn't expect that from them" kind of reaction. Both Melanie and Shawn tend to make snarky comments to each other in presentations. The children they see think it's hilarious.

• Can you both react to the influences of the moment? Things will go wrong, or the plan you have for your outing will need to be changed to create a better flow. Trust each other to make adjustments as each sees fit without breaking your rhythm.

Personalities and Interests Checklist

Do you and your teammate have to have all the characteristics of the Shawn and Melanie partnership? Probably not. Do you want to have the exact same team as Shawn and Melanie? Again, probably not. This is just to get you started thinking about how people who are so different can work together. Then you can decide what characteristics are important to you.

Some characteristics depend on the age group(s) you'll be visiting. Because Shawn and Melanie see preschool through high school out in the community, there are a wide range of interests and behaviors they need to have to be successful with the different age groups. Additionally, some things are probably more important because of the community within which MPL is located. However, you'll notice gender isn't on the list! It's great if you can have a male/female team visiting children in your community. However, it's more important to have two people whose interests and strengths complement each other.

Know the Challenges of Team Outreach

It's easy to talk about the wonderful things that come with team outreach, but there are also some real challenges you have to consider if you are going to commit to this. Shawn and Melanie especially struggle with these problems because team outreach just "happened" for them without a plan ahead of time. Dealing with the challenges as they come up is harder than knowing and preparing for them ahead of time. There are two types of challenges: those the team faces within the library from colleagues and those faced by the teammates themselves.

• Collegial jealousy. It's easy for your library colleagues to feel jealous of you and your teammate. By being out and about in the community, you may have a different work schedule to accomplish your duties. This may seem more advantageous than someone else's schedule who doesn't do outreach. You may travel places with your partner for training or get to meet and interact with people who are outside the normal library spheres. It can cause colleagues to wonder if teammates are trying to be superior to those remaining in the library. If there are newspaper articles or some other media acknowledgment of the team's activities but nothing about what is going on within the library building, that can cause hard feelings among colleagues. Why is the team getting recognized and not them?

• Misunderstandings between partners. On the way to being able to trust each other, there can be many misunderstandings between you and your teammate. Just like small children who need to be sent to separate corners when they can't get along, sometimes you and your teammate just need some alone time. You are building your team, but not everything is going to be perfect all the time. And for colleagues, if it looks like teammates are fighting, they can get worried that this will affect their work routine, or they may simply dislike dissension in the library.

• Exclusion of other library colleagues. You spend a lot of time together, inside and outside the library building. When you're at the library, you may be planning for outreach activities together. When you're in the community, you're sharing experiences with your teammate that colleagues who stay in the building don't know or understand. It can seem like you have formed an exclusive club no one else can join. You may know each other so well that you can finish each others' sentences. If you have preexisting partnerships with other colleagues for other projects, it may appear that you have dumped those relationships for this newer one.

• Trust in the team. If each of the teammates isn't fully committed to the team, it will fail. Each person must be rock-solid in his or her belief that the team is the best thing for the library and for the children the library reaches. Otherwise, it is too easy to walk away from the team when any type of challenge arises.

Talking Points for Convincing Administration of the Team Approach

You have found someone at your library who is your perfect complement. You both are ready to attract tons of children to your library. The problem is you need to convince your administration this is a good idea!

• Are you located near a school? Being in close physical proximity to a school means you already have or really should get a good relationship with that school. That means visiting! The older the children are in the school, the more you need a partner. Tweens and certainly teens are more judgmental and more set in what they like and don't like. Two people with very different interests are likely to find more children who identify and agree with what they are saying.

• Do you need local support for the library? Children may not be voting yet, but their parents do. Children can be some of your greatest supporters, and they have power within their families. Also, children grow! They may not be voters yet, but they will be soon. Make sure they have a positive impression of the library right from the very beginning.

• Can the team members still get their "regular" work done? Sometimes this means enlisting the help of other staff members. Remember, there are some people in your library who would rather have a root canal than do outreach to children, even if they love doing programming at the library. They may be very willing to cover teammates' other activities if that means they don't have to ever leave the library building.

• Do you have a "routine" that will work with your intended audience? For example, many children respond to the "snarky brother and sister" routine. Shawn and Melanie use that with all their visits to places outside the library. It works for them and their partnership. It seems to work particularly well when visiting middle school and high school. Everyone can identify with either the "snotty boy" or "bratty girl." Shawn or Melanie continually try to "one up" the other or just make snide comments when the other is talking. It dances on the edge of disrespectful, but it is also clear to the children that Shawn and Melanie genuinely care for each other. So the comments they make to each other are not mean.

• Have you acknowledged the challenges you will face as a team from colleagues within the library? One of the jobs of library administration is to keep all the staff relatively happy. Knowing that a partnership can cause jealousy among staff members, the team and the administration have to at least acknowledge this may happen. You can talk about ways to mitigate some of these hard feelings that may develop among staff. Make sure you can list more reasons why team outreach is good for the library as a whole than why people within the library may not like it.

The Administration Said You Could Have Your Team ... Now What?

You're ready! Pound the pavement, drive the car, do whatever you can to get to where the children are. You and your partner are ambassadors for your library. Remind the kids that if the two of you work at your library, then there must be something pretty fabulous about it! That's what Shawn and Melanie do. Madison Public Library must be a pretty special place if there are two awesome librarians like them there. And it's true! MPL is an amazing library, and so is yours.

And even more important than that, remember to have faith in what you are doing. Every trip out of the library won't be perfect, and even in a team, you will never reach every single child you see. But you must believe beyond a shadow of a doubt in what you are doing. If you don't believe that team outreach is the best way to bring children to your library, then the children won't believe it, either.

Good luck!

It Takes a Village
A Public and a School Library Collaborate
ANNIE MILLER

Introduction: Who We Are

Greenwich (pronounced green witch) is a rural town of about 5,000 people in Upstate New York. The library and the school are both located in the Village of Greenwich within easy walking distance of each other. As in many rural areas, the school district is larger than the town itself, and many students live a considerable distance away. The public library also has patrons coming from far and wide. Located on Main Street and open evenings and Saturdays, the public library is a natural community focal point and an obvious partner for the school library.

All the librarians of Greenwich share the goal of providing the best possible service to our patrons large and small. We also share many of the same challenges: time, money, staff, etc. It only makes sense that we collaborate. Fortunately, in our small town, the public and school libraries have had a good relationship for years. Our past activities include:

- Joint Harry Potter parties coinciding with the releases of new titles
- "A Day Along the River" with music, a book swap, mystery readers, and a free book
- Second Grade Primary source workshop in the public library local history room
- Attending professional development workshops together

Plagued by the problems that a poor economy creates, our relationship has grown even stronger as we face tightening budgets and the expectation to do more with less. Rising to the challenge, we are creating a continuum of learning that extends from the classroom to the community and beyond. Our focus on working together is opening up new opportunities for the staff and patrons of both institutions. To date, we have concentrated our efforts in two areas: collaboration behind the scenes, particularly in the area of collection development, and increased outreach to our shared patrons, namely children, parents, teachers, and administrators.

The Beginning: Collection Development Becomes a Catalyst for Change

Working together more closely has caused a significant shift in the thinking and the operations of both institutions but, like most big changes, it started with a simple question: What do we do about state books? In the spring of 2010 when the annual fifth-grade state research project began and students started coming to the public library for books, the public librarians became aware of the piteous condition of the available resources. A number of states were completely unrepresented, and many of those books that *were* on the shelves were fifteen to twenty years out of date. Clearly something needed to be done, but what? These types of books, with their many photos and graphics, are expensive, and purchasing a new full set would be a major investment. They also become dated quickly and would have to be regularly replaced to keep the collection current. Could we skip the expense entirely and direct the kids to websites and databases? To find out what would best suit the students' needs, the public librarians decided to consult the local expert: the school librarian.

After discussions of what was cognitively appropriate, useful for learning research skills, and required by teachers, the decision was made to invest in books. As we answered the question of what to buy, we inadvertently started down the road of collaborative collection development. Unaware that the practice was a trend that was gaining attention, we started from scratch, thinking about creating a public library collection that complemented rather than replicated that of the school library as a way to both save money and create a more comprehensive resource. The cost of materials is the obvious issue, but shelf space is another scarce and valuable asset that can be better utilized through collaboration. More physical space is made available for a diversity of resources when there is less duplication throughout the system. We sought input from other local school and public libraries as well, both to evaluate the quality of various series and to avoid purchasing materials that could easily be obtained by either institution through their separate consortia. The process of book selection took several months because the public library has no full-time staff, and the librarian who was most involved in the project only worked 10 to 15 hours a week, with plenty of other responsibilities to attend to during those hours. By the time the first new books started arriving, state report time was coming around again.

Looking at the condition of the state books led to looking at the public library's junior nonfiction collection as a whole. The prospect was not inspiring. There were books in the collection about countries that no longer existed, "hot" tech books from the 1990s, and social issues books from the 1960s. If our public library was to be a valuable resource for students, we needed to institute an overhaul of the entire junior nonfiction collection. Recent sweeping changes to the school curriculum, most notably the adoption of the Common Core Standards by our state, have placed a greater emphasis on informational reading. Having a strong junior nonfiction collection would be the key to the public library becoming a more valuable partner for the school. In the spring of 2010, the public library started weeding hard to get rid of all that horribly outdated material. Progress is gradual (due to staff limitations) but steady. As the public library staff slash and burn their way through the subject areas, they consult with the school librarian and the teachers about what to get rid of and what materials to purchase. Again, checking what is readily available through the public and school regional systems has been part of the process. The public librarian has also been spending time in the school library stacks, looking to see what is new, old, or missing. Sometimes the public library does choose to get a second copy of a book, particularly one that would be useful to older students and adults.

To make coordination even easier, the school librarian has given the public librarian access to her TitleWave book purchasing software account. This way, the public library can see what the school has purchased. The public library uses a different purchasing system, but can alert the school to intended purchases by creating wish lists of those items in the TitleWave account.

Outreach: Going on the Road and Getting Them in the Door

In the spring of 2011, the public library had shiny new state books, but had no idea if the teachers and students knew about them. Thus was born the second part of our strategy: outreach. Our initial goal was simple: let the teachers and students know about this one new resource. The school librarian spread the word and students were soon trickling into the public library to get the new books. We all felt that we were on the right track, but we also knew it was only the beginning.

As the public collection is transformed, we have stepped up outreach efforts that bring the public library into the school. We start off by having a public librarian make a presentation on programming and resources at the school's annual kindergarten orientation for preschoolers and their families. Next, a public librarian takes part in planning and presenting the school's annual PTSA Kindergarten Reading Night, an event to welcome new families to the school and emphasize the importance of reading at home. A public librarian helps greet families, gives out public library information and card applications, makes a short plug for the public library, and takes a turn among the local luminaries reading aloud. Every child who attends receives a free book. These are purchased by the public librarian using PTSA funds. Public library participation in both of these programs provides a great opportunity to connect with young families who haven't been attending library programs.

The children see the public librarian in school pretty often after that, as she is becoming a frequent visitor to their library classes. As is true in many schools, our library media specialist has had her contact time increased to provide for teacher release time. She now has an extra awkward half hour once a week with eight third- and fourth-grade classes. The public librarian is using some of that time to come in for booktalks. These feature new items in the collection and are pretty evenly divided between fiction and nonfiction. We are all happy to have the chance to bring these wonderful new books to the attention of their intended audience and get the kids as excited to read them as we are. The first booktalk produced a checkout right after school that day and circulation of featured books has been strong.

The students aren't the only ones who get the public library message in school. In June of 2012, the public librarian presented a booktalk at a school faculty meeting. The intention was to make the teachers and principal aware of the resources available at the public library, in terms of both materials and expertise. We wanted to "bookmark" the public library in teachers' minds as a good resource for themselves and an automatic recommendation to their students. It is amazing how few think to come to the public library or send their students. There was a show-and-tell of some great nonfiction titles, audiobooks, and other resources that students and teachers would find useful. It was an excellent opportunity to make teachers aware of the wonderful new nonfiction titles. It was also a chance to explain the collaboration between the libraries and solicit input about materials or subject areas the teacher felt needed beefing up. That first meeting produced some good feedback, and we think it is no coincidence that the public library subsequently received a grant from the teachers' association to help with junior nonfiction purchases. Our intention is to have booktalks become a regular feature of faculty meetings and expand to the 7–12 school. We aren't hoping to get more money from the teachers, but we are looking for more cooperation.

We are also continuing and adding to the programs that involve bringing students to the public library for specific events or projects. Getting the kids in the door for a memorable experience can turn "the library" into "my library." Providing other school-linked activities at the public library emphasizes the connection in patrons' minds. Some of these events and projects include:

- First-grade public library tour. Classes walk from the school to the public library where they get a guided tour. Each class has collected new books to donate to the public library collection. The books get a special bookplate with the donor's name and go on display for a month before going into the collection. The kids love seeing and checking out "their books."
- YA book group. Run by a young public library volunteer with help from the public librarian and the 7–12 school librarian, this is a great structure to help students accomplish their free-choice reading assignments. We have put the word out to 7–12 ELA teachers to see if they will offer extra credit to students who attend. This event is bi-monthly *with snacks.*
- Preschool book bags. This summer, the public library was host to our primary school's version of the 1,000 books program. The school librarian created a binder for parents signing bags out and in so it was no additional work for the public library. The bags were kept on a cart for easy loading and unloading. Delivery and return took about ten minutes. We had 43 bags go out!

Programs and events that we plan for the future include:
- Teen tech tutors. This is a program we are developing in cooperation with the school tech department and our local youth center to train teen volunteers to help patrons with computer issues. We are currently seeking funding to cover public library staff time.
- Library club. Noticing a few science experiment books among the public library's purchase list, the school librarian suggested that we hold some elementary lab days after school. The school librarian will be walking students to the public library for these and other hands-on activities from cooking and craft-making books.
- 4–6 book club. Led by a public librarian with a rotating teacher co-host, members will read a book and have a supplemental activity (an author Skype, book trailer creation, etc.) at their meeting.
- A joint blog. This will serve to update all our patrons on programming at both institutions, new favorite reads, etc.

Problem Solving: An Example of a Work in Progress

One source of frustration for both the public and school librarians has been that teachers don't usually give us a heads-up before they send students in looking for specific resources. We have all been making a concerted effort in faculty meetings, official e-mails, and casual contacts to remind them that a little advance notice can make a big difference in our ability to serve their students' needs. This is particularly true at our public library, which relies heavily on volunteers to run the circulation desk. They don't always know the collection or even how to search well, which can be very frustrating for patrons. We like to pull books ahead of time to create collections based on assignments, so students can easily find what they need. Traditionally, we have relied on the kids and parents to tell us what the assignments are, which isn't very efficient. We are looking for ways to improve both communication and delivery, so that students and their parents feel that they are well served at the public library.

When teachers do let us know what they need, the public librarians are always happy to help. The school librarian is usually a go-between, but sometimes it makes more sense to work one-on-one. We have come up with some ways to make things go more smoothly, including:

- School librarians send an e-mail if they need materials from the public system, including interlibrary loans of multiple copies of books. They have public library accounts which are used to place requests and receive notification of arrivals. Teachers can pick up the books at the circulation desk and check them out on their own cards.
- The public librarians happily field e-mail requests to help teachers find books on particular topics, which includes making ILL requests. We cheerfully check all those books in and out, even when there are forty of them!
- The public librarian met with a fourth-grade teacher to discuss needs for a biography project. This was followed by creation of an inventory of available public library resources, weeding the junior biographies in the local collection, discussions with the school librarian, and searching out new books to fill gaps.

Behind the Scenes: What Librarians Do When Nobody Is Looking

As the collection development and programming aspects of our collaboration move forward, other opportunities to work together present themselves. We find that we are simply keeping each other in mind more, becoming a team behind the scenes as well as in the eyes of our patrons. It is this connection, sustained by small daily actions that become part of the job description, that we hope will maintain the partnership through changes in personnel and programming. Some examples of this include:

- We regularly pass on interesting articles, listserv posts, and meeting announcements to our school library counterparts.
- The public library has started routinely alerting the school when materials come through from other libraries that look like they would be of interest.
- The school librarian has alerted the public library to a fundraising opportunity and set up the contact.

- We talk each other up at every opportunity and recommend each other to patrons.
- At budget time, the public librarians have spoken in support of the school librarians and their programs.
- The high school librarian recently served as president of the public library board.

Collaboration: Getting Started and Making It Work

Although we are all in the same profession, we are aware of the different demands placed on each of us by our specialties. In all our interactions, we treat each other as professionals and try to understand and respect each other's needs. When working with the schools, the public librarians always contact the school librarians first, communicating directly with teachers and administrators only when it is inconvenient for the school librarian to do so. Unfortunately, school librarians often need all the help they can get to be visible and make teaching colleagues and administration aware of their important contributions to student learning. The school librarian is patient with the sometimes slow responses and limited time the public librarians can devote to school issues. In our case, the public library is a very small institution with no full-time staff and an entire community to serve. Any issues we may have about who works harder, gets paid more, or has better vacations are left outside the relationship.

We are fortunate that our small town status has thrown us together enough to make ice-breaking unnecessary but hasn't created any bad blood that would make working together impossible. If you don't know the librarians at your corresponding institution, take the first step. It can be something small. We started our collection development collaboration with a discussion about whether the public library should replace outdated state books. To get the ball rolling, you can:

- Send an e-mail and arrange a visit.
- Try to see the other person "in action" to get a feel for his or her job and its challenges and rewards.
- Come with something to work on (like the state books) so there is a compelling reason to stay in touch.
- Trade ideas for what to put on your respective websites.

What if the other librarians have no interest in cooperation? They may have had a bad group project experience (who hasn't?), be busier than you can imagine, be insecure about working with another library professional, or they may just be happy with the way things are. If you feel like cooperation would benefit your institution and patrons, you can go ahead on your own. Just make sure not to burn any bridges. Always let your counterparts at the other institution know what you are doing so they won't look foolish when asked, and never even *imply* in public that a non-cooperating counterpart is a slacker or hindrance to progress.

Conclusion: Is It Worth the Effort? Yes!

The more we Greenwich librarians work together, the more we wish we could do. The little extra effort of sending the e-mail or having the meeting always pays off. Sometimes it is the instant gratification of a kid rushing in after school for a booktalk book. Often it is being better prepared to point a searching student to the perfect resource. Mostly it is the satisfaction of knowing that we are doing a better job of meeting our community's needs. Of course, money is always nice. To date, our collaboration has netted us $3,500 in grants for materials. We are hoping to find the funding to increase public library staff time (currently our most limiting factor), and we think that our collaboration will make a compelling grant proposal narrative.

All libraries and all librarians are different, but we have the same commitment to bringing information, enjoyment, and maybe even some enlightenment to the patrons we serve. These days, we often find ourselves being challenged to prove that we are relevant, that our work adds value in our various settings. By working across institutions, we can help the public understand that the true value of libraries lies not in the buildings and books and computers, but in the expertise and commitment of the professionals who help wrest information and learning and joy from them. We can also learn a lot from each other.

Reaching Kids Who Are Experiencing Homelessness

VIKKI C. TERRILE

When you hear the word *homeless*, what comes to mind? A hard-drinking man sleeping on a sidewalk or a park bench? A woman wearing all the clothes she owns, pushing a shopping cart piled with the rest of her belongings? More than one-and-a-half million American children?

As shocking as it may be to think of children being homeless, the reality is that families with children had been the fastest growing subpopulation of people experiencing homelessness even before the Great Recession. The subprime mortgage crisis, joblessness, and the economic collapse only made a growing problem much worse. With estimates consistently at more than 1.5 million homeless children in the U.S. (NCFH 2009), these children are everywhere, but you may not know who they are when they visit your library. Unlike "street homeless" adults, the invisibility of homeless children and families is more about blending in than not being seen by the rest of the nation. It is likely, especially in libraries in the urban and suburban communities hardest hit by the recession, that you are already seeing homeless children and families without knowing it. Some of this is by design; there is an overlap between the family homeless systems and child protection systems, and fear of losing children to foster care motivates parents to mask their situation as much as possible.

Why should libraries worry about reaching kids who are experiencing homelessness? Kids who are homeless face a huge array of obstacles to learning, problems with their mental and physical health, and other barriers to success, some of which libraries can help to address. In particular, study after study has shown that students who are experiencing homelessness miss many more days of school, are more likely to be tracked into special education classes, score worse in reading and math, and are less likely to graduate than their stably housed peers (Walker-Dalhouse and Risko 2008; Noll and Watkins 2003). Some evidence even suggests that the experience of homelessness can alter brain development, particularly in very young children, a real crisis when one considers that children under six account for more than forty percent of homeless children (NCFH 2011).

What Is Homelessness?

While sleeping on the street, in a park, or in a car may be what comes to mind when we think of homelessness, the majority of homeless kids are living "doubled-up" with extended family members or friends. Another quarter are living in shelters or other temporary housing, while the remaining kids are living in hotels/motels, are unsheltered, or move between these options (NCFH 2009). The McKinney-Vento Homeless Assistance Act, the federal legislation that ensures educational rights for students, protects youth "who lack a fixed, regular, and adequate nighttime residence," including those living doubled-up, in shelters, in hotels/motels/campgrounds, in cars or on the street, and those who are squatting (living in vacant or abandoned buildings), are migratory, or awaiting foster care placement (NCHE 2002). Under McKinney-Vento, school districts must have a liaison to provide assistance for homeless children and make registration and transportation issues less burdensome for parents. The law allows children who are homeless to attend the school local to their temporary housing location or remain in the school they were attending before they became homeless, with provisions for transportation.

Finding Homeless Children and Families

Given that so many families experiencing homelessness fly under the radar, how do you find them? The first thing to do is learn both how homelessness is addressed on the state and local levels in your area and how it is experienced by families. The involvement of municipalities in providing services to people experiencing homelessness varies dramatically, with some municipalities deeply involved in the provision of services, and others not at all. At the same time, if most of the families experiencing homelessness in your community are not living in shelters or receiving services, finding them will be more difficult. To get a sense of where your state stands, take advantage of the many resources available online, including:

- The National Center on Family Homelessness (NCFH): a nonprofit that provides research, advocacy, training, and strategies for eliminating child and family homelessness (www.familyhomelessness.org/).
- The Institute for Children, Poverty & Homelessness (ICPH): an independent research nonprofit that conducts a range of analyses on child and family homelessness (www.icphusa.org/).
- *The National Survey of Programs and Services for Homeless Families: The Red, White, and Blue Book*: the results of annual surveys and research by ICPH (www.redwhiteandbluebook.org/).
- The United States Conference of Mayors: the non-partisan organization of mayors of U.S. cities with populations over 30,000; they conduct an annual survey on hunger and homelessness (www.usmayors.org/).

Another avenue for area-specific information is your local school district. The McKinney-Vento liaison may wear more than one hat, but will have invaluable information on what homeless students in your community are experiencing and where they are. At Queens Library, we work extensively with our McKinney-Vento liaisons at both the borough (county) and shelter levels, and we are regularly included in the events they host for homeless families.

You may be wondering why, if federal law mandates educational rights for children and teens experiencing homelessness, libraries need to do outreach to them and their families. There are several reasons. First, despite the mandates, homeless children and youth still face barriers to school attendance at greater rates than their stably housed peers. They tend to have much more frequent and chronic absenteeism, both because of health problems related to their poverty and homelessness, and because of problems traveling to and from school (NCFH 2009). For students opting to remain at their old schools, travel time can add up to several hours a day; imagine the toll this can take on children and what that extra time cuts into (time for homework, enrichment activities, etc.). So, while it is *possible* regular school outreach will reach students who are experiencing homelessness, it's far more hit-and-miss than it would be in reaching students who are stably housed. In addition, many of the children experiencing homelessness are not yet school-age. Outreach at shelters or through other service providers will reach parents and younger children in addition to school-age kids and teens. In case you're still not convinced that it's worth the effort, understand that several nonprofits around the country exist to provide reading and literacy programs for homeless children. They are wonderful programs, often staffed by dedicated volunteers, but while the work they do is invaluable, shouldn't libraries and librarians really be the ones doing it?

Partnerships and Policies

Once you have a good understanding of who your homeless families are and how services are provided in your community, what should the next steps be? As with all outreach, connecting with providers, schools, and families should be about forming good, mutually beneficial relationships. Key to making these relationships strong and lasting is a commitment on the library's end to provide these services and make necessary changes to accommodate them. You may need to make decisions (likely at the administrative level) about how or if your policies will need to be amended (or at least circumvented) to serve homeless families. Library card registration policies are of particular concern. If you require proof of residency or an address to get a library card, you will have to decide what you will accept from families living in temporary housing in lieu of mail, utility bills, or other proof of address. Some options are:

- Ask for a letter from shelter staff or other providers (or the homeowner for doubled-up families) verifying the family resides at a particular address.
- Bring the library card application process physically to shelters (this verifies residency, but you can still request ID).
- Work with school staff to complete library card applications for children through the school.

Be mindful that some families experiencing homelessness are in domestic violence situations and may need extra precautions to protect their privacy. Parents may be reluctant to even get library cards for fear their whereabouts will be accessible somehow. Work with social service providers, school staff, and the parents to find a viable option. For example, if the agency has a headquarters mailing address, use that in place of their residence address, or see if there is a post office box instead of a street address you can use.

You will also need to consider options for handling existing or new fees and fines for children and families experiencing homelessness. It can be difficult for stably housed families to always return all of their materials on time; think about some of the added obstacles homeless families may have. Repeated (and often sudden) relocations alone can make it difficult to keep track of library materials, but should not act as a barrier to service. Consider offering general amnesty policies or other programs to reduce or dismiss fees and fines to families experiencing homelessness. If you are not sure what policy measures would best serve homeless families in your community, ask parents and providers what would work for them. One idea, especially if your library isn't within easy distance of a shelter or service provider, is to provide a deposit collection for families there, or a collection box that families without good transportation options can use to return their materials (more on these ideas later).

It is possible some shelter or service staff may not see library services as a priority given the many pressing survival needs of the families they serve and the bureaucratic demands they face in service delivery. This is the time to be activists and advocates, not just for library services, but for the rights of homeless children and families. Remember, good partnerships work equally well for all the partners, so always frame your approach around what the library can do for providers and their clients rather than how they can help you. Many of the services that providers look for or are asked to provide to homeless families are already offered in public libraries: job readiness services, adult education and ESOL services, computer access and instructional classes, children's education and enrichment activities. Some shelters also do not allow clients (even those with young children) to remain onsite during the day; spending time in the library and attending programs fills some of that time with meaningful, engaging activities.

Perhaps the most important reason for doing targeted outreach to families experiencing homelessness is simply that it connects people to the community in a way few other services do. If nothing else, offering a connection to something as stable and respected as a public library can be a much-needed acknowledgment that families are seen and valued even if they don't have permanent housing.

Outreach Program Ideas

Once you have found your homeless kids and families and have a commitment from partners and your library, your library is all set to go. The good news is that almost anything you do in the library can be taken "on the road" to do effective outreach.

• Storytimes. Baby lapsit and preschool storytimes should definitely be part of your menu of services for family shelters and other agencies. Anything that reinforces early literacy can only help young children experiencing homelessness, and providing parents a safe space and time to interact with their youngsters in a fun and shame-free way will serve both parent and child. Keep in mind that many of the social services aimed at parents can be punitive and demeaning, so be supportive of the parents as you model reading and good parenting behaviors, the same way you would be with your other moms and dads.

• Story and craft programs. What child doesn't enjoy storytime followed by an arts-and-crafts activity? Whether for preschool or early school-age children, book and craft programs are always a huge hit. At Queens Library, we work with a very large family shelter where at least 10 to 20 of the hundreds of school-age kids do not attend summer camp at any given time in July and August. The weekly story and craft programs we do as part of summer reading has kids as young as five and as old as 15, but somehow, it works! At this particular shelter, their onsite summer program follows a thematic curriculum; in 2011 their "countries of the world"

"Carmen Miranda" portrait made with fruit candies. The craft was part of a 2011 summer reading event held at a Queens family shelter.

theme matched perfectly with our summer reading program theme, and we read stories and made crafts for each country they studied.

 • Summer reading. Many shelters and service providers have summer camp opportunities available for homeless children and teens, so summer can be a relatively quiet time to do programs. Still, not every child is able to attend, and most are not gone the entire summer. Taking your summer reading program to a shelter or service provider is another good way to reach children who are especially vulnerable to the "summer slide." Homeless children and teens are more likely than their peers to be reading below grade level (Walker-Dalhouse and Risko 2008), so be sure to structure your program in a way that supports all readers. For example, instead of counting numbers of books or pages read, use time read as your metric. Work with the kids to find books that are interesting to them and are good fits for their reading levels. Finally, be cautious about making children read aloud in group settings. Many strong readers struggle with reading aloud, never mind those who are not confident in their silent reading abilities. You never want reading to be connected with shame or embarrassment on your watch, so look for other, less stressful ways to strengthen skills or share books in groups.

• Book clubs. Older elementary-age children, middle schoolers, and high schoolers may be interested in book clubs or other reading groups. Here again, the reading levels may not be on grade, so make sure to include both the youth and the staff in picking materials for the group to read. Short stories, newspaper articles, and poetry may all be better options, especially if there is frequent turnover of participants. It may also be difficult for youth to get quiet time in their family's living space to read large chunks of a novel between sessions; in some cases, bullying from other youth or family members may even make a child reluctant to bring a book back with them. Again, these are all things your partner agency will be able to help you address if they become an issue.

• Writing programs. Older children and teens tend to enjoy writing programs even if

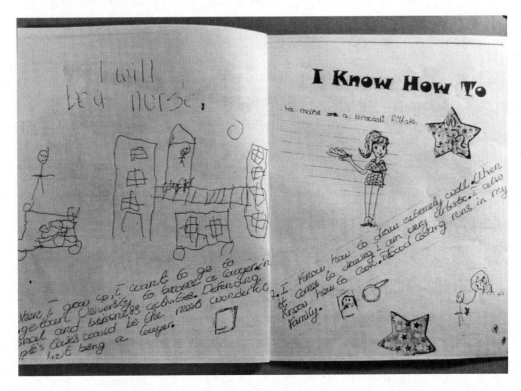

The 2011 summer reading program "zine" at a Queens family shelter.

they are not strong readers. There are many good resources for simple creative writing and poetry programs online; you don't have to reinvent the wheel! Once the writing starts to flow, consider putting together a zine or literary journal of the children's artwork, stories, and poems. Even if you don't have access to computers, have the kids copy their final drafts in their best handwriting, cut and paste a hardcopy master together, and photocopy. Done this way, they look very edgy and DIY!

Other Ideas for Shelters and Service Providers

Depending on what your shelters or service providers are looking for and able to accommodate, you can also bring services other than programming right to their site.

Some inexpensive and easy ideas are:

• Library cards. As discussed earlier, it can be difficult for parents and children who are homeless to get a new library card, depending on what you require for proof of residency. Once you have found a solution at the policy level, it may not work well in practice. Sadly, stories from parents that staff members were rude and insensitive when asking for a letter from the shelter to document their residency are not uncommon. It can be difficult enough for parents to admit they are living in temporary housing; if you cannot guarantee that they will be treated with fairness and dignity when they walk through your doors to apply for a card, consider bringing the application process to them.

• Deposit collections. Especially helpful for locations where transportation is an obstacle to regular library use, a deposit collection that is tailored to the particular needs of the site is a good way to meet an underserved population's reading needs while boosting your library's circulation. An assortment of fiction and nonfiction at the children's, young adult, adult levels should be included. Create a menu of genres and topics clients and staff can choose from to make the collection work, and experiment with the loan period to see how much time is needed to change out the collection.

• Return bins. If your library is particularly worried about lost or late materials, consider leaving a return bin or box at the shelters or service provider sites you are working with. Of course this means someone on your staff will have to pick up the returns on a regular basis, but if you are doing regular programming there, it may be worth the effort.

Ideas to Reach Homeless Families Not Receiving Services

For families who are living doubled-up or otherwise not receiving services, finding them can be especially difficult. If they have immigration or other legal issues that make them fearful of the library, it is even harder to reach them. But some simple ideas can help, and may also reach other underserved families:

• Go where they go. Take your outreach to places families have to visit regularly and for chunks of time, including laundromats, clinic waiting rooms, soup kitchens, and food pantries. Five-minute programs, especially for antsy little kids, will be a boon to parents and may wear away nervousness about the library. If you can give away books or other items while sharing information about your services, even better!

• Step-up your school outreach. If you learn that there are many homeless students attending school but not living in shelters or receiving other services, ramp up your school visits and outreach. This will increase the likelihood that you will reach as many students as possible. Consider creating packets students can take home with library card applications for the whole family, promotional materials, and other information meant for parents.

Other Ideas to Help Families

Many outreach activities aimed at homeless families will also help those struggling to stay afloat or those just getting by. The more support libraries can show to families and children, the more likely they are to keep coming back.

• Open your doors. Set up a table outside in nice weather, especially if you are on a busy street, or find out where you can have a table in a high-traffic area. Walk your neighborhood and be a good neighbor; go to PTA and community meetings, introduce yourself to shop owners and your local faith-based organizations. Be visible! At the same time, consider having an open house with light refreshments and a welcoming atmosphere.

• Collection drives. Consider hosting a collection drive for the shelters and providers you are partnering with in the library. Working with the agency staff to see what the needs are, library staff and the general public can contribute school supplies in the fall or new toys for the holiday season. Things like toiletries and laundry supplies are often needed year-round. Canned food drives are also easy to organize and, given our record numbers of even stably-housed families facing food instability and hunger, greatly needed.

• Resource fairs. If your library has a large enough meeting space, consider hosting a resource fair for homeless families, health and wellness fairs, and other events that bring services under one roof. Work with other municipal agencies, nonprofits, and faith-based organizations to find providers while adding fun activities and programs for the children. Make sure you serve food at these events (find a sponsor who will cater it for free or reduced cost).

• Task force or committee meetings. Again, if you have meeting spaces, consider hosting a meeting of service providers. If there is an existing homeless services task force or committee in your area, make sure the library has a seat at the table, and step up to be a resource for them. If there is nothing formal, build on the partnerships you have created to craft something unofficial; the more resources you and your partners have, the more you can offer your families.

In the end, anything you do to reach kids, teens, and families who are experiencing homelessness will only improve your services to other families in your community, both those you see regularly, and those who have never walked through your doors.

Works Cited

NCFH (National Center on Family Homelessness). 2009. "State Report Card on Child Homelessness: America's Youngest Outcasts." *http://www.homelesschildrenamerica.org/documents/rc_summary_004.pdf* (accessed December 19, 2012).

_____. "The Characteristics and Needs of Families Experiencing Homelessness." http://www.familyhomelessness.org/media/306.pdf (accessed December 19, 2012).

NCHE (National Center for Homeless Education). 2002. *McKinney-Vento Act* (42 U.S.C.11431 et seq.). http://www2.ed.gov/programs/homeless/legislation.html (accessed May 18, 2013).

Noll, E., and R. Watkins. 2003. "The Impact of Homelessness on Children's Literacy Experiences." *The Reading Teacher* 57 (4): 362–371.

Walker-Dalhouse, D., and V.J. Risko. 2008. "Homelessness, Poverty, and Children's Literacy Development." *The Reading Teacher* 62 (1): 84–86.

Booktalking for Incarcerated Teens
Scalable, Sustainable Success from the Hennepin County Home School
Sara Zettervall *and* Amy Mars

Once a month throughout the academic year, staff members from Hennepin County Library (HCL) in Minnesota present interactive booktalks to adolescent students incarcerated at the County Home School (CHS). HCL staff also deliver books and magazines, take student requests for future visits, and demonstrate how the public library system can help students at CHS transition back into life after incarceration. This library service is transformative and positive for the librarians and volunteers who participate, as well as for the CHS students. This essay describes:

- The unique population served at CHS
- A brief history of outreach to juvenile corrections provided by HCL
- How library staff prepare for booktalking at CHS, including tips for delivering outstanding, interactive booktalks
- How the booktalking program is evaluated
- How other libraries can modify the CHS model to implement similar programming in their communities

Population and Setting

CHS is part of the Hennepin County Department of Community Corrections and Rehabilitation, and "is a state-licensed residential treatment center for adolescent male and female offenders ages 13 to 20 who have been committed by the court" (Hennepin County 2012c). The total population averages fifty students at any given time, divided into small group homes known as "cottages." The teens at CHS are exposed to a wide range of educational and vocational programs, including an on-site school and a 5,000-volume library collection maintained by HCL Outreach Services staff. They also receive targeted behavioral therapy, which treats a range of mental health and behavioral issues and prepares them to transition back into the community upon release. The teens housed at the County Home School are sorted into three groups:

- The Girl's Focus Program consists of adolescent females who are at CHS under court order or come from social services after being removed from their homes due to neglect and abuse. They must demonstrate a history of failed community-based interventions and exhibit a pattern of acting out, resulting in harm to themselves or others (Hennepin County 2012b).
- The Short-Term Adolescent Male Program (STAMP) consists of adolescent males who come to CHS from Community Corrections and Rehabilitation and receive treatment for either 90 to 120 days or four to six months, depending on their assessed risk status (Hennepin County 2012d).
- The Adolescent and Family Sexual Health Services program consists of adolescent males who have committed sexual-based offenses and are committed to the facility to protect the public and undergo treatment and rehabilitation (Hennepin County 2012a).

Although the ethnicity and gender of the students at CHS vary, African American males typically make up the majority of students. Most students also come from neighborhoods with high rates of crime, poverty, and gang-related activity. Many come from homes where they experience neglect, abuse (physical, emotional, and/or sexual), chemical addiction, and lack of structure. Largely because of these hardships, the students at CHS have not had the benefit of a quality and consistent education and may struggle or show little interest in reading, which is why it is especially important and impactful for the public library system to reach out to them.

History and Structure

HCL has been providing library service and booktalking at the County Home School for more than fifteen years as part of a larger outreach effort called the Great Transitions program, a coordinated effort between Hennepin County Library Outreach Services, local school districts, and Hennepin County Community Corrections and Rehabilitation. The program was established to "provide access to library materials and services to adjudicated young people during and after their court-ordered stay at CHS and as they transition back to their community on probation" (Chelton 2000, 11). In addition to booktalks, students experience author visits, write and publish a zine called *Diverse City*, and participate in Read to Me, a program that introduces young parents to early literacy basics and allows them to record themselves reading a book to send home and share with their children. Prior to release from CHS, students are given an exit survey that includes questions related to reading and the library, and any fines they accumulated at HCL before entering the facility are waived.

The booktalks given by HCL as part of Great Transitions encourage students to check out books from the County Home School's on-site library or to request books from one of HCL's 41 library locations, which are then delivered to them. The goals of the booktalking program are as follows:

- Provide library services to the residents of CHS, who would otherwise experience barriers to full utilization of library materials and services due to their incarceration

- Promote interest in reading through exposure to books specifically selected to meet the interests of CHS students and reflect their life experiences
- Expand the reading interests of CHS students by exposing them to a variety of fiction/nonfiction and teen/adult materials
- Expose CHS students to the materials and services available at the public library and promote future library use upon release from CHS

Booktalking

Booktalks at CHS run on a monthly basis throughout each academic year. Scheduling begins each summer when an e-mail goes out to all librarians in the HCL system, asking them to sign up in pairs for booktalking visits. Outreach Services helps new and continuing staff and volunteers to participate in the program by providing materials on how to prepare and deliver booktalks. Each CHS booktalker receives tip sheets with guidelines for selection and presentation. Those materials address common questions and concerns, such as how to choose materials, how to deliver a booktalk, connecting with the audience, and using book trailers.

How Do I Choose Materials to Booktalk?

- Start with a list of suggested titles. HCL staff created an internal website with lists of the most requested books from CHS students over the years. Booktalkers are also encouraged to check out the "Growing Up" lists featured publicly on the TeenLinks section of the HCL website[1] (which are based on the experiences and preferences of CHS students) and to visit YALSA's website on book awards and book lists.[2]
- Avoid repetition. Check to make sure that books have not been booktalked in the previous six months. HCL maintains a database to track this information, but a smaller library system with fewer booktalkers could use a simpler self-reporting system.
- Take stock. Make sure the selected books have ample copies available in the library system. This ensures student requests can be filled in a timely fashion.
- Mix it up. Choose materials that are a mix of fiction, nonfiction, poetry, and graphic novels. Include selections from the children's chapter books, YA, and adult sections of the library.
- Be appropriate. When selecting materials for young adults, take care to avoid heavy sexual or violent content. For example, CHS does not allow any books from adult "street lit" publishers.

Surveys of CHS students have consistently shown that favorite books have fast-paced plots featuring teens battling inner demons, embroiled in intense peer relationships, and overcoming family trauma. Authors such as Paul Volponi, Coe Booth, Jacqueline Woodson, Tim Bowler, and Simone Elkeles, as well as series such as *Kimani Tru* and *Bluford High*, are sure bets when looking for material to appeal to incarcerated teens. Nonfiction subjects such as memoir, true crime, music, and sports are also favorites year after year at CHS. But even the most unlikely books can be big hits if presented in the right way. For example, one year book-talkers enthralled students by incorporating magic routines into their talks when promoting a handful of books on street magic. Another popular team of booktalkers pulled a prank with fake dog poop they baked to promote *100% Pure Fake: Gross Out Your Friends and Family with 25 Great Special Effects* by Lyn Thomas.

How Do I Deliver a Booktalk?

Booktalking is a short performance that "sells" a book to a specific audience. Much like the blurb on a book jacket, the content of a booktalk teases readers into wanting to find out what happens in a book. And it works: in responses collected over the years at CHS, students, many of whom are reluctant readers, have reiterated that booktalks help them find and connect with books they would not have thought about otherwise. The basic tips for delivering a book-talk, as stated in *Connecting with Reluctant Teen Readers*,[3] are:

- Don't booktalk a book you haven't read!
- Don't booktalk a book you don't like!
- Never tell the ending!
- Don't make it too long (2–5 minutes).
- It's okay to use notes—Post-it notes on the backs of books are good.
- Make eye contact with your audience—keep looking around.
- Give the author and title and show the cover (Jones, Hartman, and Taylor 2006, 231).

One thing to remember is that while booktalks should be clever and engaging, they can also be scripted. A booktalk that is familiar to the presenting librarian can be new to the audience and will be that much more entertaining because it has been practiced before. HCL Outreach Services has accumulated dozens of sample booktalks for use at CHS, and any library establishing a new booktalking program should plan to save its successful booktalks to share with future booktalkers. Sample booktalks can also be found on NoveList, in *Connecting with Reluctant Teen Readers*, and through other sources. The most important thing, especially with teens, is to be genuinely enthusiastic, so librarians should do what they need to do to be comfortable in front of the crowd. One of the key components of the HCL program design is having staff work in pairs, which aids comfort, creative interaction, and interest for students.

How Do I Connect with My Audience?

Teens, whether they are incarcerated or in a standard classroom, are a tough crowd. While the subjects that interest them will be diverse, they all share the fact that they are teenagers, so librarians should design booktalks with their social/emotional needs in mind. Wrapped up as they are in their own lives, teens respond well when adults demonstrate that they see them as individuals and respect their opinions. In booktalks at CHS, librarians have successfully done this by creating opportunities for choice:

- Choice of booktalks. Bring more materials than can be covered in the allotted time, and have students vote on which ones they want to hear about.
- Choice of format. Incarcerated students will likely not have access to CD players or digital music players (e.g., iPods). But when students can access audiobooks, make sure they know this is an option.
- Choice of requests. Give students a chance to request books at the end of the session. At CHS, students are allowed to borrow up to two books at a time that are delivered to them in class.

Booktalkers can also engage students in discussion by asking what they think of the books on hand, books they have already read on the similar topics, or books by the same author. Give students a chance to speak out, ask questions, and make recommendations to their friends. Invite audience members to read compelling dialogue portions aloud. Listen and respond to requests they may make for types of books to bring in the future. Being involved in the process of choosing books makes students feel respected and invested in the program.

What About Book Trailers?

HCL also uses book trailers, which are short videos created by librarians, volunteers, or publishers to promote books. Libraries that have the resources can create their own book trailers. Those that lack the time or the resources may consider using existing online resources, such as trailers found on YouTube and publishers' websites, or collaborating with library science students to create new trailers. HCL worked with students at St. Catherine University who created book trailers for CHS as part of a class on social justice in children and young adult literature. Although that collaboration took place locally, similar projects could take place at a distance or with an online program. However, while book trailers can be a stimulating addition to a booktalk, some booktalkers at CHS find that trailers can distract from the books themselves and reduce the number of opportunities for interaction and discussion with students. Trailers are great for generating excitement but should be considered a supplement—not a substitute—for in-person booktalking.

Evaluation

The success and sustainability of booktalking at CHS is due in large part to the ongoing assessment efforts of HCL staff. HCL employs two types of evaluation methods: informal interviews and surveys. Informal interviews are used to capture quotes from booktalkers and CHS students as well as gather impromptu and open-ended feedback. Separate surveys are given to the booktalkers and to the students. A mixture of qualitative and quantitative data captured through the interviews and surveys provides useful feedback to ensure that the program responds to changes in technology, student demographics, and reading trends. Continuous evaluation of the program also ensures that HCL meets its goals, responds to input from CHS students and volunteer booktalkers, and captures data demonstrating the impact of the program.

Surveys of booktalkers are primarily used to ensure that library volunteers are given all the resources they need to deliver exceptional booktalks that appeal to the unique interests and needs of CHS students. The survey data is also used to identify areas of improvement and to showcase the reasons that librarians and volunteers offer up time out of their busy schedules to participate in the booktalking program. The passion and enthusiasm shared by volunteer booktalkers can be used to validate the program's success within the library system as well as recruit other librarians to volunteer their time.

CHS students are given two types of surveys: a survey to evaluate their experience of the booktalks each academic year, and an exit survey comparing their reading habits and library use before and after entering the facility. Surveys each academic year record the students' overall reactions to the booktalks. Results show that CHS students enjoy the booktalks for the following reasons:

- Variety. Students enjoy a wide variety of fiction and nonfiction genres/categories and prefer shorter booktalks that expose them to a large array of reading material.
- Participation. Students report that being able to interact with booktalkers and choose the books they hear about is very important to them.
- Creative presentation. Students note that the interesting presentation styles, the use of book trailers, and the enthusiasm of booktalkers all contribute to sparking their interest in reading.

Alternatively, feedback about what the CHS students dislike about the booktalks has been used to make the booktalks more interactive and to advocate for letting the students request more titles at a time. These surveys also show which books are consistently popular with CHS students and reveal shifts in reading interests due to trends in popular culture and changes in CHS demographics. This information is shared with booktalkers to give them further insight into CHS students and their particular needs.

The data collected in interviews and surveys is used to measure the significant impact that booktalks are making in the lives of teens at CHS. The majority of students surveyed (ranging from just over half to more than 70 percent from 2008–2011) report reading books that they normally would not have read because they heard about them in booktalks. More than 90 percent of students request one or more books after seeing a booktalk, and 57 percent request two or three books after seeing a booktalk. Exit surveys from 2010 reveal the larger impact that booktalks have on students' lives.

- Prior to entering the County Home School, 65 percent of students report not reading any books. At the end of their incarceration, 23 percent report reading one or two books per month, and 83 percent of students report reading upwards of five books per month.
- Prior to entering the County Home School, 60 percent of students report using the library "never" or "hardly ever." At the time of release, after experiencing booktalks and other library services provided on-site, 88 percent of students plan on using the library "all the time" or "a lot."

Over time, the combined effect of booktalks, library services, and a consistent educational experience leads to students who read more while in the facility and report intentions to continue their reading habits and library use after release from incarceration.

Replication in Other Libraries

The model provided by HCL can be used by any library that wishes to provide outreach to a local juvenile correctional facility. However, there is also a great deal of potential for successful application in other situations.

- Public schools. School library media specialists looking for a way to reach out to classrooms may find they can use booktalks to promote their library internally. Or, public librarians in districts where school library services have been shut down for lack of funding could use this model to develop their own program.
- Alternative or charter schools. Often, these schools are underfunded and do not have their own libraries, so their only library contact is through the public library system.
- Community centers. At-risk teens who may not know about public library services can often be reached through local community centers. Existing clubs and after-school programs may be happy to host a monthly booktalk.
- Youth shelters. Booktalking items that appeal to homeless teens is a great opportunity to promote the library's materials and resources to a group that often lacks basic support to succeed in school.

The ideas presented in this essay are best utilized in partnership with a juvenile correction outreach program or with local schools, but not all library systems have the resources to accomplish this. Here are some suggestions for finding additional volunteers to staff the program:

- School volunteers. Many schools will have active Parent Teacher Associations or Organizations (PTAs/PTOs) that can help. If the partnering school does not have a PTA/PTO (which is often the case in schools with the most at-risk teens), they may have an existing volunteer network to tap.
- Public library volunteers and Friends groups. Library volunteers who want a break from shelving may enjoy the challenges and rewards of booktalking. Friends of the Library, who will likely be impressed with program evaluation data, can also help recruit volunteers.
- Library school students. Libraries located near graduate programs in library science can reach out for free help from students. In addition to the previous example of the HCL/St. Catherine University partnership in creating book trailers, both authors of this essay served as unpaid interns in HCL Outreach Services while they were students and were enthusiastic participants in the outreach services provided to CHS.

Above all, think creatively. Are there specific groups of teens that are in need of outreach services (like the students of CHS)? Where do teens congregate? How can the library bring its services to them? Is there someone in a leadership position at that location who can be the connection to get started? Often, the best and most lasting program support comes from partnerships with other enthusiastic organizations, such as those involved in Great Transitions. Talk to community members about creating a program like the one at CHS, and follow up wherever there is a spark of interest. At the very least, reaching out to establish a booktalking program such as the one described in this essay will help build new community connections and awareness of library services. Where programs like this one succeed and flourish, they can have a lifelong impact on the reading habits of teens.

Notes

1. http://www.hclib.org/teens/.
2. http://www.ala.org/yalsa/booklistsawards/booklistsbook.
3. This book is strongly recommended for more in-depth information on promoting books to teens, as well as for sample booktalks and more detailed instruction on reaching reluctant readers. These tips come from the section "Booktalking 101," compiled by Maureen L. Hartman.

Works Cited

Chelton, Mary K. 2000. *Excellence in Library Services to Young Adults: The Nation's Top Programs*, 3d ed. Chicago: American Library Association.

Hennepin County. 2012a. "Adolescent and Family Sexual Health Services." http://hennepin.us/portal/site/HennepinUS/menuitem.b1ab75471750e40fa01dfb47ccf06498/?vgnextoid=3f0d392732948310VgnVCM20000098fe4689RCRD (accessed October 13, 2012).

_____. 2012b. "Girl's Focus Program." http://hennepin.us/portal/site/HennepinUS/menuitem.b1ab75471750e40fa01dfb47ccf06498/?vgnextoid=a53de2aba6938310VgnVCM20000098fe4689RCRD (accessed October 13, 2012).

_____. 2012c. "Hennepin County Home School." http://hennepin.us/portal/site/HennepinUS/menuitem.b1ab75471750e40fa01dfb47ccf06498/?vgnextoid=4e38bd7d23e23210VgnVCM20000048114689RCRD (accessed October 13, 2012).

_____. 2012d. "Short-Term Adolescent Male Programs." http://hennepin.us/portal/site/HennepinUS/menuitem.b1ab75471750e40fa01dfb47ccf06498/?vgnextoid=aa2ce2aba6938310VgnVCM20000098fe4689RCRD (accessed October 13, 2012).

Jones, Patrick, Maureen L. Hartman, and Patricia Taylor. 2006. *Connecting with Reluctant Teen Readers: Tips, Titles, and Tools*. New York: Neal-Schuman.

Youth Focus Groups
Finding Out What Patrons Really Want

BRITTANY NETHERS

Why You Need a Focus Group

Outreach in the form of a focus group is a great way to get to know your target audience. I wanted to better understand what the teens in our library wanted, what they found important in their lives, and how we could help meet their needs. I know, you think you don't have time to host a focus group, but if you do not make time to fully understand your patrons and their needs, all your hard work planning and implementing programs and services could be in vain.

The best way to reach your target audience is to go where they are. Have the moderator of your youth focus groups hold the session at a local school, activity center, or other similar location. These visits are a great form of outreach since focus groups will not only get library staff out into the community, making connections, but the sessions will also provide ideas and feedback from a perspective other than that of an insider, and without the bias of being held inside of a library building.

One of the good things about having focus groups is that they are qualitative instead of quantitative, so they provide in-depth answers. For example, on an interest survey teens might answer that they want more "creative activities" in their local library, but a focus group will help explain what these "activities" consist of. Do these activities include arts and crafts, model building competitions, or enhanced technology offerings? Focus groups are great for answering these more in-depth types of questions, and they may even answer questions you did not have previously. Although the results will generally not be in a statistics-style format, they will definitely be useful.

Qualitative methods like these are helpful when diagnosing a situation, better defining a problem area, defining pliable alternatives, and discovering new ideas (Hyman and Sierra 2010). This type of exploratory study relies on smaller samples but allows for greater interaction with the consumers (in our case, patrons).

And here is why youth focus groups, in particular, are necessary: you are not a child. Even parents cannot get inside their children's heads, so how can you expect to? You do not see why kids or teens do the things they do or feel the way they feel. Getting opinions and advice directly from a child through a series of open-ended questions in a group setting may be the best way to gain insight. These group sessions work well for all ages for a variety of reasons. The group's synergy is quite valuable because the comments of one participant will trigger those of other participants, giving a variety of opinions and thoughts from the sample group. Groups consisting of six to 12 persons tend to make individuals feel more secure and allow for more validation than would an individual interview (Hyman and Sierra 2010). As a result, focus groups are necessary to continue improving library services, especially for children and teens.

Getting Started

There are some basic steps to getting started with group interview sessions. Here is a basic outline that I used for my first few focus groups.

1. Decide which customers to target (e.g., what age, sex, socioeconomic bracket).

2. Decide which library section or branch location needs feedback or patrons' opinions.

3. Decide where you want to host groups. These could be at public schools, recreation centers, or even at a market research facility.

4. Decide how many focus groups should be hosted and if this number will give you an accurate depiction of the target audience.

5. Decide how many people should be in each group. Many experts believe six to 10 participants will encourage conversation but still allow for individual opinions to be heard. Other experts think eight to 12 participants make for a better group.

6. Decide who will moderate during these sessions and what their preparation or background experience will need to consist of, or if the moderator should be a professional. Those who do this for a living will have more experience than the average library employee, and they will know what behaviors to avoid. Professionals will, however, require payment for their services.

7. Decide if group members should be compensated and, if so, how? A Businessweek article titled *How to Conduct a Focus Group* says, "If you hire a firm, a focus group can cost $2,000 to $5,000, including the $75-$100 fee paid to each participant" (Lee 2009).

8. Select the place for the session at each location, ensuring a comfortable and friendly environment, considering temperature and seating arrangements. Be aware that hosting a session at the library could give the group a bias, so this may not be the best place for the sessions.

After considering all the options, start getting together a timeline of events, contact an impartial moderator or marketing research facility, and contact area schools and parents as necessary for the target audience. Make sure to plan for a time of year that would be best for these groups. Are children in special classes at those times or on holiday breaks? Are there testing schedules to be aware of? If the sessions are not at a school, will parents generally be able to drive their children to a facility, or are they at work at these times?

Another thing to be conscious of is the target age group. It is not enough to break categories down by kids and teens; subgroups will need to be made. Is this service for the six-year-olds or the 10-year-olds? There is a big difference in interest levels. And what about teens? The 18-year-old seniors in high school will not have the same interests as their 13-year-old middle school counterparts; skill levels and topic appropriateness can be completely different, as well. Kids and teens should be grouped into smaller age ranges; six- and seven-year-olds should be placed in one group and 10- and 11-year-olds in another. A group for girls and a different group for boys may also be applicable (Guber and Berry 1993).

Youth Focus Groups 101

As you prepare for group sessions, follow these tips for effective focus groups:

• Finding participants. If a company is hired to host these groups, finding participants should be relatively easy. Participants just need to be the target audience for the service or location. If library staff will be hosting the focus groups and gathering participants, a person acting as a recruiter will be needed to screen potential participants and gather the correct group of people. If new users are your target audience, for instance, the person screening will make sure the users haven't been coming to the library for five years or more. The screener will also have to make sure that participants are the target demographics and are interested in participating. Another thing to be aware of when selecting group members is that all participants are not created equal. Overly talkative participants and those who are accustomed to supervising and directing others may not be best for your group since they may lead or dominate the session. In addition, members who attend focus groups regularly are not the ideal candidates. Those who are new to the ideas of marketing research may be the best candidates, and as a result, children often make great group members.

• Recording sessions. Find a way to record the group sessions, if possible. The personal information of participants should be completely confidential. They should be notified that they are being recorded. This does include notifying minors of audio or video recordings that will be taking place, as well as their parents.

• Parental consent for recording. Be sure to get parental consent beforehand to record any minors, preferably in writing. Make every attempt to notify parents about the focus groups ahead of time even if no recording will be taking place. Explain to parents what exactly their children will be participating in and how this will, in turn, benefit the community.

• Decide which questions to ask. Once the goals of these groups are determined, think about which questions might lead to the needed responses. For example, if these in-depth answers should explain how to get teens into a specific library location after school, the moderator may need to ask, "What do you do after school?" or "If you had less homework and more time, how would you like to spend your afternoons?" to determine what activities are enjoyable. Attempt to use language that is simple enough for a young child to understand to make sure all participants comprehend your meaning. And avoid boring the group with dozens of questions by limiting the different topics to four to 10 items.

• Be flexible. While adults, teenagers, and older children will be used to sitting at tables or desks, younger participants may feel more comfortable sitting in a circle on the floor. This is a common way children share their opinions and listen to adults. However relaxed the environment may feel, it should be made clear to both children and teens that it is very important that they pay attention. In my last focus group at a local high school, the teens and I sat around four tables that were pushed together into a square shape while the teacher sat further outside of the circle.

• Develop a script. The introductory and closing phrases for the session will need to be created, as well as questions for the groups to respond to. The moderator should read the questions out loud several times and have listeners provide feedback about the neutrality and validity of the statements and questions. After receiving feedback, readjust as need. This is where a professional moderator and a marketing research facility would really come in handy. For me, this is the most difficult part of focus groups. Deciding on the proper line of questioning, phrasing, and the proper questions to ask in order to get the needed answers can be tricky. I wanted to find out what teens were interested in using the public library for, and I was going to ask, "Why do you need the library?" but per a suggestion, instead I asked the question, "Do you need the library?" and then I encouraged them to tell me why or why not. Even this slight rephrasing will have a big effect on the answers you will receive, so be selective when coming up with your questions.

• Length of session. The amount of time spent in a focus group session will depend on a variety of factors. The age of participants is instrumental in deciding the amount of time the group can stay functional. A three-year-old has a much shorter attention span than a 12-year-old, and likewise, a 14-year-old generally has a shorter attention span than that of adults. An example of catering to these differences can be seen at the Orlando Public Library in Orlando, Florida, where story programs for preschool-age children last 30 minutes, while programs for the 18- to 36-month-olds run only 25 minutes in length, and then the programs only lasts for 15 minutes for the 18 months and younger group. These story program lengths can also be used as a rule of thumb for the maximum amount of time children can actively participate. For teens and adults, the maximum length a session should be held is one or two hours. My middle school and high school focus groups have each lasted about a class period in length, which is about 50 minutes.

• Remind participants. A few days before a group is set to take place, give participants a courtesy phone call to remind them about the upcoming event.

• Moderator as group facilitator. The group moderator is not only in the group to ask questions, but this person's job is also to move the conversation through the list of questions, keeping the group on task. In addition, the moderator should be kind but firm, act engaged and enthusiastic, encouraging all participants to respond and be specific with their comments. They must also be able to improvise depending on the flow of the session and be sensitive to the comfort level of individuals (Hyman and Sierra 2010).

• Minimize outside influences. With children and teens, you will need to have the parents and teachers away from the children during the sessions; they do not need to steer the conversation in any directions or be part of the group's synergy. Responsible adults should be close enough to watch their children, but generally, they should not be close enough to converse with or influence the group.

• Hear all voices. Give all participants a chance to speak, and do not allow a few extroverted individuals to take over the group and do all the talking. If there is an outgoing participant who is dominating the group and talking too much, he or she will intimidate the shy participants. Remember that the opinions of timid guests are also needed. In addition, some participants will not feel comfortable enough to speak up, even without one of these self-appointed group leaders. The moderator's job in this situation is to direct questions towards the quieter personalities and to make sure they get a chance to speak their minds. The moderator will also need to direct questions towards persons they think will disagree with each other in order to keep the conversation flowing and opinions being shared.

Sample Teen Group Script

Moderator Introduction:

Hi. Thanks for coming to this focus group today. I'm Brittany Nethers. You guys can call me Brittany. I work downtown at the Orlando Public Library, that big gray building. I work with everyone from babies all the way up to 18-year-olds.

I'm here today to get your feedback about the public library and what we have to offer for people between the ages of 13 and 18—we're not talking about your library here at school, but the Orange County Library System. By participating today, you are helping us continue to improve what we have available for teens, not just for you all in this room, but for teens across the county, and for future Orange County teens.

We'll get started with a few questions about you all and the library. Just give me your opinions and keep the discussion rolling. And we want to make sure everyone has a chance to chime in, so be sure to speak up!

I am going to be recording the session with this little audio recorder. The recording will not be used for anything besides my notes. I will not quote your names or use the recording for anything besides my personal use.

Does anyone have any questions for me before we get started?

Okay, here we go!

Moderator Questions:

Warm-up Discussion: What do your friends think of the library?

1. *Free Time:*
   a. *What do you do after school?*
   b. *How would you like to spend free time if you had more of it?*
2. *Library Events and Contests:*
   a. *Have any of you participated in any events or contests from the public library?*
      i. *If so, why? If not, then why not?*
      ii. *What kinds of events would you come to at the public library?*
3. *Services and Materials:*
   a. *Are there any materials or services you wish the library offered?*
   b. *We have CDs, DVDs, computers, free downloadable books, and audiobooks you can listen to. What do you feel like you need from the library?*
      i. *Do you need the library?*
4. *We have a variety of events at your public libraries, including a battle of the bands downtown every summer, and in March we are having a promotion where you can get a free ticket to the Wake Games just for checking out five things.*

What would be the best way for the library to tell you about upcoming programs and contests like these?
   a. *Now that you know what we have to offer, would you be friends with us on Facebook to stay updated? Why/why not?*
   b. *What would you like to see or do on the library website?*
5. *Last question, what are some things you care about? In general.*

Thank you for your time. I do have some little thank-you gifts for you all participating in today's group. Thanks again!

The Day Of

On the day of the focus group meeting, the temperature of the room will need to be checked to make the area comfortable. Adjust seating arrangements to make the focus group zone as friendly and inviting as possible while still maintaining a sense of structure. For instance, if there is a large conference room, make sure there are a few tables together for the group in an open circle. Be sure that all participants are checked in before getting started. Collect any photo, video, or audio consent forms, as needed. Read through the questions one more time so it will be easy to progress to the next one easily if an individual brings up a corresponding topic.

Have the moderator take notes to ensure the most value from these sessions. Even if there is a video or audio recording device, notes should be taken to attempt to capture the momentum of the conversation and any additional thoughts the moderator has during these meetings.

Be prepared for negative feedback; these are honest answers. It was quite difficult for me to hear negative thoughts from teens about my library's services, but because of my previous knowledge of focus groups, I did not try to change their minds; instead I listened closely, took notes, and asked for more responses. Based on this feedback, decisions will need to be made. If there was that much negative feedback, then the areas that were focused on may need to be seriously revamped. Of course, everything patrons suggest will not be possible, but much of it will be. This is especially true with children and teens.

As the group is discussing the questions from the script, make notes about what works and what does not. In one of my focus groups, I noticed that my contact, the school media specialist, got together a group of her frequent library users. Out of this group of 10 teens, only one had not been to a public library in our area. I made sure to note that this was a skewed group of participants and that their answers did not accurately represent the entire population of teenagers.

Interpreting Conclusions

Now that you have asked the questions, you need to decide what to do with the answers. As soon as the session ends, gather your materials and take any additional notes needed to ensure you will understand your materials at a later date. The next step is to analyze these findings; start looking for themes and ideas that stand out, and take note. A written summary of each session is a necessary step to realizing findings and being able to share this information and these recommendations with supervisors and other decision-makers. In this summary, write up what was discussed and the general feedback, along with the main points of patrons' comments. Also, describe the participants, and determine if they were a true mix of the target audience. Then make additional notes about anything else that seemed relevant or important. Congratulations! You are now prepared for a focus group of your own.

Works Cited

Guber, Selina S., and Jon Berry. 1993. *Marketing to and Through Kids*. New York: McGraw Hill.
Hyman, Michael R., and Jeremy J. Sierra. 2010. *Marketing Research Kit for Dummies*. Hoboken: Wiley.
Lee, Louise. 2009. "How to Conduct a Focus Group." Businessweek Online, October 8. http://www.businessweek.com/stories/2009-10-08/how-to-conduct-a-focus-group (accessed September 14, 2012).

Outreach to Spanish-Speaking Families
Sarah Kaufman

How can we encourage more Spanish-speaking families to visit the public library? As the Hispanic population continues to grow in the United States, it is important that libraries strive to meet the needs of these communities, especially Spanish speakers with limited or no English language skills. Data from the 2010 Census showed a significant increase in the United States Hispanic population since the year 2000. From 2000 to 2010, the Hispanic population grew by 43 percent, an increase of 15.2 million. This was four times the nation's 9.7 percent total growth rate (USCB 2011). To meet the needs of this growing population, library services to Spanish speakers are critical. Many library systems have embraced services to Spanish speakers by making it a component of their mission statements and strategic plans. Despite good intentions, however, accomplishing this goal proves challenging. Having Spanish-language books and media, Spanish-speaking staff, and even offering cultural programming is not always enough. Persistent, continued outreach must be exercised to get both continuing and new users in the door.

Cultural Assumptions

How we should refer to our Spanish-speaking communities (Hispanic, Latino, Chicano, Mexicano, Colombiano, etc.) depends on the local/personal preference of the community. The only way to know for sure is to ask community members what they prefer to be called. To use the word "Hispanic," for example, may be offensive to some populations, but not to others (Spanish Outreach 2007). For the purpose of this essay, I will be using the term "Latino" as a reference to Spanish-speaking populations. Many Latino families may be new to your community. We should not make assumptions about what they know or don't know about the library. Some may have no previous library experience in the United States. The public library tradition in the United States differs from that of Latin America. Many Latin American countries do not have a strong tradition of free public library service. A Latino patron may even refer to the public library as a "librería," meaning bookstore, instead of a "biblioteca," which is the Spanish word for library (Wadham 1999, 6). Common misconceptions about the role and function of the public library may include the following (Spanish Outreach 2007):

- Public libraries only serve the educated or those attending school.
- Materials from the library are for sale, not for loan.
- A fee is required to access the library and library services.
- Libraries will divulge personal information used in obtaining a library card to government agencies.
- Libraries only provide materials in English.

For these reasons, it is important that time be spent educating non-users about library services and how to use a library. Since we cannot make assumptions, we invite and encourage members of the Latino community to communicate their needs.

Presenting at Head Start

A significant number of Latino children enroll in the Head Start program each year; in 2009, 35.9 percent of the nationwide Head Start enrollment was Latino (NHSA 2012a). Head Start programs are located across the United States, and over 27 million children have enrolled since 1965. One of the best methods for reaching Spanish-speaking families is to contact and partner with your local Head Start family support specialist. The National Head Start Association's mission is "to coalesce, inspire and support the Head Start field as a leader in early childhood development and education" (NHSA 2012b). They rely on community partnerships to provide a range of education, health, nutrition, and family support services. These services are primarily targeted to at-risk children and their families. Visit NHSA.org to find contact information for your nearest Head Start site and family support specialist.

Once you get in touch with your specialist, offer to present at a Head Start parent meeting. Head Start family support specialists coordinate and facilitate monthly parent meetings on site. These meetings serve to update parents on school happenings and community resources. Furthermore, family support specialists will often welcome community presenters to attend and share information with families. These Latino families, having worked closely with their specialists, have come to trust and rely on them. By speaking as an invited guest, you will be viewed with similar trust.

Be willing to present a topic of interest related to children and literacy in addition to basic information about the library. Letting the family support specialist know you are knowledgeable in these areas will make you more valuable as a presenter. Head Start parents are interested in practical, effective ways to help their children succeed. For example, in recent years early literacy has been a popular topic for library outreach presentations. In addition to your presentation, there will most likely be business items to discuss as part of the Head Start parent meeting. Since the meeting may only run about an hour, it is critical that you spend your presentation time wisely. You may have as little as 10–15 minutes to present. If you bring handouts or visuals, consider setting up or distributing them when first arriving. Try to locate a table to place additional displays/materials. If a suitable surface is not present, ask your host for suggestions. In communities with high Spanish-speaking populations, meetings are typically conducted in Spanish. Bilingual (Spanish and English) meetings are also available depending on site location. Let the family support specialist know in advance if you require translation assistance. A bilingual parent from the audience can be appointed to help translate.

Presentation Topics

Help families discover how the library's resources, programs, and services can meet their needs. There are a variety of topics appropriate for parent meetings and gatherings, most of which can best be dealt with by a children's librarian:

- How to get your child interested in reading
- What are the best books for children to read
- How to prepare children ages 0–5 to learn how to read (early literacy)
- What programs/classes are available at the library

Share your presentation ideas with the family support specialist and allow him or her to provide suggestions. After some discussion, you can determine the details for when, where, and what topic you will present. Not only is a school setting already comfortable for families, but you will have a guaranteed audience. Along with the main presentation topic, be sure to provide families with basic information about the library. Include a brief overview of how to obtain a library card, what materials and resources are available, and information on locations and hours. Bring along welcome brochures, program schedules, and library card applications. Registering library cards on site, if possible, is a convenient option for families. Library staff who do not speak Spanish may feel anxious about presenting to Spanish speakers. However, the inability to speak Spanish should not discourage anyone from presenting. The site family support specialist will almost always be there during your presentation and be able to assist. While presenting in Spanish has advantages, your audience will still be appreciative if you present in English, with some translation help.

As you offer programs at your library, remember to keep your Head Start and public school contacts informed. They will be most helpful in spreading awareness of your programming to Spanish-speaking families in the community. They can also provide insight as to what families in your community need most. Attending the same school or Head Start parent meeting two or three times a year is ideal, but even once a year is better than no contact at all. Over time, you may begin to receive invitations to other schools as Head Start family support specialists recommend you as a presenter to one another.

Presenting to Children at Schools

Local elementary and middle schools can also be receptive to outreach from public libraries. Contacting the school librarian first can make the process of setting up an outreach visit much easier. Since you are both in the library business, it will likely be easier to make a connection. If available, you can also introduce yourself to the school's family resource specialist. This person is often a community expert who helps coordinate programs and events for families at the school. Back-to-school nights or parent information nights make ideal settings for outreach visits. Let the school know you are interested in participating during these occasions. Depending on the event, you may choose to read books to children or bring simple crafts or activities for children to complete at a booth. Such events often occur during the beginning of the school year.

The end of the school year, as summer begins, is also a prime time for school visits. Collaborate with local school librarians on ways to promote your library's summer reading program to students. Not only is this a good opportunity to market the summer reading program, but you can also feature booktalks, which are quick (about three minutes or less) introductions to a book. You may choose to reveal the basic plot of the book, read an excerpt aloud, or come up with another creative way to pique your audience's interest in the book. Using props or dressing up as a character from a book is also a fun attention-getter. Bring along physical copies of books as visuals. This way when students visit the library, they can describe the cover if they have forgotten the title of the book.

Customize your presentation to be appropriate for both the age and reading level of your audience. For example, make sure you are not booktalking a third-grade level book to a group of fifth graders. Also, choose those topics and genres that will have interest to your audience. If using booktalks to connect with a group of Latino elementary school students, find literature that has connections to their culture or language. As a start, I recommend exploring Latino literature by the following noteworthy children's authors: Alma Flor Ada (*The Lizard and the Sun*), Pat Mora (*Tomás and the Library Lady*), Gary Soto (*Chato's Kitchen*), Joe Hayes (*La Llorona/The Weeping Woman*), and George Ancona (*El Piñatero/The Piñata Maker*). Booktalks, when presented correctly, excite and motivate children to want to read and visit the library.

Tips for Outreach Presentations

• Keep it informal. Dress in work-casual clothing and accessories. This will make you appear more approachable to children and families. Remember, through your presentation you are serving as the face of the library. Dressing too formally may discourage some people from asking questions or connecting with you. Likewise, it is important to speak plainly and clearly. Try to avoid using complex words since audience members may not understand their meaning. When presenting, look for opportunities to solicit input and questions from your audience.

• Keep it low-tech. There is a time for fancy PowerPoint presentations and laser pointers, but unless it is really necessary, try to keep your outreach demonstrations low-tech. Outreach presentations should have a genuine, human element to them. Don't use technology as a substitute for good face-to-face communication. Utilize "attention-getters" and ice breakers such as reading a short story or sharing a quote or jokes from a joke book to keep your audience engaged.

• Bring handouts/freebies. Never come empty-handed to a presentation or community event. Even though information about your library is most likely available online, keep in mind that not everyone has easy access to a computer or the Internet. Bringing library pamphlets or contact information to distribute is important. If your library has any other freebies (e.g., pencils, key chains, notepads, magnets), bring and distribute those, as well.

• Establish yourself as a contact. Let your audience know what you do for the library. Share your contact information so they can get in touch with you directly should they have questions after the presentation. Invite your audience to visit your library and ask for you specifically. If you don't speak Spanish, offer the name of a coworker who does. Having the name of someone they can request for assistance will put Spanish speakers at ease. If you are asked a question you cannot answer, either refer them to another individual or agency that might know, or take their contact information and follow up with them once you find an answer.

• Make it interactive. In her book *Going Places with Youth Outreach,* author Angela Pfeil makes this valid point about outreach: "Marketing children's library services is not just sitting at a booth at an exhibit or event telling people who happen to stop by about your services.... If your plan specifically uses the words educate, learner, successful, or outreach, then your staff will need to be more active than simply sitting at a booth" (2005, 29). Should the opportunity to have a booth at an event arise, look for ways to entice people to stop by. Providing an activity, game, drawing, or demonstration of how to download e-materials on a cell phone or portable electronic device will attract attention.

• Be enthusiastic. Convey enthusiasm and knowledge for your presentation topic. Even if you have already presented similar presentations several times before, remember that the information you are now presenting is new to this audience. Smiling and using friendly body language will also help your audience connect with you.

Programming at the Library

At the library, celebrate Hispanic culture with library programs. Culturally diverse programming at the library appeals to Spanish-speaking families, but it also enriches the community as a whole. Some simple and popular ideas for programs at the library include:

• Día de los Niños/Día de los Libros (Children's Day/Book Day). This event is celebrated on April 30th each year. The event focuses on children, culture, books, and literacy. Typically, Día de los Niños events include storytimes, crafts, outdoor activities, games, food, and even author visits or book giveaways. Of course, not all Día de los Niños events need to be this large-scale. Even a bilingual storytime and craft makes for a simple, fun afternoon celebration, as well. For additional programming ideas, visit www.reforma.org.

• Tardeada (afternoon dance/party). A tardeada is a social dance typically held on Sunday afternoons. The purpose of the event is to celebrate Hispanic heritage and bring the community together. For a library program, consider offering a sampling of food, music, entertainment, and dance that reflects the culture of the community. Local businesses may be interested in donating materials or food for the event if asked. You may also consider collaborating with other city or county departments to pool resources and sponsors to produce a large-scale event. Every year the City of Tempe, Arizona, produces a tardeada festival that lasts all afternoon and into the early evening. While the City of Tempe Diversity Department coordinates this event, several city departments, including the library, help staff the event by hosting a booth with information and activities for families to enjoy.

• Spanish and English bilingual storytimes. Take advantage of the variety of songs and books available in both languages. Many English speakers will also appreciate the opportunity to expose their children to the Spanish language. Sharing bilingual books increases children's comprehension of a second language while building their confidence and understanding in using that language (Byrd 2005, 26). Many traditional children's books are available in Spanish translation or even bilingual format. Familiar folktale classics such as *The Gingerbread Man, Jack and the Beanstalk,* and *Goldilocks and the Three Bears* lend themselves well as bilingual read-alouds because many children are already familiar with the structure of these stories.

- Guest presentations. If funding is available, consider hiring a professional presenter who will appeal to Spanish speakers. There are many options to explore. Some ideas include mariachi bands, flamenco dancing, Mexican folk dancing, and even academic lectures pertaining to Hispanic culture. If your programming budget is limited, do not hesitate to ask performers what they can do given your budget limitations. Most performers will be flexible and work with you on cost.

- Puppet shows. Even with a lone performer, a simple and entertaining puppet show is possible. You may choose to pre-record an entire play ahead of time or speak the parts in front of a live audience. Puppet shows help bring books—especially folktales—to life for children. There are a variety of folktales from Latin American countries that can be adapted for puppet shows. "Trickster tales" featuring a character that uses cleverness to defeat or outwit others are especially amusing to children. *Borreguita and the Coyote* by Verna Aardema and *The Tale of Rabbit and Coyote* by Tony Johnston are examples of popular Mexican trickster tales. They also adapt well to puppet show format. For very young audiences, consider using puppets to recite simple bilingual poems and rhymes.

- Spanish/bilingual book displays. Promote your library's bilingual collection with attractive shelving or dedicated displays. This will help families locate materials and it will also increase circulation. When showcasing award-winning Latino literature, seek out books that have been awarded the Pura Belpré Award. This award was named after the first Latina librarian at the New York Public Library. The award was established in 1996 and is presented annually to a Latina/Latino author and illustrator whose work "portrays, affirms, and celebrates the Latino cultural experience in an outstanding work of literature for children and youth" (ALA 2012). Displaying these kinds of books not only demonstrates good selection in children's literature, but it sends a message to the public that Latino culture is valued and supported by the library.

- Implement best programming practices. The American Library Association (www.ala.org), Reforma (www.reforma.org), and WebJunction (www.webjunction.org) provide many resources and ideas for planning cultural programs and events. Choose to provide events and programs that involve the entire family. This makes it easier for Latino families to bring along children of different ages. "Single caregiver/single child programs are rarely successful as they are not an option for Latino parents with larger families" (Wadham 1999, 14). If possible, seek out community members from Spanish-speaking cultures who have an interest in helping to plan or assist with events (Byrd 2005, 34). Keep in mind not all programming needs to be holiday-themed. Programs designed to help new Americans/immigrants adapt to and understand their new communities can be successful. Possible adult programming topics and classes might include English as a second language, finding a job, housing and tenants' rights, and citizenship study classes (Byrd 2005, 38).

Partnering with Other Community Leaders

Setting up informal interviews with teachers, business leaders, church leaders, community center directors, and other community leaders can help further your knowledge about what is going on in the Spanish-speaking community and how the library can help (Byrd 2005, 10). Remember, seeking out advice is not a sign of weakness. Rather, it demonstrates your library's priorities and values. "People love to reconnect to their cultural heritage if those ties have been severed or the cultural tradition has been lost. The library can act as a resource for people wanting to reconnect to or know more about their cultural traditions" (Byrd 2005, 36).

Whether you are eager to try new programs and services that you think will appeal to Spanish speakers or improve existing ones, it is highly advisable to consult local community experts and leaders from the Spanish-speaking community. Many community leaders will be pleased you are asking for their input and will try to be helpful, knowing you are working to improve services to community members.

Works Cited

ALA (American Library Association). 2012. "Welcome to the Pura Belpré Award Home Page." http://www.ala.org/alsc/awardsgrants/bookmedia/belpremedal (accessed September 9, 2012).

Byrd, Susannah Mississippi. 2005. *¡Bienvenidos! ¡Welcome! A Handy Resource Guide for Marketing Your Library to Latinos*. Chicago: American Library Association.

NHSA (National Head Start Association). 2012a. "Head Start Mission Statement." http://www.nhsa.org/about_nhsa/mission_statement (accessed September 9, 2012).

_____. 2012b. "Head Start Program Fact Sheet." http://www.nhsa.org/about_nhsa/mission_statement (accessed November 12, 2012).

Pfeil, Angela B. 2005. *Going Places with Youth Outreach: Smart Marketing Strategies for Your Library*. Chicago: American Library Association.

Spanish Outreach Libraries Workshop. 2007. "Empowering Library Staff to Reach Out to Spanish Speakers and Increase Their Access to Technology." February 21. Presentation at Scottsdale Public Library, Scottsdale, Arizona.

USCB (United States Census Bureau). 2011. "The Hispanic Population: 2010." http://www.census.gov/prod/cen2010/briefs/c2010br-04.pdf (accessed May 31, 2013).

Wadham, Tim. 1999. *Programming with Latino Children's Materials: A How-to-Do-It Manual for Librarians*. New York: Neal-Schuman.

Reaching Out to LGBTQ Youth

Jamie Campbell Naidoo

Lesbian, gay, bisexual, transgender, and queer/questioning (LGBTQ) youth (children and young adults) are present within every state and almost every county in the nation. Chances are an LGBTQ child or young adult or one with an LGBTQ parent/caregiver has visited your library this week.[1] These youth comprise the daily patronage of our school and public libraries, yet they often go unrecognized until tragedy strikes. Recently the amount of bullying and hate crimes directed towards these youth or suicide attempts by these youth have escalated. Numerous news stories have profiled LGBTQ youth who have ended their lives because they were ostracized by friends and family members or victimized by peers. According to the most recent report by the Gay, Lesbian, and Straight Education Network (GLSEN), 63.5 percent of LGBTQ youth experienced bullying because of their sexual orientation, and 43.9 percent were victimized by other youth because of their gender expression (Kosciw et al. 2012). Youth with LGBTQ parents/caregivers are also victimized and bullied because of their parents' sexual orientation. Almost half (42 percent) of these youth are the object of verbal ridicule because of their family composition, and one out of five have been discouraged from talking about their families by teachers, librarians, and other educators (Kosciw and Diaz 2008).

Libraries hold a unique opportunity to reach LGBTQ youth by creating welcoming environments that acknowledge them and celebrate their differences. By providing developmentally appropriate books and materials that represent LGBTQ topics, libraries validate the experiences of these youth, afford opportunities for them to make literary connections, and assist all youth in understanding themselves and the world around them. The purpose of this essay is to provide information for librarians on how to reach out to LGBTQ youth via high-quality collections, inclusionary services, exciting programs, welcoming environments, and online resources. Examples of youth outreach programs are highlighted along with recommended professional resources for developing services for these populations.

Informational Needs and Welcoming Spaces

Many LGBTQ youth may not be out—publicly open about their sexuality or the sexuality of their parents/caregivers—and the ability to identify them to meet their needs is problematic for many youth librarians. Nonetheless, LGBTQ youth have informational needs similar to other youth. Privacy is the most important of these needs and can take the form of confidentiality in patron records for LGBTQ youth or discretion when helping them locate materials.

Access to current, accurate information about LGBTQ families, health concerns of LGBTQ youth, and local LGBTQ organizations serving youth are all highly important to LGBTQ youth. Similarly, libraries striving to promote understanding of LGBTQ cultures will want to provide access to recreational materials—such as audiobooks, films, youth literature, music, and magazines—that positively and accurately portray LGBTQ-themed topics.

Of equal importance is the ability to locate this information within the library's collections. Outdated subject headings can deter youth from finding materials about LGBTQ topics. More often than not, the most common problem related to access is the complete lack of subject headings or keywords that indicate LGBTQ content. Without adequate and accurate terminology in the MARC record of a library item, youth will have difficulty locating information and materials about themselves and their families. This is particularly problematic as some LGBTQ youth will not engage a librarian to assist them in locating gay-themed materials, nor will they likely use materials in LGBTQ-labeled sections of the library. LGBTQ subject headings have been updated over time, so librarians should ensure that their MARC records reflect LGBTQ content.

Another need of LGBTQ youth is access to a welcoming, safe environment where they can explore their educational and recreational needs. This inclusive environment should be free of homophobic attitudes and practices. Often librarians do not realize that by choosing only books about nuclear families or with straight characters to use in library programs and by having filtering software on their computers that suppresses information about LGBTQ topics, they are perpetuating unintentional heterosexism (the suppression of information about LGBTQ topics) in the library. Inclusive environments benefit everyone, not just LGBTQ youth. Librarians could consider contacting local LGBTQ organizations to identify parents and youth in their neighborhood who are open to assisting with the creation of library environments inclusive of the LGBTQ community.

Displaying posters that are inclusive of LGBTQ youth helps to normalize their presence in society while suggesting that the library is a safe place for them. A wonderful resource for librarians looking for children's posters inclusive of LGBQ families or for suggestions on including these families in early childhood programs is The Rainbow Families Council, a volunteer community organization based in Victoria, Australia. Their website (http://rainbowfamilies.org.au/) contains vibrant information sheets and posters that can be used in the library. The information sheets can be placed in LGBTQ-friendly displays in the parenting and/or youth section of the library, and the posters can be used in programming rooms.

An equally useful resource for librarians reaching out to older LGBTQ youth are the You Belong @ Your Library posters created by the Sacramento Public Library in 2012 for National Library Week. These posters, funded by a Scholastic Library Publishing National Library Week Grant, feature a diverse group of LGBTQ youth reading, rollerblading, computing, etc. Posters can be freely downloaded from the American Library Association (ALA) website and customized. Available: www.ala.org/advocacy/advleg/publicawareness/campaign%40your library/you-belong-your-library.

The ALA also created a toolkit, "Out in the Library: Materials, Displays and Services for the Gay, Lesbian, Bisexual, and Transgender Community," which contains useful information for librarians interested in designing welcoming environments for all LGBTQ patrons. The toolkit includes information about LGBTQ materials in school libraries as well as LGBTQ youth books. Available: www.ala.org/ala/aboutala/offices/oif/iftoolkits/glbttoolkit/glbttoolkit.cfm.

Selecting LGBTQ Youth Materials

When librarians select and use high-quality youth literature that accurately and authentically represents diverse cultures, they assist youth with their identity development. Well-chosen books can celebrate the diversity within the LGBTQ community and normalize experiences of LGBTQ youth. Some librarians may not feel qualified or comfortable selecting LGBTQ youth materials. Fortunately, many resources are available. Librarians may also find it useful to engage the services of their youth advisory groups to help them select entertaining, relevant, and current materials. Below are a few resources for locating quality books as well as links to awards for LGBTQ youth literature.

• *Gay, Lesbian, Bisexual, Transgender and Questioning Teen Literature: A Guide to Reading Interests* (Webber 2010) is a timely collection development tool for locating LGBTQ young adult fiction and nonfiction books.

• *The Heart Has Its Reasons: Young Adult Literature with Gay/Lesbian/Queer Content, 1969–2004* (Cart and Jenkins 2006) provides selection guidelines, historical information, and annotated bibliographies of LGBTQ young adult books.

• *Rainbow Family Collections: Selecting and Using Children's Books with Lesbian, Gay, Bisexual, Transgender, and Queer Content* (Naidoo 2012) offers librarians an extensive listing of children's books and non-print resources with LGBTQ content. Evaluation criteria, programming suggestions, and a history of LGBTQ children's literature are also covered.

• Lambda Literary Awards. Presented by the Lambda Literary Foundation, these awards celebrate the best in literary fiction and nonfiction books that represent LGBTQ experiences. There are several categories of annual awards for adults and one for children's and young adult titles. Available: www.lambdaliterary.org/category/winners-finalists/.

• Rainbow Books. Awarded annually by the ALA's Social Responsibilities Round Table and Gay, Lesbian, Bisexual, and Transgender Round Table (GLBTRT), this booklist includes fiction and nonfiction youth titles that authentically portray LGBTQ topics. Available: http://glbtrt.ala.org/rainbowbooks/rainbow-books-lists.

• Stonewall Children's and Young Adult Literature Awards. Presented by the ALA's GLBTRT, this award recognizes youth books that positively and accurately represent the experiences of LGBTQ youth and families. Many members on the awards selection committee self-identify as LGBTQ and are knowledgeable about the daily experiences of LGBTQ youth. Available: www.ala.org/ala/mgrps/rts/glbtrt/stonewall/index.cfm.

Planning Programs and Services

When LGBTQ youth see reflections of their lives in library programming, their existence is validated and they understand that librarians value and respect them. At the same time, programs and services respectful and inclusive of LGBTQ youth counteract homophobic sentiment and normalize their experiences, thereby providing a window into their experiences for other youth. This section provides ideas and considerations for librarians planning programs and services for LGBTQ youth.

One of the most common types of programs for younger youth is the library storytime. When considering the informational and recreational needs of LGTQ youth and families, librarians have the option of planning "out and proud" storytimes that focus on LGBTQ books and topics, or planning "inclusive" story programs that use inclusive language. In this latter type of storytime, librarians do not need gay-themed youth books; instead, they change pronouns while reading a book with androgynous animal characters to be inclusive of LGBTQ families/characters. Another alternative for inclusive programming involves using story starters to begin a narrative and then allowing youth to finish the story by inserting their own personal experiences. Additional inclusive story program alternatives incorporate family composition books (books about various types of families, including LGBTQ families) or ask youth to create their own stories representative of their lives and family structures. Youth can share their stories with each other during the library program.

For older youth, librarians can include LGBTQ youth literature alongside other titles in themed book discussions in which youth read books on broad general themes and then discuss with each other. An example of this would be a book discussion with supernatural or science fiction themes, allowing queer young adults books such as David Levithan's *Every Day,* Perry Moore's *Hero,* Malinda Lo's *Adaptation*, and Diane DeKelb-Rittenhouse's *Immortal Longings: A Vampire Novel* to be included alongside Suzanne Collins' *The Hunger Games*, Stephenie Meyer's *Twilight*, and James Dashner's *The Maze Runner.*

Librarians interested in reaching LGBTQ youth via "out and proud" storytimes and programs have several options, as well. The most simple and basic option for this type of programming would be designing a storytime program with picture books centered on LGBTQ characters or families. Alternatively, LGBTQ-themed books could be included along with other books in a program that celebrates diversity, individuality, or a general topic such as animals. For instance, if the librarian wanted to design a winter-themed program around the topic of penguins, then Justin Richardson and Peter Parnell's *And Tango Makes Three* could be used with Polly Dunbar's *Penguin* and Jean-Luc Fromental and Joelle Jolivet's *365 Penguins*. When planning "out and proud" programs for older youth, librarians could invite LGBTQ young adult writers such as Alex Sanchez or Julie Anne Peters for an author visit. For those librarians concerned about funding or anti-gay community sentiment, virtual author visits via Skype are a great way to include LGBTQ authors into programming.

Multiple public libraries around the world host "out and proud" programming for LGBTQ youth and families. Here are a few examples:

• In April 2009, the Central Public Library in Gandia, Spain, partnered with diversity and anti-discrimination organizations to deliver a weeklong series of LGBTQ-themed programs celebrating diverse families. These programs incorporated LGBTQ Spanish picture books along with numerous hands-on crafts and activities. A detailed description of the program (in Spanish) along with examples of marketing posters are available at www.lgtb.es/item.php?id=123 and the activity sheets to accompany the LGBTQ children's books are available at www.lgtb.es/descarrega.php?id=405&arxiu=Pintem_families_diversitat.pdf.

• In May 2011, the Communication Studies Department at San Francisco State University partnered with the Office of Children's Services at the San Francisco Public Library to offer a program for and about LGBTQ families that integrated eight LGBTQ children's books with performance arts. The program ("Dragons & Dresses & Ducklings—Oh My!") highlighted various gender expressions and families to promote love, diversity, and acceptance.

• In June 2012, the District of Columbia Public Library participated in the DC Pride Festival to offer a pride booth for LGBTQ youth and families. Programming included LGBTQ reading lists for youth and adults, LGBTQ trivia questions with prizes, and a young adult craft activity at the booth. Librarians used iPads to issue library cards and brought carts of LGBTQ materials to circulate.

Several online and print resources are available to assist librarians in reaching LGBTQ youth with ready-made, adaptable programs and lessons plans using LGBTQ children's and young adult literature. Selected ones are listed.

• Children's author and lesbian mother Vicki Harding offers educators and librarians a useful teacher's guide, *Learn to Include Teacher's Manual: Teaching and Learning About Diverse Families in a Primary School Setting*, that complements her beginning reader series of LGBTQ children's books. The manual is designed for youth in kindergarten through third grade to help them learn more about family diversity and normalizes the experiences of youth with LGBTQ families. The guide includes hand-on activities, discussion prompts, and reproducible worksheets. Available: www.hotkey.net.au/~learn_to_include/pdf/revised%20manual%20 Sept%2005.pdf.

• Sponsored by the Human Rights Campaign Foundation, the Welcoming Schools website is a comprehensive resource filled with lesson plans, bibliographies of recommended LGBTQ youth books, and resources for creating welcoming environments for LGBTQ youth. Video clips of younger youth talking about what it means to be LGBTQ are included along with a free 93-page resource guide. Particularly appealing for librarians are tip sheets about inclusive libraries for LGBTQ youth. Available: www.welcomingschools.org/.

• An international nonprofit organization supporting LGBTQ youth, Safe Schools Coalition is a clearinghouse for librarians and other educators dedicated to creating welcoming, safe places for all youth. The websites includes bibliographies and lesson plans divided according to age group and hotline information for LGBTQ youth. Available: www.safeschoolscoalition.org/.

• TransActive Education and Advocacy supports gender nonconforming and transgender youth and their families. The organization's website includes lesson plans, training information, links to community resources, and other relevant information related to promoting understanding of transgender youth. Available: www.transactiveonline.org/index.php.

• Around the Rainbow is a Canadian project providing support for LGBTQ and two-spirit youth and their families. Their website features French and English toolkits for parents and educators, curriculum guides, bibliographies divided by age level, and links to online sources for serving LGBTQ and two-spirit youth. Available: http://familyservicesottawa.org/ children-youth-and-families/around-the-rainbow/.

• *Serving Lesbian, Gay, Bisexual, Transgender, and Questioning Teens* (Hillias and Murdock 2007) is one of the best resources for librarians interested in developing programs, collections, and services for older LGBTQ youth. The authors provide recommended annotated bibliographies of young adult books, suggestions for booktalks, and ideas for LGBTQ youth programs.

• "Opening the Gate: Booktalks for LGBTQ-Themed Young Adult Titles" (Parks 2012) provides several ready-to-use booktalks of LGBTQ young adult titles along with suggestions on how librarians can reach older LGBTQ youth.

Public libraries across the nation use the promotional materials and programming themes provided by the Collaborative Summer Library Program (CSLP). The CSLP also equips librarians with information on how to plan programs and services for specific populations. The section of the CSLP website dedicated to library services for alternative families lists recommended LGBTQ books for programming under "GLBT Family Resources" (accessible: www.cslpreads.org/alternative-families.html). Other ideas for library outreach programs inclusive of LGBTQ youth are:

- Events in conjunction with LGBTQ Heritage Month in June
- Outreach in LGBTQ events: LGBTQ family picnics, Parents, Families and Friends of Lesbians and Gays (PFLAG) meetings/events, etc.
- Partnerships with Gay-Straight Alliances at local schools or local gay youth organizations
- Family films series that include gay-friendly films
- Visits from gay-friendly youth authors or illustrators such as Jacqueline Woodson, Todd Parr, David Levithan, Maya Christina Gonzalez, and Patricia Polacco, who have created a variety of youth books with and without LGBTQ content

Online Outreach in the Community

Some librarians with a passion for serving LGBTQ youth may live in rural, secluded, or socially conservative communities that make it difficult for outreach inclusive of LGBTQ topics and themes. The mission of any library is to reach youth where they live. If "out and proud" outreach is not possible, librarians have the option of online outreach. Numerous online resources can be made available to LGBTQ youth via online pathfinders and bibliographies. Youth can access these materials privately anywhere Internet connectivity is available. The pathfinders can provide information on a variety of social and informational topics of interest to LGBTQ youth and can provide links to online communities for LGBTQ youth to connect with one another. An important aspect of these online pathfinders is providing information for crisis and hotline sources that can offer counseling to distressed LGBTQ youth. Suggested resources for pathfinders are listed below.

- Outbeat Youth: A Radio Show For and About Queer Youth. Available via streaming audio, this radio station highlights LGBTQ youth who have made a difference in the world, provides information on LGBTQ topics of interest, and showcases the talents of LGBTQ youth. Available: www.outbeatyouth.org/.
- YouthResource. Created by Advocates for Youth, this dynamic website explores sexual health and current issues of concern to LGBTQ youth and includes special sections for LGBTQ youth from various cultural backgrounds. Available: www.amplifyyourvoice.org/youthresource.
- Ambiente Joven. A project of Advocates for Youth, this Spanish-language website provides a wealth of information and networking opportunities for LGBTQ youth in the United States and Latin America. Available: www.ambientejoven.org/.
- Rainbow Riot (for young adults) and Rainbow Rumpus (for children). Developed by

lesbian mother and writer Laura Matanah, these sister websites are online literary magazines for young adults and children with LGBTQ parents. Available: www.rainbowriot.org and www.rainbowrumpus.org.

• It Gets Better Project. Originally started by columnist, advocate, and author Dan Savage, this project provides over 50,000 motivational web streams for LGBTQ youth meant to encourage them that life will get better despite bullying from peers. Available: www.itgetsbetter. org/video/.

• The Trevor Project. Established in 1998, this national nonprofit organization is dedicated to suicide prevention, crisis intervention, and support education for LGBTQ youth. The comprehensive website includes various types of communication and social media venues. Available: www.thetrevorproject.org/.

• COLAGE: People with a Lesbian, Gay, Bisexual, Transgender or Queer Parent. National support group for youth with LGBTQ parents/caregivers. The website contains bibliographies of recommended LGBTQ youth literature, online resources and activities for youth of LGBTQ parents/caregivers, and much more. Available: www.colage.org/.

Offering bibliographies online allow youth to access lists of recommended informational and fiction LGBTQ youth materials in the privacy of their homes. They can then visit the library to find these items. Ideally, librarians would use their collections to develop bibliographies relevant to their local populations. However, if librarians are concerned about highlighting their local LGBTQ materials, they can list links to online bibliographies and encourage youth to search the library holdings for items of interest. Below are a few examples of bibliographies and review blogs of LGBTQ materials:

• "A Rainbow Celebration: Gays & Lesbians in Books for Children." Created by The San Francisco Public Library. Available: http://sfpl.org/index.php?pg=2000154901.

• "I'm Here, I'm Queer, What the Hell Do I Read?" Created by writer and speaker Lee Wind. Available: www.leewind.org/.

• "Queer YA: Fiction for LGBTQ Teens." Created by librarian and book reviewer Daisy Porter. Available: http://daisyporter.org/queerya/.

• "Gay-Themed Picture Books for Children." Created by school librarian and book reviewer Patricia Sarles. Available: http://booksforkidsingayfamilies.blogspot.com/.

• "Transgender Resource Collection." Created by The Oak Park Public Library (Illinois). Available: www.oppl.org/media/trc.htm.

Concluding Thoughts

In an ideal world, librarians would not experience problems when providing outreach to LGBTQ youth. Unfortunately, the reality is that many librarians have good intentions and work hard but meet resistance from their administrators and local community. Nonetheless, it is vitally important to ensure that all youth have access to LGBTQ materials and services that provide windows into the LGBTQ culture. Meeting the needs of this population will not be easy, but hopefully some of the information in this essay will help you along the way as you determine the best way to provide outreach to the LGBTQ youth in your community.

Note

1. For the remainder of this essay unless specified otherwise, LGBTQ youth will be used to represent youth who are LGBTQ or who have parents/caregivers that are LGBTQ.

Works Cited

Cart, Michael, and Christine Jenkins. 2006. *The Heart Has Its Reasons: Young Adult Literature with Gay/Lesbian/Queer Content, 1969–2004.* Lanham, MD: Scarecrow Press.

Hillias, Martin J., and James R. Murdock. 2007. *Serving Lesbian, Gay, Bisexual, Transgender, and Questioning Teens: A How-to-Do-It Manual for Librarians.* New York: Neal-Schuman.

Kosciw, Joseph G., and Elizabeth M. Diaz. 2008. *Involved, Invisible, Ignored: The Experiences of Lesbian, Gay, Bisexual, and Transgender Parents and Their Children in Our Nation's K-12 Schools.* New York: GLSEN.

Kosciw, Joseph G., Emily A. Greytak, Mark J. Bartkiewicz, Madelyn J. Boesen, and Neal A. Palmer. 2012. *The 2011 National School Climate Survey: The Experiences of Lesbian, Gay, Bisexual and Transgender Youth in Our Nation's Schools.* New York: GLSEN.

Naidoo, Jamie Campbell. 2012. *Rainbow Family Collections: Selecting and Using Children's Books with Lesbian, Gay, Bisexual, Transgender, and Queer Content.* Santa Barbara: Libraries Unlimited.

Parks, Alexander. 2012. "Opening the Gate: Booktalks for LGBTQ-Themed Young Adult Titles." *Young Adult Library Services* 10 (4): 22–27.

Webber, Carlisle. 2010. *Gay, Lesbian, Bisexual, Transgender and Questioning Teen Literature: A Guide to Reading Interests.* Santa Barbara: Libraries Unlimited.

Early Literacy Outreach for Teen Parents

CORINNE SANCHEZ *and* XELENA GONZÁLEZ

Anyone who works with teenagers knows that a fun-yet-thoughtful approach to programming must be taken lest you lose your audience. This is particularly true when presenting to teens who also happen to be parents. Many of them are still striving to finish school themselves, so preparing their little ones for the world of reading can seem a daunting task.

For this reason, the Little Read Wagon has developed a reliable method for reaching teen parents and introducing early literacy techniques in a way that is simple, straightforward, and highly interactive. This essay describes our process, shares our personal experiences, and outlines best practices.

Who We Are

The Little Read Wagon is the San Antonio Public Library's early literacy outreach initiative, designed to support the development of young children's love of books, reading, and learning. Through a variety of programs and outreach efforts, we provide foundational literacy information and materials to parents, extended family, and caregivers of children ages birth to five years. Services are provided free of charge at public libraries, childcare facilities, schools, and nonprofits. Our mission is to empower the community with an increased awareness of early literacy skills and to provide the tools needed to support those skills.

Teen parents have been a part of our target audience since our program's inception in 2002. In 2010, we began to experiment with new ways to reach this group, designing an early literacy program specific to their needs and interests. This effort arose from various school districts' requests for campus visits. But we also hoped to address a pressing need within our particular community. Our county consistently reports a teen birth rate that is nearly 50 percent higher than the national teen birth rate. We recognized an important opportunity to work with our city's youngest parents, whose learning styles and modes of communication are unique.

Over the last ten years, our program has expanded to reach nine school districts in the San Antonio metropolitan area and Bexar County. In 2011–2012, we provided 99 programs, serving 582 teen parents on 26 public school campuses. In 2011–2012, the San Antonio Public Library received funds from the City of San Antonio to expand early literacy services, resulting in the addition of four part-time employees. Based on community demand, we anticipate further growth and development of our teen parent program.

Our Approach

Most of our parent/caregiver programs are structured around the early literacy strategies promoted by the Every Child Ready to Read (ECRR) project of the Association for Library Service to Children and the Public Library Association. Their updated early literacy practices are simple enough for most parents to commit to memory: Talking, Singing, Reading, Writing, and Playing.

Our teen parent program has developed "make-and-take" activities that correspond to each of these early literacy practices. They allow our young parents the opportunity to create something meaningful for their children. Throughout the process, we share ideas and suggest simple at-home practices that build upon each strategy. Students are therefore engaged in hands-on activities while remaining receptive to the information being presented.

A central principle to the Little Read Wagon's programming is using inexpensive or recycled materials. We want parents from all walks of life to feel confident in creating fun learning experiences for their children without having to spend much money or any money at all. The make-and-take activities we present can therefore be easily replicated on a small budget.

In addition to bringing home a handmade gift for their child, each participant is allowed to choose a board book to add to their personal collection. All we request in return is an evaluation at the close of each session. These evaluations gather data requested by our funders. They also gauge the effectiveness of our programs in delivering the message of early literacy importance and realistic practices. According to our numbers and written feedback, we are consistently effective in delivering this message.

Introducing the Five Early Literacy Practices

The Every Child Ready to Read campaign offers a bounty of helpful toolkits, PowerPoints, and materials to help spread the message of early literacy made simple. It is a worthwhile investment to become familiar with their methods of presentation, and we rely on these strategies as the backbone for most of our outreach efforts. The difference in working with teen parents is that you are dealing with shorter attention spans and competing for attention in a culture that is overstimulated.

We've found that appealing to the highly visual and tactile learner is the best approach when introducing the early literacy practices of Talking, Singing, Reading, Writing, and Playing. Rather than stand before a group and present the way we would with traditional parents, we put materials into the hands of our teen participants as soon as possible. We talk while they work. The eye contact we're accustomed to in a regular presentation isn't always there, but the audience tends to remain actively engaged and listening.

The following five sections will describe the make-and-take projects we introduce for each practice. We'll also provide tips tailored for a teen audience. Each of the projects listed below takes approximately 45 minutes or less to complete.

"Reading" Make-and-Take: Book Tote

Purpose: Always having a book on hand is the easiest way to make reading a daily habit. Encourage reading on the bus, in waiting rooms, at bedtime, and at bath time. Remind par-

Personalized book totes enhance print awareness and encourage library use.

ticipants that modeling reading is also important: at snack time, baby can watch mom or dad complete homework. The personalized tote bag also gives new library users a place to keep their borrowed books together. We often highlight reading in our initial presentation because it allows us to promote the many library resources available to teens—both as patrons and as parents. Remember to bring promotional materials and library card applications for participants to carry home in their totes.

Supplies:
- Blank canvas bags (we use bags that have our library's logo on one side)
- Fabric markers
- Stencils

Steps:
1. Distribute blank canvas bags and markers. Encourage students to use their own personal touch and creativity in decorating bags. Recommend that parents print their child's name to help develop print awareness.

2. For those who are not comfortable drawing freehand, offer a variety of stencils (basic letters and shapes). Penciling an outline before using markers also works well. Remind them that fabric marker designs remain after washing.

3. Since participants in our programs always get to choose a board book for their child,

the totes can be used immediately for books and for any other library materials you've distributed.

"Talking" Make-and-Take: Look Tube

Purpose: The look tube is a variation of the kaleidoscope. It encourages parents and children to play "I spy" games and to focus on one item at a time. As adults, we tend to forget how fascinating it can be to notice the tiny details of leaves, shells, feathers, and rocks. Bring a variety of props that encourage talking: magnifying glasses, flashlights, play phones, and recycled water bottles filled with various objects. Encourage parents to talk to their children about their day. If it happens to be a bad day, suggest they ask questions instead or wonder about the world together. Make up a story—perhaps one that imagines a positive solution to their particular situation.

Supplies:
- 10" cardboard mailing tubes
- Mirrored poster board (cut into 10" × 3½" strips)
- Sheet protectors (cut into circles 3" in diameter)
- Contact paper (cut into 10" × 5½" sheets)
- Clear tape

Look tubes are homemade kaleidoscopes for observation and "I spy" games.

- Stickers
- Markers/crayons

Steps:

1. Score two lines lengthwise along mirrored poster board at one-inch increments, segmenting (but not separating) the poster board into three columns.

2. Fold along the scored lines with the mirrored surface facing inward, forming a triangle tube. Use clear tape to fasten poster board ends together, keeping triangle tube shape.

3. Slide mirrored triangle tube inside the mailing tube.

4. Tape sheet protector circles to each end of the mailing tube, forming the "lenses" of the look tube and keeping the mirrored triangle contained inside.

5. Use crayons, markers, and stickers to decorate the outside of the tube. Personalize it with the child's name.

6. Slowly peel backing of the contact paper and cover the body of the tube. This will protect the stickers and tape from tiny hands that like to peel.

"Singing" Make-and-Take: Songbook

Purpose: Your participants may not be familiar with traditional children's songs. Bring plenty of examples to share, and don't be shy about singing. (We want to remind them that you don't have to have the best voice for baby to appreciate your singing.) Also, bring children's music from your library's collection to play while participants work. Elicit examples of popular songs to illustrate the point that repetition and rhyme appeal to listeners of all ages.

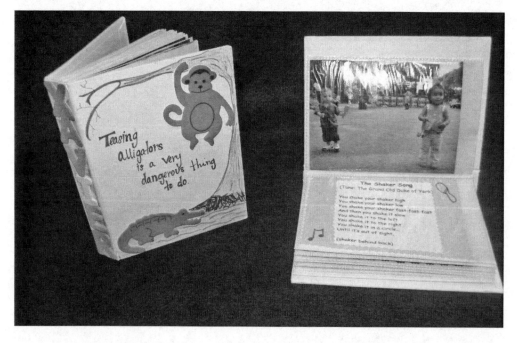

Songbooks store lyrics to inspire singing, while family photographs also encourage talking.

Supplies:
- Blank white photo albums
- A variety of colorful cardstock sheets (pre-cut to fit photo album pages)
- Song sheets
- Markers
- Crayons
- Scissors (regular and those that cut unique designs)
- Variety of stickers
- Foam shapes
- Glue sticks
- Pre-made songbooks to show as examples

Steps:
1. Before the presentation, format song sheets (8.5" × 11") to fit six songs per page. Songs can include anything from classic children's lullabies to finger plays, rhymes, and chants. Include a list of online song resources for participants to reference for new song ideas and to hear the tunes/lyrics of songs learned in class.

2. Participants begin by cutting each song and gluing it to a cardstock sheet. This provides a colorful border for each song.

3. Slide mounted songs into the photo album pages, leaving adjoining pages empty. These can be filled later with photos of participants' children and family, as well as their own favorite songs and rhymes.

4. Decorate songbook cover and pages with markers, crayons, stickers, and foam shapes while presenter sings songs and demonstrates finger plays. Encourage participation among willing participants.

"Writing" Make-and-Take: Gel Board

Purpose: Perhaps the most popular project from our teen program, the gel board, works in the same way as an Etch-a-Sketch, but it is appropriate for even the youngest writer who is just learning to develop his/her fine motor skills. While they're working, we remind parents that many of the activities they already do with their children are considered early writing: gripping and manipulating toys and puzzles; making marks with chalk, crayons, and finger paints; even allowing playtime on computer/phone keyboards.

Supplies:
- Sturdy cardboard or foam core project board (cut into 10" × 12" sheets)
- Re-sealable food storage bag (gallon size)
- Clear hair gel
- Duct tape (various colors/prints)
- Clear packing tape
- Scissors
- Food coloring
- Contact paper (cut into 10" × 12" sheets)
- Spoons

Gel boards provide a fun writing activity for both teens and their children.

Steps:

1. Place approximately 2 tablespoons of clear hair gel into food storage bag. You'll need just enough gel to coat the inside of the bag.

2. Add 5–8 drops of food coloring to the gel inside the bag.

3. Seal your storage bag, leaving a small opening to allow air bubbles to escape. Gently spread the gel and food color mixture into every corner of the bag, working the gel from the bottom of the bag to the top, so that air bubbles escape out of the small opening.

4. Once you have worked out most of the air bubbles, seal the storage bag completely.

5. Secure the gel-filled bag to the foam core board using two 8" strips of clear packing tape. This can be done by wrapping the re-sealable portion of the bag around the top edge of the foam board and taping it to the back of the board. The gel bag will hang a bit longer than the foam board. Wrap the extra length of the bag around the bottom edge of the board and tape it to the back of the board.

6. Slowly cover the entire storage bag and exposed board edges with the pre-cut sheet of contact paper. This will extend the life of your gel board by protecting it from sharp nails and objects.

7. Make a border for your gel board using duct tape of your choice. Two 10" strips and three 12" strips will cover all exposed edges of the storage bag and board (including the exposed seal on the back of the board).

8. If time allows, decorate the back of the board using markers and stickers. Personalize it with the name of the child who will enjoy pre-writing fun.

For an easy-to-follow tutorial with photos and additional tips, please visit: http://little readwagon.blogspot.com/2012/05/gel-writing-board-tutorial.html

"Playing" Make-and-Take: Play Dough

Purpose: Playing incorporates all of the early literacy practices, especially when it comes to making and manipulating play dough. There are many easy-to-follow recipes that allow opportunities for reading and print awareness. Children can talk about what they are sensing and creating as the play dough changes form. Songs like "Pat-a-Cake" and "Happy Birthday" may come to mind. Early writing occurs when children cut, roll, stamp, or pinch the dough, exercising their fine motor skills. They can also shape the letters of their name with "snakes" of dough. Remind parents that playtime is the *one* time when their children are in charge. Reach the child's level of carefree fun, and any interaction that takes place is beneficial for their blossoming minds.

Supplies:
- Measuring cups
- Measuring spoons
- Large bowl
- Mixing spoons
- White flour
- Cooking oil
- Salt
- Water
- Food coloring
- Storage containers

Steps:
1. Pour ¼ cup salt into your bowl.
2. Add 2 tablespoons vegetable oil.
3. Measure ½ cup *plus* 2 tablespoons water and mix with spoon.
4. Add 5–10 drops of food coloring.
5. Stir the ingredients in your bowl for one minute.
6. Measure 1½ cups of flour and stir it into your mixture.
7. When the dough becomes too thick to stir, use your hands to mix the dough until it forms a ball.
8. If the dough is too sticky, add flour. If it's too crumbly, add a tiny bit of water.
9. Play! Your dough will last for about a week. Keep it in an airtight container between uses.

Getting Started

Although we believe this program can be duplicated with success in most settings, it is important to assess what resources you have available. The Little Read Wagon has several funding sources that have afforded our outreach team three full-time employees, four part-time employees, materials for programs, plus two customized minivans used to transport staff and materials to off-site locations. Be realistic about how you can customize this program to fit your needs. Starting small is always a smart approach. Finding the right point of contact for each outreach location is crucial. In schools, this could be a social worker, a teacher, or another faculty/staff member who organizes a pull-out program for teen parents. Scan the school's or district's website and make phone calls until you find the right person. School principals typically have their hands full, so if you start your search there, you might be placing yourself in a long line of callbacks. If possible, partner with other agencies who are already working with teen parents on campuses or in community centers. Start a discussion to see if your message of early literacy falls in line with the purpose of their program. A partnership may not always be mutually beneficial, but if reaching teen parents proves a difficult task, it is worth your time to find out who may already have an established relationship with this group. Sometimes schools have a teen parenting program already in place. They may even discuss the topic of early literacy with their students. Yet you still have information worth sharing. Often students need to hear the same message—with a new spin—from someone outside their school walls.

Once you have established contact with the right person, set up a meeting at the program site. This will allow you to gauge which projects will be possible to conduct within the space. At the meeting, make clear the mission and structure of your presentations. Don't commit to a full series unless you've established a solid relationship with the outreach site. Try offering an initial presentation that gives an overview of the five early literacy practices. If the test run proves successful, set up subsequent visits.

Here are other important questions to ask prior to visiting any new campus:

1. What kind of teen parent program do you have in place (if any)?
2. How many participants do you have, on average?
3. Do you meet with multiple groups/classes?
4. How often do the teen parents convene?
5. Do you meet in the same space each time?
6. What is the room setup (desks, rows, tables, etc.)?
7. Will there be a teacher (or other established authority figure) present at each session for the entirety of the presentation?
8. Will we be visiting during a regularly scheduled class time, or will you need to send out passes ahead of time?
9. Can we have five to 10 minutes immediately before and after each presentation to set up and break down our equipment?
10. Where can we check in on campus? Should we be prepared to show identification? Will we need to complete a background check before the visit?
11. Should we call/text a contact person upon arrival?
12. Where is the best place to park? Are ramps and elevators accessible for hauling heavy equipment from the parking lot to the presentation site?

Best Practices

• Maintain a healthy level of respect for your participants. You are not there to pass judgment on them or the choices they have made. You are there to help them prepare their children for the world of reading.

• Just because you offer respect does not mean you'll get the same in return. Don't take personally any perceived disinterest or rudeness from your participants. Be patient—they're still green.

• Some teen parents face heavy problems in their personal lives. Avoid offering advice beyond your expertise. Use your skills and discretion as a librarian to direct them to proper resources as the situation requires.

• Addressing behavioral problems should not be your main responsibility. If you are conducting the program within a school, ensure ahead of time that a teacher or other established authority figure is present during the entire presentation to assist in classroom management, should that become an issue.

• Invite participation but be prepared to proceed without it. At times you may be singing a song all alone, and that's okay. It's better than putting someone on the spot who might grow defensive.

• Teen parents are often bombarded with unsolicited advice. Avoid the stance of "This is what you *should* do...." Rather, take the approach of someone there to share ideas: "This is what you *can* do...."

• Allow your participants to lead the direction of the conversation. Like any parents, they will want to talk about their children's habits and milestones. This gives you a chance to encourage healthy habits that are already in place, and it puts your audience at ease.

• Talk about your own children—the ones you have at home, the ones you have already raised, or the ones you have worked with. This lends a personal touch to your presentation and helps participants feel more comfortable talking about their own parenting experiences.

• Don't take yourself too seriously. We find our participants are more willing to listen and share when we are not afraid to show our silly side. After all, our subject matter is play dough, puppets, nursery rhymes, and games. Have fun with it!

• Whenever possible, coordinate with the childcare centers that serve the teen parents you work with. In several instances, we have had the privilege of working with parents while also delivering regular storytimes to their children at nearby facilities. This establishes trust and builds rapport with your participants, especially when you're able to recall their children's names and discuss the songs or books they enjoy during storytime.

• Working with your participants' children may also provide opportunities for expansion of your program. For instance, our newest effort includes coordinating an early literacy playtime that features stories, songs, and sensory experiences for our teen parents and their children.

Adapt this program to fit the needs of your community. It may not look exactly like ours, but be assured your efforts are necessary and will be greatly appreciated. Good luck!

Using (Free) Technology to Reach Out ... and Bring In!

AMANDA NICHOLS HESS

Considering library outreach ideas? Poetry at the public library comes to mind. Or a "battle of the books" at elementary school media centers. Or even Facebook pages full of content for academic libraries. Each library uses different outreach techniques to reach their patrons. In many cases, outreach is public, highly visible, and highly promoted. Sometimes, though, outreach is more discreet, behind-the-scenes work to change attitudes or perceptions and encourage engagement.

My school library media center, located literally in the center of a junior high school, served 1300+ eighth and ninth graders and 70+ staff members. When I began there, it suffered from an identity crisis. It strove to be user-centered and meet students' and staff members' needs, but fell short. I was lucky to have a captive audience—the patrons were already in the building, and I just had to get them through my doors. So my outreach needed to change attitudes, perceptions, and views *first*, and engage *second*. I found several free, easy-to-use technology tools that helped me make these changes seamlessly as part of a broader program redesign.

Beginning at the Beginning: The Web Page

The library media center's web page was one of the first areas I identified for a major shift. When interviewing for the position, I'd checked out the web page and, at first blush, had ideas to make it more customer-centric. However, once I was *officially* in and started digging, I found a myriad of things in need of changing or discarding. This might not seem like a traditional outreach project, but today's students are "drawn to digital resources" (Johnson 2005, 26), and as such, the library media center should provide resources available digitally. I was working to change perceptions, and the way patrons viewed e-resources was an important part of those perceptions. Furthermore, studies have shown middle school students want greater access to their library (Bleidt 2011, 79); one way to expand access was through increased availability of online resources. So, to reach students, I started by making the library media center's virtual presence something they were drawn to, or could at least use effectively.

I began with the web page's look. In an assessment of library media center web pages, the best pages offer inviting and welcoming interfaces with conveniently arranged and aesthetically pleasing information (Baumbach 2005, 9–10). When I began, the library media center web page missed those marks. Instead, there were boilerplate templates, frequently changing fonts and colors, and no consistent theme or style. To elevate and simplify the design, out went the numerous boilerplates and in came a graphically stylized picture of the *actual* media center as a consistent page header. Haven't been to the *actual* physical space? Here's what it looks like. Out went the inconsistent fonts and colors—in came a single design, complete with universally used fonts and text colors (the school's colors, of course). By carrying this design scheme out on all library media center pages, any online visitor would know they were visiting a library media center web page.

Part of changing the look and feel of the web page involved simplifying and clarifying the available information. Once the web page had a cohesive design, I moved to simplifying the listed resource links and sub-pages in the navigation sidebar. When I first began, many of these links directed patrons to short, specific pages. This meant a few things.

- There were many sub-pages—too many, in my estimation.
- Sub-pages listed in the navigation sidebar caused continual scrolling on each and every page.
- Sub-pages had no logical or alphabetical organization.

I imagined this from a teenager's perspective. If I found information organized this way, would I use it? Would I consider it helpful, convenient, or effective? The answer was a resounding "no," so I condensed and logically reorganized information. Individual pages for each community library were condensed into a single "Local Libraries" page. Community organization listings cluttered up the site and could be simplified into a one-stop-shop page of local links. While this information was useful, it was infrequently used and became unnecessary clutter on the navigation sidebar. So, these important-but-rarely-used links shifted to the library media center's home page and off the navigation sidebar (and off of every page). The last step was, of course, to alphabetize these reorganized and consolidated resources.

Simplification and streamlining scratched the surface, but to *truly* revamp the library media center web page, I had to evaluate the site's content and make it more purposeful. I started superficially; the previous library media specialist had loaded the home page down with link after link and, while well-meaning, this had created a "scroll of death." After all, "people do not come to the Internet to read," and as such, library media center web page design should incorporate indents, bulleted lists, and "eye magnets" for ease of use (Warlick 2005, 14). So, I worked to identify what information was critical to read and how non-critical material could be condensed. Links to the library catalog and databases? Important and front-and-center. An expository paragraph on a rarely-used interlibrary loan service from the intermediate school district? Not as important. Off of the home page it went. I also made use of formatting tools, using two- and three-column tables to condense text, use more of the page, and eliminate excess white space. This way, the essential information fit on the library media center home page without any page scroll at all.

Finally, I rephrased information on the library media center's web page with user-centric terminology. The library's online public access catalog (OPAC) and database listing were two places where I focused this work. In one examination of library media center web page terminology, 58 percent of students using school library media center web pages look for the word "books" to signify a library catalog, but only 2 percent of school library media center web pages surveyed use "books" to connote a library catalog (Jurkowski 2007, 389–390). Furthermore, 49.4 percent of students looking for articles on school library media center web pages prefer the word "articles," but none of the library media centers surveyed used that terminology (Jurkowski 2007, 390–391). The disconnect between jargon and everyday language can impede student use. In my effort to reach out, I used everyday language instead of discipline-specific terms. Out went the "Library Databases" and "OPAC"; in came the direct and easy-to-understand "Find Articles" and "Find Books."

Once the school year was underway, I used this refreshed resource in overt outreach efforts. Specifically, I integrated the new web page into library media center orientation by creating an online scavenger hunt students had to complete in teams (for prizes, of course). This scavenger hunt, done completely online through Google Forms (more on this later), asked students to find information across the library media center's online resources and helped them learn about the many information retrieval tools available to them. Every eighth grader (and some ninth graders) were exposed to the new web page, and this project equipped students with library knowledge while fulfilling my web-page-redesign-as-outreach-tool efforts. And as I worked with classes across the curriculum, I witnessed firsthand how a more user-centered web page helped me achieve the library media center's goals and affect students' research habits. As an added bonus, the district's technology director even told me how much he liked it!

Just Google It

Another free technology tool I employed for outreach was Google. Now, this may sound like a nontraditional route for a library media specialist to take, but I used Google Apps for Education to reach students *and* staff. The school district switched to Google Apps for Education just as my tenure began. While this panicked many and caused more than a few hiccups, Google Apps' enormous tech toolkit gave me a myriad of free outreach tools.

One caveat of Google Apps for Education: it offers many of the same (if not *fewer*) options compared to a standalone Google account. This means accessing a broad range of free, easy-to-use web tools could happen just as easily with a free Gmail account. So, libraries or school districts without organizational access to Google Apps for Education can use these ideas, too.

One tool I used extensively was Google Docs and its various file types (documents, spreadsheets, presentations, etc.). Tools like Google Docs can help students understand how to create their own learning products and share their research and work with others (Naslund and Giustini 2008, 64), so these tools can be used effectively with students to impact their learning experiences. I used this feature—and particularly the ability to collaborate online—to my advantage. Google Docs allowed the creation of simple, clean documents for sharing with students and staff. And, Google Docs' unique "Publish to the Web" option—which enables automatic updates to a document that has been "published" (shared or embedded) online—meant students, staff, and parents had access to up-to-date information. Up went reading lists, informational handouts, and presentations with a few clicks of the mouse rather than uploading files, and they were always current.

Another frequently used tool was Google Forms. In fact, it became a critical and constant companion throughout my work, particularly in outreach. Through Google Forms, I did the following:

• Created student engagement/feedback forms. These encouraged student participation in the library media center's culture. For example, an online book recommendation form embedded in the library media center web page allowed students to voice their opinions and help shape the popular reading collection. This form also connected the virtual space to print resources.

• Built instructional and knowledge assessment tools. Forms, such as the library media center online scavenger hunt, asked students to participate in their own learning rather than sit-and-get information. Forms also saved evidence of student learning and understanding for further review and remediation.

• Developed easy-to-use, on-the-spot program evaluation tools. Visualizing outreach project data became simple and automatically compiled, so I could course-correct or continue with clarity.

In all situations, Google's back-end computing power automatically added and tabulated form entries in a Google Docs spreadsheet. Google's automatic chart and graph options meant data could be visualized, worked with, shared, or manipulated in other ways.

Integrating Google Apps into my practices also became a way I connected to and worked with teachers and students. Teachers saw the power online document creation offered their students, so my work parlayed into collaborative classroom instruction. This use of, and leadership in, technology allowed me to be an instructional partner and show students another way the library media center extended beyond its four walls. In turn, students recognized how Google Apps could simplify their work, and as I helped them use these tools, I demonstrated the value and usefulness of library-based services in their own lives.

Putting It in Writing

Blogging was another part of my tech-centric outreach plan that happened through Google Apps. Blog posts are opportunities to forge meaningful connections with patrons (Foote 2010, 41), and a blog can be a key opportunity for school library media specialists to reach parents (Byrne 2012, 17). So, I created a regularly updated media center blog to increase external communication and web presence, encourage online dialogue, and reach out to students, staff, and parents.

Midway through the year, I switched from an internally created blog to Blogger, a free tool provided through Google Apps. With this switch, blogging as outreach became easier and more powerful. Because it was integrated into my Google account, I needed no additional account or login information. Blogger's features made routine updates much less of a chore. I could create a post and schedule it to be published later; this meant I could write posts when I had a spare moment, not the moment a post needed to go online. These features helped eliminate the time commitment, which can be a downside of this communication method (Foote 2010, 42). Blogger also let me authorize *other* users to publish to the blog, so instead of offering weekly book reviews from *my* perspective, I engaged students in the reading, writing, and publishing process. Blogger allowed me to incorporate videos, polls, pictures, and feeds from other sites to increase engagement in content.

In addition to frequent posts on important or interesting information, I used recurring, scheduled posts as outreach tools. Each Friday, I'd post a book review of a title from the library media center shelves. These brief reviews (never negative) encouraged students to check out a particular title and helped me connect the virtual and physical library media centers while simultaneously encouraging reading and resource use. On Tuesdays, I posted technology tips directed at teachers, administrators, and building staff. These tips addressed technology needs or tools relevant to staff; however, tech-savvy students could often use these tips, too.

In addition to technology instruction outreach, I moved into virtual, asynchronous instruction with technology how-to videos. Even among media specialists, use of Web 2.0 tools in schools can be limited by lack of informal professional development and learning time, and by a dearth of relevant training opportunities (Baumbach 2009, 15–16). These issues can prevent educators from gaining the necessary knowledge to use and integrate Web 2.0 tools into their programs. To counter this problem in my own building, I created short, to-the-point videos using Jing, a free screencasting program from TechSmith. Dubbed "Two Minute Technology," these videos addressed teachers' FAQs. They were embedded into the media center home page, and these screencasts of instruction offered a judgment- and pressure-free way for staff members to get technology help while making help resources convenient and accessible anywhere with an Internet connection.

If a Picture's Worth a Thousand Words, What Does That Mean for a Video?

This project reinforced that images and video offered an avenue for significant instruction. Video can be a powerful and useful tool to reach students in the Millennial generation (Naslund and Giustini 2008, 63), and as I worked with video production for instructional purposes, I ventured into using it as an outreach tool, as well.

In February, I began representing library statistics in video form. I thought this would be a more meaningful way for building and district administrators to understand what the library media center offered to students. I put together a brief, three-minute-or-less video with an eye-catching theme, music, and significant statistics for the month, which included:

- The number of books acquired/added to the collection
- The number of students visiting the library media center on their own
- Circulation statistics
- Class usage and instructional collaborations
- The types of technology training offered

To do this, I used a simple video creation tool: Animoto. Because it is web-based, Animoto allowed me to work on the video from any computer at any time. The price was right—free!— and, as an educator, I received an expanded (or "Plus") account. This educational option allowed me to create longer videos and gave me access to more themes and music to use in my productions. Because these themes and music are built into Animoto itself, I never had to do any design work or find the right copyright-friendly tune. Creating these promotional videos, then, was as simple as uploading and arranging video and images, entering text, and selecting a theme and music. A powerful product resulted from minimal effort.

Originally, this video was directed at higher-ups, and I distributed it via e-mail. But as an afterthought, I began to loop it on the library media center televisions through the building's closed-circuit channel. Both students and staff were drawn to the video as it played throughout the day. When I created the monthly video report for March, I used it as an opportunity to engage students. I filmed their thoughts and perspectives on the library media center and made *that* the backbone of the video. Then, as the video played in the library media center, students watched it *and* looked for themselves *in* it. This technology endeavor, originally intended as an outreach tool for administrators, became a more powerful outreach tool on all levels, achieving three goals:

- Bringing students into the media center
- Engaging students in the media program
- Demonstrating student engagement to administrators and key stakeholders

Expanding the Student Library Media Center Experience with New Technology

As the school year progressed and I got to know the student population, I identified other tech-centric ways to reach out and bring students in. One way was through the use of QR codes. Librarians can use QR codes to offer high levels of support, interactivity, and engagement to patrons (Harris 2010, 12), and I viewed this as an engagement opportunity for my library media center. Nearly all students had access to their own cell phone or iPod Touch, so QR codes were something they could access. To represent library media center information around the school, I integrated QR codes into—or often used *instead* of—text. This was primarily intended as a curiosity-piquing tool for students who didn't use the library media center regularly or weren't aware of the tools and resources available.

One particularly effective use of QR code for outreach was for a monthly book club meeting. Instead of putting the book cover on the flyer—as was standard practice—I inserted a QR code in its place. By scanning the code, students reached a web page with the book's title, cover, meeting information, and even a video book trailer. The QR code, then, allowed me to share more information than I had previously. By incorporating the book trailer, I reached students through a medium that engaged them.

Just as with the monthly reports, I used free and easy-to-use tools available online to create this project.

- I created a base web page for the book club information.
- I shortened the web page's link using bit.ly—shorter links make for less-pixilated QR codes.
- I pasted the shortened link into Kaywa's QR code generator, and—*voilá!*—a QR code appeared.
- From there, I saved the QR code as an image and used it on outreach materials.

This new and unique way of representing information generated interest in and higher attendance at the meeting, and again demonstrated to students that the school library media center was a place for *them*. Many students, even those who didn't use the library media center, asked or commented about the QR codes around the school.

So, technology—and especially free resources—helped me with outreach throughout the school year. By the end of the year, student visits to the library media center were up over 100 percent; using technology tools to make the library media center visible, current, and accessible influenced this increase. Furthermore, technology allowed me to increase the library media center's visibility within the district and throughout the community. Technology helped me reframe the library media center's space—both virtual and physical—and what library services mean for a new generation of patrons.

Works Cited

Baumbach, Donna J. 2005. "The School Library Media Center Web Page: An Opportunity Too Good to Miss." *Knowledge Quest* 33 (3): 8–12.

_____. 2009. "Web 2.0 & You." *Knowledge Quest* 37 (4): 12–19.

Bleidt, Shirley A. 2011. "How Students Utilize and Perceive their School Library." *American Secondary Education* 39 (3): 67–85.

Byrne, Richard. 2012. "The Best Tools for Reaching Out to Parents: Maintaining a Blog and using a Variety of Mobile Services Will Foster Important Connections." *School Library Journal* 58 (9): 17.

Foote, Carolyn. 2010. "Putting Your Best Foot Forward." *School Library Journal* 56 (1): 40–42.

Harris, Christopher. 2010. "QR Codes in the Library: Use 2-D Barcodes to Offer the Coolest Services Ever." *School Library Journal* 56 (10): 12.

Johnson, Doug. 2005. "A Vision for the Net Generation Media Center." *Learning & Leading with Technology* 33 (2): 25–26.

Jurkowski, Odin L. 2007. "School Library Web Site Terminology." *Library Hi Tech* 25 (3): 387–395.

Naslund, Jo-Anne and Dean Giustini. 2008. "Towards School Library 2.0: An Introduction to Social Software Tools for Teacher Librarians." *School Libraries Worldwide* 14 (2): 55–67.

Warlick, David. 2005. "Building Web Sites that Work for Your Media Center." *Knowledge Quest* 33 (3): 13–15.

Creating and Running a Digital Bookmaking Fair for School or Public Libraries

STACY CREEL

Making books with children and teens is not a new idea for librarians. Many libraries still make books, especially with kids and teens, like scrapbooks, memory books, accordion books, etc., but libraries may not have experience with making digital or electronic books. Making electronic books can be done in any type of library with any age group, but this essay focuses on creating electronic books (e-books) in school and public libraries for youth.

You may wonder: why should libraries take the bookmaking trend into the digital format? There are several things to consider. Electronic books are a growing part of the publishing industry. Although additional academic research needs to be done, early studies indicate children prefer digital books, and libraries are typically about embracing technology, so this seems like a natural progression (Greenfield 2012). Libraries often have circulating collections of digital books, so this activity is a natural fit and a way to promote part of the collection. Creating e-books with youth provides you with the opportunity to host a creative, safe learning environment, while encouraging self-expression. Plus, the idea of writing workshops for youth is not new and has been popular for decades in public and school libraries. A good example of a multi-session writing workshop for teens that ends with a public sharing is *Write Here, Write Now: Holding a Creative Writing Workshop Series at Your Library* by Heather Pritchard (2008). The idea of the electronic book fair takes a traditional writing workshop into the next stage using today's technology.

E-book making fairs are also an excellent way to support The Common Core Standards by integrating literacy and blending in research and media skills. Students need to have the "ability to gather, comprehend, evaluate, synthesize, and report on information and ideas, to conduct original research in order to answer questions or solve problems, and to analyze and create a high volume and extensive range of print and non-print texts in media forms old and new. The need to conduct research and to produce and consume media is embedded into every aspect of today's curriculum" (CCSSI 2012). Since e-books can be created by students on a variety of topics and tied to any subject, they are a perfect fit. Depending on the topic, participants may need to do background research and synthesize that information into manageable content. They have to use technology to "present their ideas and knowledge in an individual and meaningful way" (University of Houston 2011).

But what does it take to get started? There are six basics steps for hosting a digital book-making fair in your school or library.

Step 1: Before Getting Started

First, see if you have access to the following:

- Computers
- Headset with microphone
- Ability to download free programs
- Digital camera and/or scanner
- Web page to host files and/or storage device to keep them all together
- Materials for brainstorming, writing, and designing
- Volunteers willing to judge
- Award certificates
- LCD projector
- Permission/release forms

Computers will be used for teaching the software, creating the project, and showing the final e-book. If your IT department uses blocking or filtering software that prevents downloads, you may need to meet with them to explain the project and gain permission to download specific programs. The digital camera or scanner will be necessary if participants are interested in creating their own original artwork or are interested in using printed photographs. Disposable digital cameras can be found online for around $10 per camera. Finished projects may be shared for a limited time or indefinitely through your library website depending on the type of e-book program you use. Some programs may require you to house the project on a storage device like a CD-ROM or jump drive.

Basic materials like paper and writing/drawing utensils are necessary for the early stages of creating the e-book. Certificates of participation and appreciation should be considered for participants and judges. Judges may be teachers in the school, library staff, administrators, or regular library users. If at all possible, judges should not have family participating in the e-book fair. The LCD projector will be helpful in two stages—the teaching of the software and in showing the completed projects. Some participants may want to create e-books but not submit them into the fair. Those who decide to participate in the e-book fair should obtain parental permission, including a permission to publish form. You should establish some guidelines for language, images, and content. Identifying information should be limited; for example, no last names, addresses, ages, birth dates, etc.

During this stage, you should establish your schedule; the entire process should take about two months. In the first week, you should take time to investigate the different software platforms available. After you have selected one, make an appointment with IT if necessary. Even if your system allows downloading, you might want to give them a heads-up anyway in case they have some extra expertise or insight to share. In the second week, you should work with your fellow librarians, staff, teachers, etc., to identify three workshop dates and the date for the e-book fair, and then reserve the appropriate rooms. If hosting the fair in a public library, this is also the time to begin advertising the e-book writing workshops. Flyers should make it clear that it is a multi-week process. It may be helpful to have participants register so that you can send them e-mail reminders of the project and help increase their participation for the entire process.

You will need to make the decision as to whether or not walk-ins will be allowed. The downside of walk-ins is that they may not be in for the entire process, but there is no guarantee that registered participants will be, either! The upside of walk-ins is that even in week one, they'll have a good time and learn something. If the program is taking place in the school library setting, this is the time that you should be working with the collaborative teacher to schedule computer time and coordinate if the e-books need to focus on specific topics.

The third week will require identifying potential judges, contacting them, and getting confirmation. This is also a good time to consider any collaboration that can take place. Do you have a local community college or university close by? Not only could they serve as potential judges, but they also may provide experts to help teach the technology or help with writing tips or sessions. Many academics have community service outreach as part of their job expectations. If there's not an academic resource close by, you should check to see if you have anyone in your community participating in writing associations, like the Society of Children's Book Writers and Illustrators. They may be able to provide some support for writing or illustrating during the participant workshops.

Is there a local newspaper? It never hurts to call and see if they can provide a local reporter to come out and talk about writing. A perk of having a reporter come is that you will be more likely to get some press coverage at the end for the actual viewing. During this third week, you should become familiar with the platform and develop the training and corresponding tools and aides.

Workshops should take place in weeks four, five, and six. The first workshop is initial training. This will most likely involve story writing and the introduction to the software. The second workshop will primarily involve uploading projects and providing assistance; 75 percent of the project should be complete at this time. The third and final workshop is when participants will be finalizing projects. If you are doing this in a public library and do not have enough library regulars for three weeks of workshops, you might consider partnering with a local school, after-school program, or youth center.

During the sixth week, in addition to the final workshop, you will begin advertising the e-book fair, inviting participants and parents to the e-book viewing. As a technology-based event, it makes perfect sense to advertise the program through your social media outlets. You might even consider highlighting some of the books on the website or Facebook in the weeks leading up to the fair. Advertise the event at local schools, libraries, technology stores, and local media outlets. Radio shows, local news shows, and community websites are great places to advertise. During week seven, judges will have access to projects and submit their votes. In week eight, you will host the e-book viewing and celebration, announce winners, and present certificates.

Step 2: Getting Started

First, you must pick the software platform you are going to teach and ask participants to use. While many participants might have access to more sophisticated programs at home or be willing to pay for programs, it is important to use a single platform for your e-book fair for two reasons. First, it creates a level playing field—participants will be judged on the same standards on the same platform. Second, it allows you to guarantee that the e-book will run on your library's system because you will have tested it out and downloaded the program prior to getting started. Before selecting a program, be sure to read the terms and conditions of the site or program. Programs/tools typically fall into one of the following categories:

- Slideshow
- Timeline
- Mixer
- Comic
- Scrapbook
- Mapping
- Photo
- Audio
- Video
- Presentation

Some free tools by type can be found through Alan Levine's wiki—50+ Web 2.0 Ways to Tell a Story (http://50ways.wikispaces.com/). This wiki provides a variety of tools in each category that should be investigated. Some free programs or website applications that you might consider are:

- iMovie (Mac only)
- Microsoft Photo Story 3 (PC only)
- Windows Movie Maker (PC only)
- QuickTime Pro (Mac and PC)
- Picasa (Mac and PC)
- PhotoPeach (Mac and PC)
- TikaTok Pearson (Mac and PC)
- VUVOX (Mac and PC)
- Animoto (Mac and PC)
- Universal Design for Learning (Mac and PC)
- RockYou (Mac and PC)
- OurStory (Mac and PC)
- ToonDoo (Mac and PC)
- Wayfaring (Mac and PC)
- Flickr Tell a Story in 5 Frames (Mac and PC)
- SlideShare (Mac and PC)

A quick Google search will reveal that there are many more digital publishing or digital storytelling platforms available. While some are free, there are many that offer a free trial or are relatively inexpensive. Whatever you opt to use, you might start by searching for video tutorials before playing with the program. Programs that have tutorials available will be beneficial for you when teaching the program to participants and for afterwards when participants need a reminder. After you have selected the program to use, take time to learn it and then create a step-by-step lesson for e-book fair participants. Be sure to locate some exciting examples to open the lesson with so they are aware of what can be accomplished.

Step 3: Creating Their Story

Even if tied to a particular subject or activity, participants should start by brainstorming ideas for their story. The story should be between 10 and 15 "pages" long. If stories become overly long, you might encounter problems hosting or uploading them. Once they have written the story, it is time to brainstorm what images would fit their story. They may opt to draw and scan the images or to take pictures with a digital camera for uploading. However, if these two options do not appeal, they may find royalty-free images at Flickr Creative Commons, 4FreePhotos, FreePhotoBank, Morguefile, and many more. Some of these sites require credit or a link be provided back to their site, so be sure to read the terms and conditions.

Depending on the age of the participants, you might want to have them create a storyboard. A storyboard is an organizational tool that helps the writer visualize the sequences. It typically contains a place for the image, the text, and any sound or extras. There are lots of free templates online, like Printable Paper or The eLearning Coach's Storyboard Depot. Another quick Google search will result in plenty of choices. Once they have laid out the story and images, it is time to edit. Is there anything that needs to be changed, clarified, or removed? Are sentences grammatically correct and free of spelling errors? Have they met the overall goal of the project? Once editing is done on paper, participants are ready to try their hands at the technology. It is expected at this first workshop that only a handful of participants will get to the technology stage. This is especially true for younger participants.

Step 4: Supporting the Process

Whether you are in a public or school library, it will be beneficial to host several sessions for participants to have access to computers and to you. After your initial session, participants may need a reminder, so helpful hints sheets on the process will be beneficial. Follow-up sessions will also provide participants access to the scanner and help with editing if needed. It might be helpful to establish a password and username protocol so that they do not have to struggle to remember the login and password. You might consider usernames to be first name and last initial (mine would be StacyC) and passwords to be your library's name and the participant's birth month and day (such as USM0114). At the second workshop, participants should be between 75 percent to 100 percent done. Encourage those who are completely finished to attend the third and final workshop to help their peers. Anyone not finished by the third workshop should be encouraged to finish their project to be included in the final viewing but should not be included in the judging. A cutoff date is necessary so that judges can have sufficient time to view all of the projects. Completed projects entered into the e-book fair should be uploaded to the website or made available through storage devices.

Step 5: Judging the Projects

The easiest way for your volunteers to judge the projects is to use a rubric or a scale. If you have enough participants over a wide age range, then it is appropriate to break the judging into groups. You might even separate participants into categories like biographical, nonfiction, fiction, etc. The rubric should cover the following areas:

- Is the story unique, original, or creative?
- Is the grammar correct?
- Do the images appropriately reflect the story? Are the images clear?
- Does the story flow? Is it organized?
- What is the sound quality of music and/or narration?

The ideal judging setting is to have all of the judges there on a specific day during set hours to view the books at your location. This limits potential issues with technology and allows you to provide support if issues do arise. It also speeds up judging since the e-books will be running on multiple computers. If this is not possible, you can post completed books on a closed website for viewing.

Judges should record their responses and return them to you for tallying. The responses and points should be kept confidential; even the winners do not need to know the scoring/ranking. Once judging is complete, certificates of participation for the winners should be created. You might consider asking the judges if they prefer a thank-you letter or a certificate for their files. In addition to inviting them to the celebration and e-book viewing, be sure to ask for feedback on the process, areas of improvement, etc., formally or informally.

Step 6: The Viewing and Celebration

Now comes the really fun part. Participants and their families get to see their work projected on the big screen. You get to promote the library as a place that bridges technology and books, and all for very little money—the cost of certificates and snacks. Be sure to test out the technology before the program begins. To make things look more high-tech, have multiple viewing stations (laptops) around the room as well as the big screen. This allows guests to view the books in less time and with less crowd congestion. A slideshow of pictures from the workshops can be included on the big screen. If you have enough time, showing every e-book on the big screen is ideal. Giving participants certificates makes them feel special and is cost-effective. Winners should receive something additional, and what that means will depend on budget. Using ribbons for the winners costs very little. If your budget can handle more, trophies or plaques work well. If at all possible, you may consider going "all out" with e-book readers for top prizes.

Be sure to send press releases to the media and get pictures for your own website and publicity. Having a brochure with the book titles, author information (first names only), and brief summaries will give the participants something to take home as a souvenir. If you have multiple viewing stations, you might try listing them first by viewing station. Don't forget to do a book display. Include books on bookmaking, and print out covers of e-books in your collection to promote them.

Conclusion

Creating e-books and hosting a digital bookmaking fair highlights technology, creates publicity buzz, creates involvement opportunities, and can be accomplished with very little expense. There are very few issues or problems that you might encounter. The issue of allowing walk-ins versus signing up is one issue, and project completion is another. Even with sign-ups, there is no way to guarantee everyone completes the project. One tried-and-true way to increase participation is snacks, but you would want to do a scheduled break because of computers and equipment.

Another issue that might arise is your level of involvement in assisting participants. If they are unable to do something, are you going to step in and help them complete it? Using volunteers may help those needing more one-on-one attention. It may also help to brainstorm ways to modify what they are doing. If you take the time to investigate the technology you choose and practice it on your computers, you should not encounter any real technology problems; however, things like Internet connection speed or outages are outside of your control. If at all possible, have IT on standby. Even with these minor issues, the six basic steps for running a digital or e-book fair can be accomplished in about eight weeks.

People are familiar with science fairs and social studies fairs. Some schools even have geography and math fairs, but not everyone is familiar with the idea of an e-book fair. Creating e-books incorporates technology in a meaningful way, and hosting a digital bookmaking fair is inexpensive, educational, and involves staff, children, parents, and teachers.

Works Cited

CCSSI (Common Core State Standards Initiative). 2012. "English Language Arts Standards; Introduction; Key Design Consideration." http://www.corestandards.org/ELA-Literacy/introduction/key-design-consideration (accessed January 29, 2013).

Greenfield, Jeremy. 2012. "For Reading and Learning, Kids Prefer E-Books to Print Books." *Digital Book World,* January 9. http://www.digitalbookworld.com/2012/for-reading-and-learning-kids-prefer-e-books-to-print-books/ (accessed January 19, 2013).

Pritchard, Heather. 2008. "Write Here, Write Now: Holding a Creative Writing Workshop Series at Your Library." *Young Adult Library Services* 6 (4): 19.

University of Houston. 2011. "Educational Uses of Digital Storytelling." http://digitalstorytelling.coe.uh.edu/page.cfm?id=27&cid=27&sublinkid=30 (accessed May 24, 2013).

Preschool Outreach
Small Public Library Programs
REBECCA D. RICHARDSON

When I first began working as the director of the Cresson Public Library, I was warned from my predecessor not to expect much in the way of program participation. At first I thought nothing of it and began planning away what programs we would like, including the standard preschool storytime. I jumped right into planning the storytime—stories, songs, crafts. I talked with parents about the types of programs they would like to see the library have for their children. When the school year started, I advertised the beginning of storytime through word of mouth, flyers around town, and press releases. I was the only person who showed up the first week.

Anemic attendance continued for some time, and it didn't change until we started a library outreach program. After implementing the outreach effort, we had a total of nine storytime programs and more than 100 unique children every month. Not only did our storytime statistics increase, we also experienced a small but measurable increase in our patron base as students from the preschools would insist that their parents bring them to the library to see "The Library Lady." The cost for the overall outreach program was minimal, with each individual program lasting approximately 15–20 minutes, and it was easily accomplished with our staff of two.

Scenario

The Cresson Public Library is a small, rural library in Western Pennsylvania. It has a collection of approximately 10,000 titles, a patron base of 1,500 individuals, and a staff of two part-time workers. It is a stand-alone library that is part of the Cambria-Somerset Consortium. The annual budget of less than $50,000 a year is used to cover facility costs, wages and benefits, collection development, and programs and outreach. As one might expect, programs and outreach costs are kept to a minimum in order to maintain the building, etc.

The Cresson Public Library operates within five miles of two other public libraries that provide established preschool storytimes. When I spoke with parents about attending our storytime, I was told by many that while they came to the Cresson Library to check out books, they had been attending the storytime at one of the other local libraries for years and felt it would be disloyal to the librarian there if they were to begin attending our storytime. We purposely ran our storytime on a different day than the other libraries, but parents still felt it would be disloyal. By the end of the first month, I was up to four children. These same children came every week. We had a total of four programs every month with a total of 16 children (it was the same four children at each program).

I had received good feedback from the parents of those who attended the program. The children seemed to have a good time. But still, it was the age-old problem of having a great program with few participants. Throughout the fall, I asked patrons who brought their preschool-age children to the library for books why they never came for storytime. The answer was usually that they would either feel disloyal to the library where they had gone to storytime in the past, or they were working. So, I began to ask, "If I were to move storytime to an evening, would you be able to come?" The answer was generally, "No, by the time we get home from work, we're tired."

I did not necessarily want to "steal" patrons from other programs, so I decided to focus on the children of the working parents. I began to ask myself: where are these children? Who takes care of these children during the day while the parents are working? In the Cresson area, many of the children were in one of four preschools/daycares in the area.

I started doing some research into outreach programs. Most of the articles I found involved larger libraries or school libraries (Vandersteen and Baker 2008; Cahill 2004). None of them fit my needs exactly, so I began to pick them apart to garner ideas I could use to develop my own program.

From Questions to Answers

Once my research was done, I came away with five key questions:
1. What do I hope to accomplish through my programs?
2. Where do I want to go?
3. What would I want to include in the program?
4. How long would my program last?
5. How much money would this program cost the library?

The answer to the first question seemed rather obvious to me. I hoped to increase the number of participants in my preschool storytime. While I enjoyed the children who attended our programs, I wanted to reach more.

In tackling the second question, I looked at the community and decided that I would focus my program on the two daycare providers and the two organized preschools within Cresson Borough. I did receive requests to take the program into other communities, but I declined because they were within the service area of a different public library. I did not want to turn my program into a competition between libraries.

The next two questions on my list were tied together—how much I could include in my program was fairly dependent on how much time I had with the children. I decided to keep it fairly simple, with no more than two stories or a story and a finger play. I chose not to give a full-length storytime.

The final question dealt with cost, which was the biggest issue I faced with this program. Cost covered everything from staff salaries, mileage to get to and from programs, and supplies.

I decided to apply for a grant to help cover any costs. Finding a grant was not difficult. Cresson, Pennsylvania, is in a depressed area, and there are many literacy grants out there compatible with low-income areas. The grant I applied for and received was a Target Early Childhood Reading Grant for $500 (Target Corporation 2012). I initially planned my program as though I had no outside funding because the recipients of the grant were not notified until August, and I wanted to begin my program at the beginning of the school year in September. However, the Cresson Public Library did receive a separate grant of $500, which helped to offset costs and allowed me to purchase a book for each student involved in the program.

Cresson is a small town, so many of the teachers I wanted to offer the program to were patrons whom I saw regularly at the library. I had begun a program where they would call me with a theme they would be covering in the classroom, and I would pull a number of items from the shelves for them to go through. Once I had received approval on the project from my board of directors, I began to speak with teachers about hosting my program. While they were receptive, it quickly became apparent that I needed to go through the building administrators (preschools) and owners (daycares). These teachers gave me a key phrase to use when talking to their administrators: early childhood literacy standards.

Not all administrators were immediately receptive to my coming into their buildings and offering a program. They already had librarians. I had to assure the building principals that I was not intending to take the place of their staff, but I would offer a helping hand by conducting an additional storytime to their students. I also had to stress that I would be working within the teachers' curriculum plans. The daycare and preschool owners/operators were quite happy to have the programs brought to them. It gave them something else they could use as a selling tool for their facilities.

Getting Started

The program finally got off the ground, though it kicked off a month behind schedule due to issues with gaining entrance to schools. In total, I added five storytimes a month in four off-site locations (one location had two storytimes because they had different students every other day). I offered these programs on two set days a month. I chose Tuesday and Wednesday because there are very few school holidays in the middle of the week, and I was trying to become a part of the students' routine. It also fit well with the storytime schedule offered within the library on Thursday mornings.

I tried to keep the cost of my storytime minimal while still providing the students/teachers with a program worthy of my coming into their classrooms. On my first visit, I would introduce myself and we would have a small discussion about libraries and what they could find there. I would also leave some flyers and pamphlets for the students to take home to their parents. After that first visit, a typical program would include a reminder about who I was, what the library had to offer, and at least two stories or a story and a finger play. I would also leave either coloring sheets or a simple craft that could be done when the teacher needed a filler activity.

As far as staffing, when you are a library with only two employees, you tend to get creative. The Cresson Public Library is open beginning at 1:00 P.M. daily. The late opening allowed me to conduct the programs in the morning, typically around 10:00 A.M. Each program lasted approximately 15–20 minutes. In the event that I was not able to conduct the storytime myself, I would schedule my assistant to do them.

There were some problems that occurred with this program, but nothing that we could not overcome. Most problems were weather-related. The school would occasionally have a snow delay or closure. If they were delayed, the students would be arriving just at the time I was scheduled to read to them. After the first occurrence, we would schedule a "snow date" in the event of a cancellation due to weather.

Another issue was with the books I brought with me. I found that sometimes I would bring a book they had already read, or a book the teacher had been planning to read to the students later. We solved this problem by having me either call or e-mail the teacher in advance with the titles I planned to read to be sure there would be no double coverage. This would also allow me to find out what themes the teacher had in her classroom that month and give me the chance to find materials that would supplement her lessons. I found that most preschool programs have similar themes throughout the year.

I also made the mistake of bringing the same book to the parochial preschool and the public preschool. I had to do some quick rephrasing in order to make the book more acceptable to a secular audience. After that, I would double-check my titles and bring a book to switch out if the book for the parochial school was something unacceptable in a public school.

When I analyzed the results of the program in light of the first question I asked myself (What do I hope to accomplish through my programs?), I concluded that the storytime outreach was a success. I set out to increase the number of children participants in our preschool storytime program, and I accomplished this goal. Instead of the usual four distinct children each month, we were reaching more than 100 distinct children. When added together, this figure blew our previous years' statistics out of the water! In addition, many of the children whom I saw in the schools came to the library building with their families, and they became library patrons. Thanks to the Target grant, we were able to provide every child who participated in our preschool storytime for the year a free book. For several, it was the first book they had ever owned.

Important Steps to Consider When Providing Programs to a School or Daycare

When Figuring Your Costs:
• Calculate the wages of library employees and decide if you will pay them for a set amount of time or from the time they leave point A until they return. I recommend setting a time frame. It helps people to be prompt and not linger too long in the classroom they are visiting. Teachers are busy, and the students have a schedule. While you may think you are being helpful by offering extra stories or songs, you could be hindering the schedule of the day.

• Calculate mileage (if applicable) and where mileage will begin. Do you begin counting miles from the employee's departing location or from the library building?

• Calculate the cost of supplies. This includes books you plan to purchase and any craft supplies you intend to leave with the teachers.

• Calculate a separate "wish list" of items you would like to add to the program if the funding opportunity arises.

• Look for funding opportunities. Target, as I mentioned earlier, offers Early Childhood Reading Grants. Walmart (2012) and Family Dollar (2012) offer similar community-based grant opportunities.

When Approaching a School or Daycare about Providing Programs:
• Ask permission from the school principal or daycare operators to approach their teachers about a recurring outreach program, and use the word "partnership." Partnership is an important word in the world of funding.
• Stress that you do not intend to replace the school librarian, and that you plan to conduct your storytime program only with the preschool class. Often school officials feel that since they have a librarian of their own, it is not necessary to bring in one from outside the building and that you could have some nefarious plot to take over their school library program.
• Ask each school office what the rules and procedures are for visiting the school. Nearly every school requires visitors to check in and to be identified to their staff as a visitor.
• Ask if you will be considered a volunteer and if you need any child safety clearances.
• Once you have the permission of the school administrator, approach the teacher to find out if he or she is interested in having a recurring program.

Once You Have Approval from the School Administrator and the Teacher:
• Plan a time that works for both you and the teacher.
• Obtain the teacher's contact information: an e-mail address for any questions that can wait until the teacher has time to respond and a direct phone number for times when you need to speak with the teacher immediately.
• If possible, set the date of your program for the same day each month. I found it worked best for me to plan two mornings a month for the preschool outreach and do all the programs on these two days.
• Ask about the teacher's preferences for days when there is a delay or when the school is cancelled due to inclement weather. It is better to have this information far in advance of an actual occurrence so that you can have a plan in place.
• Be flexible. The success of the program is highly reliant on the cooperation of the teacher/school. While you may like to think you are doing them a favor by bringing the program to their classroom, they are actually the ones doing you the favor by allowing you to conduct your program and raise your participation numbers.

Planning the Program:
• Make a list of the books you intend to use for your in-library storytime and e-mail them to the teacher of the preschool for final approval. This is useful because you don't want to repeat the books they either (a) have already read to the class or (b) plan to read to them in the future.
• Find a coloring page (these are often available free of charge online) or a simple craft to bring with you that goes along with your theme.

Conducting the Program:
• Introduce yourself to the children on their level. Most schools require students to refer to teachers with some sort of respectful title, such as Mr., Mrs., Ms., or Miss. I asked the children to call me Miss Becky because it was easy for them to pronounce and remember. Do not be surprised if they call you something like "The Library Lady."

- Have the children gather around you close enough to see and hear but far enough away that you are not crowded.
- Introduce the story, the author, and the illustrator. I do this at every storytime because it helps cement the idea in their heads.
- Because the time in the classroom is fairly short, if the students would like a story read a second time, give them the option of reading the second book you brought or repeating the first.
- If a child is acting out, distracting you or the other children, do not stop your story. When the story is over, ask the student to please sit in the chairs away from the group, but close enough to hear the story. If it happens more than once, speak with the teacher privately about possible solutions. Do not attempt to discipline the student yourself; this is the responsibility of the classroom teacher.
- Mostly, smile and enjoy the celebrity of being a guest reader in a classroom of three- and four-year-olds.

While librarians may be going into the school with the goal of raising their program statistics, the program is about much more. It is the same reason we offer preschool programs in our libraries. It is about instilling a love of books and literacy in children. It is about exposing children to the joy of hearing someone read to them. It is about opening a world of thoughtful imagination that comes from sharing a good story and reaching out to children in your community.

Works Cited

Cahill, Maria. 2004. "Meeting the Early Literacy Needs of Children through Preschool Outreach Storytime Programs." *Knowledge Quest* 33 (2): 61–62.

Family Dollar Stores. 2012. "Giving Back." http://corporate.familydollar.com/pages/givingback.aspx (accessed September 24, 2012).

Target Corporation. 2012. "Early Childhood Reading Grants." http://sites.target.com/site/en/company/page.jsp?contentId=WCMP04-031821 (accessed September 24, 2012).

Vandersteen, Beth, and Susan Baker. 2008. "Preschool Outreach the Rapides Way!" *Louisiana Libraries* 71 (2): 3–5.

Walmart Stores. 2012. "Local Giving Program." http://foundation.walmart.com/apply-for-grants/local-giving (accessed September 24, 2012).

Taking Your Show on the Road
STEM and Early Literacy Storytime Outreach
Josie B. Hanneman

Outreach storytimes and activities are an invaluable way to reach patrons who do not walk through your library's doors. By reaching your public where they are, at events, in preschools, and in other public places, you strengthen the impact you have on your community. By providing early literacy storytimes, and those that include science, technology, engineering, and mathematics (STEM), you help to grow readers, future scholars, and the next generation of library users.

In this essay, I will first discuss the specific logistics of contacting groups to do outreach storytimes. This could be with specific institutions, at community gatherings, and in other possible settings. Next, I will consider various props for the different venues. In some cases, you need nothing more than you and your books; in others, you might want to prepare for a stage show or outdoor event. Finally, I will share specific programs that I have found useful and fun, and suggest ways to replicate them in a variety of settings.

Making First Contact

In every community there are preschools, daycares, and events that will welcome a talented, enthusiastic, and free storytime provider. While we'd like to visit them all, in reality we all need to look at our schedules and the demands on our time and select the options that work best for us. Before contacting groups, organize your thoughts on what you'd like to offer and what sort of time you have to commit to the endeavor. There are major differences between a one-off storytime, a monthly or weekly storytime, or hosting a daylong kids' corner at your local Fourth of July celebration. Once you know what you can offer, start making a list of potential outreach locations. If you've been in your community for a long time, you're probably aware of quite a few child-serving institutions and gatherings that can populate your list. If you're new to a place, be sure to brainstorm with coworkers, community shareholders, and anyone else you come across! A few sure-fire places to start would be a community calendar provided by your Chamber of Commerce (or a similar group), local event guides, parents you see in the library, and a quick Google search. Elementary schools will also have knowledge of the local daycares or preschools that feed into their student bodies.

After you've made an exhaustive list, prioritize which groups you can reach with the greatest impact. Keep your specific library's mission and goals in mind as you decide which ones to contact for outreach. And do not throw the complete list away! Some of the groups or events you visit in your first round will be problematic (more on this later), and you'll want to fill in the empty spots with other opportunities.

Preschools and Daycare Centers

Preschools and daycare centers are great places to start your outreach journey. For the most part, they have organized schedules, professional staff, and many of the same goals as the library. The first step is gathering together a list of these groups in your community and prioritizing which ones you'd like to reach. In a small town with limited offerings, this can be fairly easy; in a larger city, you might not be able to make an exhaustive list. Don't worry! You can always update your list and reevaluate as you go.

Most of these institutions will have readily available contact information on the Internet, in the phone book, or via your Chamber of Commerce. Making the initial contact might be a little challenging as teachers and staff are often busy during the work day and not physically in the building after the school day is over. Keep trying; you'll make contact with someone eventually! Make sure your offer is well "packaged" and ready to sell when you dial the number or type in the e-mail address. Your skills are important, and children will prosper from being exposed to your knowledge. If you don't communicate this effectively, you'll never get the opportunity to share.

Each librarian and library will need to prioritize based on their mission, goals, community, and individual strengths. Working within the framework of my library district, I select preschools and daycare centers based on their need, size, access to the library, and their target students' possible status as high-risk. In practice, this means that I put Head Start programs at the top of my list, then put local special-needs preschools into my calendar, and finally find room for those places that are larger and geographically distant from the library.

One special circumstance worth mentioning is the preschool or daycare center in your neighborhood that is capable of attending your regularly scheduled programs within the library. Many schools are within easy walking distance, or even on the same community campus. Others have transportation that makes it possible for them to visit you. These options need to be explored if you are to make the greatest impact and reach a larger number of children with fewer library resources.

When you do preschool and daycare visits, be sure to bring something that the children can take home with them. This has two benefits: it lets the parents know that the library is active in their children's lives, and it can give them further activities to do in the home, strengthening the positive outcomes of the original session. At my library, the custom is to bring a "rhyme sheet" that lists the rhymes we did and the books we read during our storytime. On the back, I often put a coloring sheet, in-library storytimes and locations, or other pertinent library information.

Community Outreach at Events

In my district, there are many yearly events that are a natural fit for the library. These are often one-day or weekend events that help get the library's message out to an unconventional audience. The people who see you at community events might be a different crowd than those who attend your in-house programs and use the library's services. Furthermore, attending kid-friendly events will provide children and parents with fun and educational activities that may entice them to visit their favorite librarian in the library at a regularly scheduled program. Finally, attending and participating in local events is another method of raising community awareness of the library and its resources.

Most community groups want to get the word out about their events and programs. Check local papers, the Chamber of Commerce, community calendars, and longtime inhabitants for leads on different things going on. Continue checking these sources regularly. If you find out about an event too late this year, you can put it on your calendar for next year.

Once you have a list, evaluate the entries to see if they fit with your library's storytime goals. We have events where we can set up our small, portable puppet stage and have live theater. This is a good fit for us. At other events, the audience and the layout are just not conducive to storytelling and science fun. They can remain on your outreach list if they meet another goal but might not be appropriate for sharing early literacy and STEM activities.

Other Institutions in Your Community

You may want to consider visiting other groups in your community. During the summer, many food banks provide free lunch to children through partnerships with local entities, including schools and libraries. Check with local groups to see if you can provide storytimes and activities at these regular meals. There are summer schools that serve migrant populations. These might be a good fit for a STEM activity. Some businesses have places to drop off children while their parents shop. A quick storytime could work during busy hours. Homeless shelters and battered women's homes may also have children in need of your talents. These latter two will require a high level of sensitivity, and they might ask for a background check or confidentiality agreement. Brainstorm for more ideas specific to your community.

Evaluating Continuation with a Group or Event

At some point, you may need to make the difficult decision about continuing to visit a group or event. There are a few very important aspects to consider when evaluating visits or attending an event in a professional capacity:

• Need. Can the staff of an institution or event provide equal or better service than you can with your visits? Do they really need you to augment their offerings?

• Organization or discipline. Is the school so chaotic or the event so poorly organized that you cannot effectively reach your goals? With schools, this can be difficult; often those with the least-prepared staff are the ones that need your help the most. It's a challenging decision, with no "right" answer.

• Fit. Is visiting a specific group or event really effective in reaching your library's early literacy and STEM goals?

• Staffing. Can another library staff person or volunteer attend the event? If handing out flyers is all that's needed, for example, try to send a volunteer.

Props and Supplies

Bringing realia, props, and specific hands-on activities can enliven any early literacy or STEM-focused storytime. Some proficient storytellers can bring their tale to life with nothing more than their bodies; I am not that gifted and prefer to bring books, felt boards, toys, puppets, or other objects to enhance my stories and activities.

If you've created storytimes and programs in your library, the above accessories are probably something you are already aware of. Taking the show on the road, however, requires more. Depending on the situation, you may need to be able to transport all of the items yourself in one trip, keep an eye on all your materials, or even be able to hold them in your hands for the duration. Situations like this call for a luggage cart that fits boxes, and perhaps bungee cords to hold them on the cart. You might need a backpack or other specific carrier. Some items might require a hand truck. If you are going to attend events, be sure to be prepared for the weather. In summer, a popup tent is useful for shade; in winter, dressing properly is vital. Events will provide varying levels of support, so be sure to check with the organizers. Some things you might want to have on your checklist include:

• Will a table or chairs be provided? Some events will have them, others will not. In the latter situation, a sturdy, lightweight folding set will serve you well. Be sure you can transport them in terms of carrying and vehicle size.

• How much space will you receive? Is there room for that portable puppet theater? Or will you be limited to a chair, or something similar?

• Will there be access to water for STEM activities? Will It Float (see below) is one of my favorites, but I wouldn't do it at an event where I needed to bring my own water!

• Will you be near an electrical outlet for possibly sound or other uses? If you need it, check for Wi-Fi, too.

• If you're at a preschool, will the setting fit your needs? Take into account your own abilities and comfort levels. If you have difficulty sitting on the floor for storytime, for example, be sure to arrange for a chair.

• Luggage carts, hand trucks, garden wagons, boxes, crates, book bags, and backpacks may be necessary for transporting your materials.

You will also want to consider what early literacy and STEM-specific props you will need. This might require a large investment, so prioritize for your library. Here are a few ideas of what you might want to accompany you to events and outreach storytimes:

• Traveling felt board. This can be as small as a 1' × 1', and as simple as a sturdy piece of cardboard covered in felt. Larger ones are useful with a big crowd, but will also have hauling and transporting challenges. In a pinch, wear a fuzzy sweater and use yourself, or a volunteer from the audience, as a felt board!

• Portable puppet stage and puppets. These are great for independent play at events. Children will create their own stories and make new friends with little direction required. Alternatively, you can read a story that has the same characters as your puppets; for example, you might use a wolf and other forest animal puppets for the adaption of a classic Latin American song by Claudia Rueda, *Let's Play in the Forest While the Wolf Is Not Around.*

• Tubs for water; measuring tools; magnifying glasses; sandpaper and velvet for texture exploration; rocks, bones, and feathers, for scientific exploration. There is a never-ending list of items you could use for self- or librarian-led STEM activities.

Specific Programs

The following specific programs can be used in a variety of settings. I will include a basic plan, plus suggestions for extending the activities and resources. Use your own creativity to mix, match, and expand on these ideas. One major takeaway that I hope everyone remembers: don't shy away from using difficult science-related words; this does double duty of introducing participants to science concepts and enriching their vocabularies. Even if they don't remember the word the first time, it will stick better with subsequent uses.

Will It Float?

Many stories are a great accompaniment for floating experiments. The purpose of this activity is to practice predicting outcomes, forming hypotheses, creating real-life experiments to test these hypotheses, and observing the results of your experiments. You can also add classification to lengthen and discuss the activity. Using books to introduce the ideas of sinking and floating connect the library's literacy goals with a fun science activity. In the classic title *Who Sank the Boat?* by Pamela Allen, the audience can experience boating and falling into the water. Allen's book also has great rhyming lines, and can also be used in the activity below.

Who Sank the Boat?

In this idea adapted from an activity done by Wilsonville (OR) Public Library staff, begin with the story *Who Sank the Boat?* This is a very flexible story that can be told using the book, performed with felt characters prepared beforehand, or with the use of audience participation. In the last option, bring some very basic props to label the volunteers: you can give the cow volunteer horns, for example. Also have some sort of boat for them to sit in. Something as simple as a colored cardboard cutout or a blanket spread on the ground will work fine. This book's repetitive, rhyming text helps reinforce language play. Point out and emphasize the rhymes to help children develop early literacy skills. For example, when you've told the story, ask, "Did you hear the rhyming words? They said flutter and it rhymed with 'the pig who was as fat as...' what? 'Butter!'"

There are many other titles that have boats, floating, sinking, or water in them that would work for this activity. In the book *Jonathan and the Big Blue Boat* by Philip C. Stead, there is a near miss with sinking, for example. Read *Mr. Gumpy's Outing* by John Burningham for a fun overboard mishap. Use the one with which you are most comfortable. If you'd prefer a longer storytime, bring the children back together after the experiment, discuss it, and read a second book.

Buoyancy Experiment

After telling one of the above stories, discuss who sank the boat, how it happened, or what it means to float and sink. If you'd like, introduce and explain the words "density" and "buoyancy," and explain how they determine what will sink and what will float. Next, have several tubs of water available. I prefer clear plastic so that people can see things from the side view.

In a school setting, you can work with the whole class or have them in smaller groups with a staff member. Arrange several items next to the tub. If you're working with the whole class, hold an item up and ask them to hypothesize, or guess, if it will sink or float, then drop it in your tub. If there are smaller groups, have the staff person do the same. (It's easier for a smaller group to communicate their opinions openly, but the institution might not have enough support staff to make this work well.) In smaller groups, you can also practice sorting as part of your hypothesizing. You can sort the items you have into two categories: those that students think will float and those that they think will sink. After each item (perhaps 4–6) has been put in the water, have the students report on their observations. For example, "Did the chalk float or sink?" Wait for their responses and move on to the next item. You can add another sorting activity: those items that sank and those that floated. If you have time, brainstorm about other items. "What else could we drop in the water? Would it sink or float? What's your hypothesis, or best guess?"

If you're doing this activity at an event, rely on parents to hypothesize with their children, but be available and aware to help out when needed. Read the book, or tell the story as above, and then explain the process to the audience for experimentation. This is a great project for outdoor summer events. If people get a little wet and messy, it's all part of the fun!

Plant Growth: Biology, Ecology, and Measurement

Watching a plant grow from a seed is an amazing process, and there are plenty of books that illustrate and entertain with this concept. First, find a book that shows some aspect of the process (see the list below for inspiration). Read that book, and then show a prepared, growing bean sprout. It's best to have it in a plastic bag with a little bit of soil so that the children can see the roots under the dirt as well as the leaves above the soil. Be sure to point out the different parts of the plant (roots, stem, and leaves) and discuss how plants need sun, water, and soil to grow. Beans are one of the easiest things to grow and have a quick germination time, so they are very useful for this experiment.

Some good book titles for this activity include:

- *And Then It's Spring* by Julie Fogliano, illustrated by Erin Stead
- *Sunflower* by Miela Ford
- *Flora's Surprise* by Debi Gliori
- *One Watermelon Seed* by Celia Barker Lottridge, illustrated by Karen Patkau
- *Koala and the Flower* by Mary Murphy
- *To Be Like the Sun* by Susan Marie Swanson, illustrated by Margaret Chodos-Irvine
- *Pumpkin, Pumpkin* by Jeanne Titherington

For a takeaway craft, there are two options: messy and clean. For the messy path, fill a few tubs with potting soil, provide bean seeds, trowels (or large spoons), small plastic zipper bags, permanent markers, and masking tape. Follow these steps:

1. Have each child write his or her name on a piece of masking tape, then place it on the bag. You, parents, or staff can also write their names for them, explaining what you're doing as you go. This will help with letter recognition and print awareness.

2. Have each child fill a bag with about 2–4 inches of dirt, and place 1–2 bean seeds just below the top of the dirt.

3. Explain that they will have to water it lightly, just like in the books you read previously, and allow it light to grow.

For the cleaner version, have pre-filled bags, but still have children write their names, and place their beans inside.

Please note that in the long-term, this is not the best gardening idea as lack of drainage will allow for rot to occur. If you'd rather use pots or old yogurt containers with holes poked in the bottom, the plants will grow longer with the added benefit of drainage. This variation will make it impossible to see the roots, however. Clear plastic cups would work as a good compromise: they are steadier and allow for drainage, but it will be more difficult to see the roots and leaf development. Sunflower and basil seeds are useful for other growing projects if you plan on keeping the plants around for a longer period; they also germinate fairly easily and quickly.

Wrap-up

I hope I have conveyed the importance of providing STEM outreach storytimes. These acts will enrich a wider audience and expose more children and parents to the possibilities of literacy and STEM activities at a young age. There are some minor challenges in providing these services outside the library, but they can be overcome with planning. The inconveniences of taking your show on the road are well worth the benefits of deepening your library's service to the wider community.

After-School Storytimes
Activities for Elementary School Outreach
Krissy Wick

After-school programs for children in elementary school provide fantastic outreach opportunities for any library, but they pose some unique challenges. The groups are often large, the ages are often mixed (including kindergartners through fifth graders), and the time and space are often short. What's a librarian to do? The following programs have all been done with groups of elementary students ranging in age from kindergarten through fifth grade and in number from small groups (10–20 kids) to very large ones (100–150 kids). They are easy, they are fun, and they work!

Before You Start

Before you enter into any outreach partnerships, here are some things to ponder:
- What is the setting like? Will teachers or group leaders be present in the room while the program is going on, or will I be expected to lead alone? What is my library's policy on this? What is the school's?
- What resources are available at the outreach site? Will I have a TV with a DVD player? Will I have craft materials to use?
- What is the space like at the site? Can I get up and move with the kids? Will I have table space for a craft project?
- How many kids will I be working with, and what is the age breakdown?
- How often will I be expected to come? Is that sustainable given my current level of programming?

In order to maximize your time, it can be helpful to create one elementary school outreach kit each month to use at multiple locations. It can also be helpful to set aside parts of your schedule that are devoted solely to outreach. Once you have a kit, you can shop your services around to other programs in your area. People are amazed when you call and say, "Hi, I'm from the library. I'd love to come once each month and do a storytime with your kids. And, my services are absolutely free." If you prefer, you can wait until groups call you and ask for specific themes or programs, but in my experience, being proactive and letting groups know exactly what you can do for them has allowed me to significantly increase my number of outreach partners while keeping my planning time to a minimum.

Book Checkout Outside of the Library

After-school programs, even those taking place in schools, often do not have access to lots of books. Many are constantly on the lookout for giveaways and grants to spruce up their collections, but they are still in need of material to keep kids engaged during academic or free reading times. So, providing book checkout to these programs is a must. Several methods can be successful:

• Create a rotating collection at the site. For many of my outreach sites, I select books myself for the group, check them out on the group's organizational card, and then bring them to the location with my trusty handcart. The sites do not let kids take the books home, so loss rarely happens, and the kids still get new books to read every month.

• If you are able to check books out remotely, bring a selection of books to the site and then let kids go through and choose one that will be their special book for the month. Again, it's best not to let the kids take the books home in order to avoid loss and big fines on the organization's card, but the kids still get the experience of choosing library books and finding something that will interest them.

Providing outreach sites with book checkout isn't always easy—hauling those buckets around can be a little hard on the body. However, the children benefit so much from having new, exciting books to read each month that it is entirely worth it. Plus, it will up your circulation numbers and give you a free workout. It's a win, win, win!

Picture Book Programs

No matter what ages you have in your group, you can still use picture books. Many picture books are meant for older children to begin with, whether they have dense text or twists and turns that older readers can appreciate much more easily than younger ones. For a 30-minute program, I often turn to picture books and short films based on picture books. When watching films, I like to read the picture book first and then view the film. This helps kids understand the importance of the written word. The book (or the script) is always written down before it is acted out (or animated)—it has been amazing to see how many kids do not understand that concept! Here are some themes I like to use with sample titles and DVDs:

• All About Anansi. This tricky spider's tales are always a treat. I prefer Eric Kimmel's versions, such as *Anansi and the Talking Melon*, *Anansi Goes Fishing*, and *Anansi and the Magic Stick*. Live Oak Media has a DVD collection of these stories turned into films, as well.

• Caldecott Winners. Give a short history of the Caldecott Award, and then read some aloud. Really, any of the winners will work (except for *The Invention of Hugo Cabret*), but I like to mix it up between wordless books like *Tuesday* by David Wiesner and those with longer stories, like *Officer Buckle and Gloria* by Peggy Rathmann. Weston Woods has a whole DVD dedicated to film versions of Caldecott winners, so there are lots of quality viewing options, too. This is such a fun topic, you could do a series on Caldecott books by including Honor books and lots of discussion about how to evaluate picture books. You could even end the series with a Mock Caldecott event!

- Fractured Fairy Tales. *Falling for Rapunzel* by Leah Wilcox, *The Three Pigs* by David Wiesner, and *Beware of the Bears*! by Alan MacDonald are some of my favorite picture books to use on this topic, just to name a few. Add in the DVD of *The True Story of the Three Little Pigs*, and the kids will be begging for more!
- Jon Scieszka. A wonderful author to feature, Scieszka's tales always get kids giggling. *The Stinky Cheese Man and Other Fairly Stupid Tales*; *The Frog Prince, Continued*; and *The True Story of the Three Little Pigs* are fun read-alouds, while an additional showing of the film version of *Robot Zot!* will have the kids clutching their sides.
- Magic. *Probuditi!* by Chris Van Allsburg, *Anton Can Do Magic* by Ole Könnecke, and *Strega Nona* by Tomie DePaola are perfect picture books about magic, and the film version of *Sylvester and the Magic Pebble* is very well done.
- Mo Willems. An author study on Mo Willems is a hoot. Use his books that appeal to older readers like *Edwina, the Dinosaur Who Didn't Know She Was Extinct, Goldilocks and the Three Dinosaurs*, and any Elephant and Piggie story. Cap it off with any one of his award-winning Weston Woods films, and you'll have a surefire success on your hands.
- Mysteries. After discussing what makes a book a mystery (and giving some hints about how to solve one), try reading *What Really Happened to Humpty?* by Jeanie Franz Ransom, *Detective LaRue* by Mark Teague, or *The Wretched Stone* by Chris Van Allsburg. Then, show the film version of *Mystery on the Docks* by Thacher Hurd. Your little sleuths may shock you with their detective skills.

If time allows, a craft is the perfect addition to these programs. If Google searches, Pinterest, or publisher's and author's websites don't provide any inspiration, simply having the kids try to create pictures in the style of one of the illustrators can be an incredibly worthwhile exercise. Not only do kids learn to appreciate the skill illustrators have, they also get a chance to experiment with different craft materials and styles.

Chapter Book Programs

If your group is on the older side (mostly kids in third through fifth grade), or if you just feel that your group is ready for chapter books, an incredibly easy and fun program is a book and movie club. Depending on the amount of time you have and the number of weeks you will be conducting your program, the club can consist of several parts.

- Reading the book. Generally speaking, with 30 minutes of reading time, you can read 20–25 pages (depending on font size and spacing). An average book takes six to eight sessions to complete. If your program is monthly, you can choose shorter chapter books or movies based on picture books (like *Jumanji* by Chris Van Allsburg or one of the many movies based on a Dr. Seuss book), or check with group leaders and see about them continuing the program weekly, even in your absence. Oftentimes, if you lay out the program for them and come once or twice each month to help out, they will be happy to continue the reading and viewing for you.
- Viewing the movie. After reading, show 15–30 minutes of the movie, or wait until the last few sessions and show it in its entirety. Challenge the kids to find details in the movie that

were not in the book and vice versa. Ask them why things may have been added or deleted in the movie version. You'll be amazed at how closely they were paying attention when you were reading!

• Related craft or activity. If time allows, you can do related crafts, word searches, or crossword puzzles. Publisher's websites, author's websites, and simple Google searches are great places to find craft and activity ideas, and several free word search and crossword puzzle creators exist online, so you can create your own.

When choosing books and movies, keep in mind the makeup of your group. While it is great to use your club as an opportunity to introduce kids to the classics, it is also important that kids are able to identify with the main characters and have the book/movie speak to them. If your first book is a classic, make the next one contemporary. Read an animal story and then a science fiction story. Always keep your audience in mind, and always leave time for discussion. Also, make sure to view the entire movie before you show it. Ratings today are not what they used to be, and inappropriate language may surprise you in movies rated PG (and cause problems with the leaders of your group). The following list includes books and movies that I have used or considered:

• *The Bad Beginning* by Lemony Snicket
• *Because of Winn-Dixie* by Kate DiCamillo
• *Bridge to Terabithia* by Katherine Paterson
• *Charlie and the Chocolate Factory* by Roald Dahl
• *Charlotte's Web* by E.B. White
• *The Cheetah Girls* by Deborah Gregory
• *The City of Ember* by Jeanne DuPrau
• *Coraline* by Neil Gaiman
• *Diary of a Wimpy Kid* by Jeff Kinney
• *Freaky Friday* by Mary Rodgers
• *From the Mixed-Up Files of Mrs. Basil E. Frankweiler* by E.L. Konigsburg
• *Harry Potter and the Sorcerer's Stone* (or any Harry Potter book) by J.K. Rowling
• *Holes* by Louis Sachar
• *Hoot* by Carl Hiaasen
• *How to Eat Fried Worms* by Thomas Rockwell
• *The Incredible Journey* by Sheila Every Burnford
• *James and the Giant Peach* by Roald Dahl
• *The Lightning Thief* by Rick Riordan
• *The Lion, the Witch, and the Wardrobe* by C.S. Lewis
• *The Mouse and the Motorcycle* by Beverly Cleary
• *Peter Pan* by J.M. Barrie
• *Prince Caspian* by C.S. Lewis
• *Runaway Ralph* by Beverly Cleary
• *Stuart Little* by E.B. White
• *The Tale of Despereaux* by Kate DiCamillo
• *Tuck Everlasting* by Natalie Babbitt
• *The Witches* by Roald Dahl
• *The Wizard of Oz* by L. Frank Baum

Reader's Theater with a Twist

Reader's theater can be an enjoyable program, but doing it in an outreach situation can be tricky. Oftentimes, children's reading levels in these group settings vary widely (with some having abilities well below their classmates), some kids may be too shy to read in front of others, and still others may simply not be able to read and act things out. To avoid these issues, I like to do a different type of reader's theater. At my library, we call them participation stories. Here are some examples:

• Using *Falling for Rapunzel* by Leah Wilcox, I type out the text of the story in script form and have three children act with me (one as Rapunzel, one as the maid, and one as the prince). The kids don't have to say anything, they just act out the parts by listening to me read (and occasionally getting some gentle coaching from me). I also bring props. For this particular story, I print out pictures of the things Rapunzel throws out of her tower. Then, I have the student acting as Rapunzel stand on a chair and throw the pictures down when I cue her.

• For *The Three Little Pigs*, I put up pictures of a straw house, a stick house, and a brick house. I wear a necklace with a Big Bad Wolf picture on it, and the kids wear necklaces with little pigs. Then, all of the kids act as the pigs together while I narrate the story and act out the Big Bad Wolf's part. The kids love to say the "Not by the hair of my chinny chin chin" line together, and watching them run from house to house is a riot.

• *Goldilocks and the Three Bears* is another classic story that the kids love to retell. Using three different-sized bear puppets and a necklace with a picture of Goldilocks, I narrate the story while the kids act out the parts. Because the story is so familiar, they are often able to chime in with the lines, even though I don't ever require it of them.

• *Caps for Sale* by Esphyr Slobodkina is another easy and funny tale to tell as a participation story. I have monkey necklaces for all of the kids and a stack of flannel hats. I act as the narrator and the peddler, and the kids take my hats and act like the monkeys.

• *The Enormous Turnip* (any version will do) gets kids laughing as they all gather around my giant paper turnip and try to pull it up. Again, necklaces or puppets serve as the costumes for the characters, and I narrate the story while the kids act it out.

• Another story with a royal theme is *The Prince Won't Go to Bed* by Dayle Ann Dodds. This story's fantastic repetition will have all of the kids joining in by the end. I narrate and children act as the prince, the princess, and assorted castle folk. A few props such as pillows, blankets, and a pretend bowl of pudding round out the show.

• *The Baby Beebee Bird* by Diane Redfield Massie is a hilarious story to tell with puppets and a librarian narrator. The Beebee Bird's continuous (and annoying) cries crack the kids up, and the variety of animals is a treat.

The number of stories that can be modified into participation stories is unlimited. It just takes a little creativity, a few puppets, and some clip art. By going deeper into the story and truly engaging with the characters, kids are able to uncover layers of enjoyment in books many did not even know was possible. I have been absolutely delighted while doing participation stories to see previously timid children come out of their shells and normally naughty ones (often boys) use their energy in a positive way as they ham it up in front of their classmates. And the next time I visit, they are clamoring to get a part and perform a new story.

Beyond Books: Creation Programs

Besides book or story-based programs, several other programs can work well in an outreach setting (and can still incorporate books, albeit in a lesser way). LEGO clubs work perfectly as an outreach program. You just need a bucket of LEGOs, and you are ready to go. I generally do LEGO clubs around a particular theme each month. If my theme is cars, I will print off pictures of LEGO car creations and pass them around, and I will have books (nonfiction and fiction) about cars to serve as inspiration. Then, I dump out the LEGOs and let kids build. I also take pictures of the kids' projects and post them on our library's Flickr page, which gets a great response from kids and parents. To keep things tidy, a coworker taught me that using a parachute under the LEGOs makes cleaning up a snap.

Creating art projects out of recycled materials can be a great outreach program as well, although it does require hauling a lot of stuff between the library and your outreach site. Using old CDs to make flashy ornaments, magnets, or picture frames can keep kids occupied for hours. Toilet paper tubes, construction paper, and glue make great binoculars. Rubber bands and shoe boxes make lovely sounding guitars. The list goes on and on (and ideas abound with simple Google searches or some time perusing Pinterest). The true beauty of recycled material crafts is that it can inspire kids to look around them, in their own homes and schools, and use things in a new and creative way. It doesn't matter if they don't have a lot of traditional art supplies at home because they learn that they can make art out of anything. To incorporate books into this activity, you can bring craft books to display and talk about what nonfiction has to offer kids.

Making Outreach Work for You

In tight economic times, it can sometimes be difficult to convince managers that outreach is worthwhile. While library outreach programs are good for kids because they promote literacy and strengthen kids' relationships with the library, outreach is just as good, if not better, for the library. Outreach programs increase your program and attendance numbers since you are often working with larger groups than may normally attend individual library programs. They also increase circulation (if you are doing book checkout with the site). And most importantly, the partnerships you establish through outreach can be life-sustaining if your library budget is threatened. No better library advocates exist than outreach collaborators. Their willingness to speak up for your services is invaluable. So don't wait—buy a handcart, and get on the phone to those after-school groups. Your new partners are waiting.

Traveling Summer Reading Show

Carol H. Waxman *and* Susan M. Hansen

What do you do each year to excite the children in your town about coming to the library during the summer months and completing their reading assignments? After visiting each kindergarten through fifth grade classroom in each of the eleven elementary schools (264 visits!) during the hot, humid month of June, a group of exhausted children's librarians groaned, "There has to be a better way to motivate the kids to come to the library to get their books and complete their summer reading requirements! Hey, let's put on a show!" The idea had worked in the classic Mickey Rooney/Judy Garland movies, but could a show solve the West Hartford (CT) Public Library's summer reading dilemma? In a word: yes! Twenty-three years ago it solved the problem and it continues today as an annual event that engages and excites every school-age child in town along with their media specialists and teachers.

Producing the Traveling Summer Reading Show takes a significant time commitment from five members of the children's staff at the West Hartford Public Library. Starting in January, we begin meeting to discuss ideas for the show to be held in late May/early June. Each year we choose a different theme. Often, we use current topics like the Olympics, a popular movie or game, or a news event; other times an idea for a plot evolves after a creative discussion and a flurry of brainstorming. Once the plot is chosen, it's time to write the script. One member of the staff usually takes on the task of writing a first draft; the objective is to create an entertaining show that will last approximately thirty minutes and entice the children to visit the library, get their books, and read, read, read!

In early spring, the staff meets again to review the draft of the script. This is the time for suggesting changes to the plot, adding new ideas, developing the characters, and crystallizing the storyline. Sometimes there is a complete rewrite at this point, but since everyone has been thinking about the proposed plot through the winter and early spring months, the new ideas usually fall into place quickly and the show takes its first big step towards becoming a reality. By April, the staff have their completed scripts in hand and begin to learn the dialogue.

In addition to the script, another important element of the show is background music. If you've ever watched a movie or television show with the sound turned off, you know how critical music is to setting the atmosphere. In the past we used cassette tapes and CDs; we'd bring a portable player with us to the schools and hook it into the school's sound system or turn the volume all the way up if there was no system. Now we customize a playlist on an MP3 player and use that with our library's own portable sound system. We play music while the children are assembling in the auditorium, include musical interludes during the show while we change sets, and always find a catchy theme song to play at the end to get everyone up out of their seats and singing along. We have used music ranging from the Olympic theme to "Monster Mash," and even Katy Perry songs! Music adds an extra dimension to the show and helps give our performance a more professional feel. It is gratifying to us when children who have seen the show come to the library and sing the songs they heard. The show's music seems to dance in all our heads for many months afterwards! In fact, one of our members can still sing the words to our very first theme song from 23 years ago!

Who Are the Stars?

The same five children's staff that created the script are also the "stars" of the show. Even the shyest among us gradually loses that feeling and becomes more confident after the first time on stage. In past years we have been pirates, Angry Birds, visitors from foreign countries, contestants in game shows, campers, science professors in laboratories, riders in a hot air balloon, Olympic contenders, sea creatures, and characters from children's literature. We have discovered talent in ourselves that we never knew we had. The Traveling Summer Reading Show has brought us a greater understanding of the capabilities we have when we let go of our inhibitions in order to excite children about reading. We know that we remain as characters in these children's minds for a very long time.

If you work in a smaller library with fewer staff members in the children's department, perhaps staff in other areas of the building would be willing to join you. You never know who can act, sing, and/or dance! It also might be possible to use volunteers from your community, such as college students, members of civic organizations interested in education and literacy, or PTA members who might like to join you in visiting the schools. You never know until you ask!

Costumes and Set

We are also the set designers, costume creators, sound technicians, and road crew! Each year we pool all of our crafting skills and other talents in order to utilize whatever we have at hand to design and make our costumes and set. This may mean a trip to the local thrift shop, craft store, big box retailer, or raiding the attic or basement at home to turn up amusing bits and pieces that can come together for the costumes. They can be as simple as our own "play" clothes; children who always see us in our work clothes don't recognize us in a baggy sweatshirt, jeans and sneakers, or a funny hat. Even a funky pair of sunglasses adds drama!

Foam core board is the basis for the background sets as it is lightweight, easy to work with, and cut into just the right shapes. The background is drawn on the board, painted, and then can be embellished with paint, glitter, feathers, etc.

We find the most appropriate props we can from a variety of places, whether they are "artifacts" from foreign countries or game show stunt props. We leave no stone unturned, and will search the Internet for bargains and unique items if our catalogs and contacts let us down.

In the past, we have used a papier-mâché volcano, fake doors, a wooden pirate ship, and the wonderfully cozy flying house with balloons from a popular movie. Your imagination is limitless—use it and watch what happens.

Plot

It's all about the story! Putting on a show is nothing more than a dramatic storytelling opportunity, and we know how children love stories. Our shows always focus on the concept of summer reading; often one of the characters is in a difficult situation and needs help to get home and get his/her summer reading finished. One year the plot revolved around a girl who had spent her birthday visiting the aquarium and was accidently locked in after the closing time. Some of the kindergartners were visibly frightened at first, but as soon as they saw all of the "sea creatures" come to the rescue, they sat back and enjoyed the show. In 2011, the story was based on the national summer reading theme "One World, Many Stories" and featured the main character from the flying house movie who traveled the world meeting people from other cultures while earning badges along the way. His long trip home was filled with adventure, mystery, and fun. Many of the plots emphasize friendship and using cooperation to solve problems.

Sometimes we travel to foreign countries and are exposed to the culture, traditions, and dress of that country. We often use a game show format that poses questions about children's books to the contestants. The staff tries to work in as much humor and action as they can. We often use interactive elements like asking the audience to help us guess the answer to clues or getting the kids to stand up and sing along to our songs. And most importantly, we always have a happy ending and remind students to do their summer reading.

Flying house with balloons set from the "One World, Many Stories" show.

Cost

The largest cost of this production is the staff time. Our children's librarians need time away from their regular duties to write the show, create sets and costumes, and program music in order to make it a success. We stop our children's programming in late spring so we will have the time to put finishing touches on the show as well as time to visit each school and perform. As big a challenge as it is, presenting a show to the entire school body is far more effective than visiting each classroom; that was less exciting for the children than attending a live show in the auditorium with their classmates.

The non-personnel cost to produce the show usually includes ordering a few props, purchasing material for costumes, buying foam core board for the set, and getting some paint and special props. We try to reuse, recycle, and repurpose items from previous shows when we can. Although we have been fortunate enough to have a limited budget to help us out (usually less than $200 on each production), the show can be done for next to nothing. Empty book cartons (instead of foam core board) can be painted for use as props. One year a staff member visited a thrift shop, purchased a wedding gown, and made several costumes from it! Remember that the children will be hooked by your character, not your outfit or the set design. Keep it as simple and comfortable as you can, and focus instead on involving your audience in an exciting story.

On the Road Again

Taking the show to all eleven of our elementary schools is a huge challenge. We have sets and sound systems to transport and need every inch of cargo space our cars have. We try to use an SUV or the largest car our staff members own. Sometimes it's possible to borrow a van to use. We recruit some of our younger staff members to help us carry equipment and set up at the schools. We often do two shows in one day, so we have to set up, break down, pack up, grab a quick lunch, and hit the road again to set up at another school. Some schools have large auditoriums with wonderful lighting systems that we use; some only have large multipurpose rooms like a gym or cafeteria, and we are left to do the best we can. None of the schools we visit has air conditioning, and that's an important factor. In early summer you don't want to be in a heavy costume under bright lights in a hot auditorium. We usually need an hour to set up and a half an hour or more to break down and pack the set afterwards. It is possible to do two shows in one day, and we often do as we attempt to visit all eleven elementary schools in the course of six days.

Our show literally leaves the children on their feet—jumping, laughing, and shouting for more every year. Following the performance, we play music and dance down off the stage and up through the aisles. We invite the teachers to dance in the aisles with us, and that delights the kids even more! We greet all the children we know from the library, and they treat us like celebrities for the next three months. The children can't wait to rush into the library to tell us how much they enjoyed the show. It's a completely energizing experience for everyone involved! Those children who may not have been excited about reading before usually have a change in attitude after the show.

Parents have told us when they ask that everyday question that comes up in most homes in the evening, "What did you do in school today?" that they get a very excited answer from the children who have seen the summer reading show. Instead of the usual one word answer "Nothing," children enthusiastically embark on a re-telling of the plot of the show. For them, the characters have come to life, and they want to share this experience with their parents. It is amusing to staff who are shopping after work in the supermarket or when they are at another local venue to hear children whispering from the aisles, "There's Miss Nelson!" or "She got out of the zoo!"

Public Library/School Relations

In our town, the public schools and public library work together to formulate a plan for summer reading. When the library staff decides on a theme for the show, we share that idea with the library media department supervisor for the public schools for her approval. The library's graphic artist designs the reading lists and reading records with our logo for the summer reading theme. Each year, the summer reading list suggests titles and authors for each grade, preschool through fifth. The list, which is developed by the children's librarians, offers many new titles and series as well as traditional choices. The children may read books from this list or any other books of their choice.

The graphic artist also designs special stickers for the children to place on their reading record, the form they use for recording how many times during the summer they read and what books they read. After the show is presented, the children are given the lists and records by their schools to take home for the summer. Library staff validate the reading records with the stickers as children bring them in all through the summer. The children return these records to their classroom teachers in September, when each school holds an assembly to honor all the children who participated in the summer reading program.

Post Performance

For the past few years we have used the library's website and social media sites to advertise the success of the show and to keep it on the children's minds all summer long. A library staff member attends at least one performance and takes photographs. These photos are put in a Shutterfly or YouTube slideshow and linked to our library website. Some of the photos are printed to display in the library so that the children can share them with their parents when they visit. If we can get someone to shoot a video of the show, we play this in a loop on a monitor near the door to the children's library. This year we created a Pinterest board about the show and used the services offered at Shutterfly to create a large autograph book with pictures from the show. As children visit over the summer, they are asked to sign the book and tell us which elementary school they attend.

These ideas are easy to adapt, even if you consider yourself "low-tech." You can make an autograph book yourself by printing some of your photos on a color printer and placing them in a binder. You can pin some of your pictures on a bulletin board and let children write their names on index cards and pin them on the board, too. The year that we did the show about an aquarium, we placed some of the scenery in the library and made it into a "photo booth."

Children posed in front of it all summer, sometimes pretending they were being threatened by the shark, or on a foam surfboard, and we took their photos and added them to the online slideshow. Documenting the program and later activities with photographs and video not only allows the children and their families who may have missed the show to enjoy part of it, it is also a great way to show your library board the impact you have made through this important outreach to your community. Activities that remind the children of the show and allow them to interact with the story keep their enthusiasm high all summer.

Your Own Show

While taking on all of the work to write and stage your own show may sound daunting, it is an idea that is easily scalable and replicable in any size community, even if you work in a small library. If you have the support of the local schools, the only other things you really need are time to prepare and a desire to bring your storytelling skills to a whole new level. Yes, it can be a bit frightening, and a bit daunting, but it really isn't that scary. Your inhibitions and doubts will fade quickly once you begin the process.

Start thinking and planning, and soon the excitement will carry you along. Originality isn't really important; some years we have used the state or national summer reading theme, like the theme for 2012: "Dream Big." Remember that children often want to hear the same

Entire cast of the "Dream Big" show (left to right, kneeling: Dee Williams, Kari Ann St. Jean, Jane Breen; standing: Carol Waxman, Elliott Mara, Janet Murphy).

story over and over again; a somewhat familiar storyline may feel more comfortable, especially to the younger students. During the year, take note of important news events, weather conditions, famous people, and popular new books—virtually anything can give you an idea, a focus, and the beginning of a plan. Once you have the theme in mind, the rest seems to flow naturally; it is exciting to be creative with costuming, designing, scoring the music, and finding fun things to use in the show.

We seasoned (and yet still amateur) actors have been through it all, and we keep coming back for more. We have been through soaring heat waves, rain and wind, sound system malfunctions, prop breakage—you name it, it has happened to us! Even the flying house with balloons we so lovingly created fell down with a loud bang (to the delight of the crowd who thought that was hilarious!) during the show and the actors had to stand by it and hold it up while conveying their lines. We have persevered through it all because the "show must go on" for the children. We want to excite children about reading and instill a lifelong love of reading. The numbers of children who walk through the doors of the library after seeing the show in their schools attest to the fact that our mission has been accomplished. To all of you: have fun! We wish you nothing but the best of luck. If you are ever visiting West Hartford, Connecticut, in late May or early June, please stop by to see a show!

Overnight at the Library

Tami Morehart

At the Wagnalls Memorial Library in central Ohio, something wasn't working. The majority of our juvenile patrons should have been drawn from our local school district, but they just weren't coming. After all, the district's Intermediate School (serving grades three through five), is located within walking distance of our library. The students obviously didn't view Wagnalls as another available resource for their studies, so I began to look for ways to encourage them to visit on a regular basis. The question was how to get them here.

After some careful consideration, I came up with a contest that would not only bring in the students, but their families, as well. It needed to be something that my two part-time staff members and I could handle beyond our regular programming. That's how our "Overnight at the Library" contest was born.

Overview

To put it simply, the Wagnalls Memorial Library developed a lottery-type contest that allowed students to "win" a spot in an overnight program at our library. Our current requirements are that the student must attend our local school and be in the third grade.

To be entered into the lottery, third-grade students would need to visit the library one time each month with their families to check out materials. I intentionally wrote the program to include the whole family so I could talk about other programming the library offered for both children and adults. As the family visited, I used this time to do some booktalking and introduce the students to chapter books. When the students had chosen their items, they took them to the children's desk where the contest sheets were kept. Each time students visited the library and brought their families with them, they got their contest sheets stamped. We kept our contest sheets alphabetized in a three-ring binder at the desk for ease of use. At the end of the contest, all completed entries (i.e., entries with all stamps received) were placed in the drawing, and the winners were selected from the completed entries. The winning students were announced at the school.

Eligibility

In order to be eligible for the drawing, third-grade students had to visit the library once a month for a set amount of months. I suggest starting the program in September and ending it in March. This gives you the month of April to choose the dates of your overnight at the library. We made sure all contest sheets were filled out by the last day of the month that the program ended. All fully completed sheets were entered into two random drawings: one for the boys, and one for the girls. I chose fourteen boys and fourteen girls; this was easy to manage for our space, though you may choose to have a larger or smaller number of contest winners.

Developing Relationships/Collaboration

The following is a list of contacts you should make during the course of your program:
- Director. Go over your idea with him or her. This is an overnight event. Be sure it has library board approval. Have everything in writing to present to your director. Provide a copy of flyers being sent to students, costs involved, staff needed, rooms to use, and waivers for liability.
- Staff. This is a two-night event. One night will be just for the girls, and one just for the boys. Be sure you have one staff member per night to be in charge and at least two other volunteers to help (to keep costs low, I took comp time to cover four to five hours I was up with the students). Your volunteers could include parents or teen volunteers. Maintenance staff should be informed about any alarm system that might have to be disengaged for the area of use, and they must ensure that the security of building can be maintained. This must be a "lock-in" event for the safety of everyone involved.
- School principal. Contact the principal at either the end of the school year or early in the summer to meet and discuss what a great opportunity this program will be for both your library and their school. Give them printed materials to go over and let them suggest a date for the overnight event at the library that doesn't conflict with school events.
- Teachers of the students. After talking to the principal, get the teachers involved. This should be done as soon as school starts. Set up a time for the classes to visit the library to find out about the program. Get the teachers' e-mail addresses so you can stay in contact with them. Use this contact to encourage teachers to utilize the library for their own teaching needs, subject requests, or project assistance.
- Parents. A parent must come to the library and register his or her child at the first visit. Go over the rules again with all parents, encouraging them to actively participate in their students' library visits. Using the information on the student stamp sheet, get an e-mail address for each parent/student. Use this to contact them halfway through the month via a bulk e-mail reminder to come in each month.
- Volunteers. After winners have been announced, send out an e-mail to all of the parents asking for at least two volunteers per night. You could also use a teen volunteer each night who would play games and help out with activities.

Related Activities/Incentives

To make sure that everyone gets registered, hold a class-by-class contest. The first class that had everyone registered at our library got a prize for their classroom. Prize ideas might be books or other library-related materials. It should be something popular that the kids will really want! Maybe suggest a class-by-class competition to see who reads the most books. The "winning" class might get a special "day" trip to the library, and you could have some fun activities planned for them on that day.

Contest Structure

Date Selection

I have found that May is a very busy month for schools, so it is best to hold the overnight event in April. A back-to-back Friday and Saturday night (for both groups) is best. If you have enough room, it's possible that you could hold both of them on the same night in different areas. I would recommend the two separate nights and not have girls and boys together for safety issues. I was able to use our program room right off of the library floor. This way, we had access to the library for our flashlight scavenger hunt and the restrooms.

Student Stamp Sheet

To make the student stamp sheet:
- Use white copy paper and a three-hole punch so you can keep the stamp sheets in your handy three-ring binder (much easier than having the students keep up with it themselves).
- Include the student's and parent's names, homeroom teacher, phone number, and e-mail address.
- Make a small square for each month of the contest.
- Use a seasonal or library-related stamp each month and a different colored stamp each time to make the sheet fun and colorful.
- Include a parent permission line for the student to participate.

Student Information Flyer

After you have made contact with the principal and teachers, print off a flyer to go home with the students. Take a few copies over to the school and give one to the principal and one to each of the teachers whose classrooms are participating. The teachers can make copies and send the flyer home with the students. The students can then bring the flyers with them to the library when they sign up on their first visit. I also put a copy of the student information sheet on our website. Be sure to put the registration deadline in bold! If you plan ahead, you might be able to participate in your school's back-to-school night. Check ahead with the principal and ask if the school has one and if you could set up a table to pass out information. This way you can introduce yourself to the students' parents and answer any questions they might have. Give out any of your library's other fall programming information at this time as well.

Your flyer should contain:
- Your library's name, address, phone number, website, and hours
- Dates of deadlines and final program
- Time of overnight (8:00 P.M.–8:00 A.M.)
- Types of food provided—popcorn, soda pop, donuts, chocolate milk, juice, and bottled

water for each child. List what you are providing in advance in order to accommodate any food allergies.

- The requirement of monthly library visits with their families
- Mention of games/activities/crafts/booktalks/prizes
- Maybe a picture of sleeping kids, pictures from last year's event, or any other pictures of kids having fun!

E-Mail List

After registration, set up your e-mail group of parents and send out a welcome e-mail. Include your name, e-mail, and phone number. Give them the information again about coming once a month and getting their stamps. Include (in bold!) the last day of the contest and the overnight dates.

Announcing Winners

Once you have randomly drawn out the names of your predetermined number of boy and girl winners, write up an announcement to use at the school. Going over to the school and personally announcing the winners would be best. Check with the principal in advance to see how he or she would like to handle this. In case you are not able to go, send over an announcement to be read by the principal over the loudspeaker. Send congratulation e-mails to each winner's parent with overnight information the same day as the announcement is made. Be sure to include in this e-mail that at least one parent must drop off the student at the overnight in order to sign a permission slip for the child to attend.

The BIG OVERNIGHT!

1. What students should bring:
   - Sleeping bag, pillow, pajamas if they want (many of our students simply slept in their street clothes), and a snack to share if you need to cut costs. They might also want to bring a stuffed animal.
   - NO electronic devices of any kind were allowed. We assured all parents and students that if they required use of a phone to call home, they would be permitted to use the library's phone.
   - Flashlight
2. What volunteers should bring:
   - Sleeping bag or small blow-up mattress, blanket, and pillow
   - Any toiletries they may want
   - Flashlight
   - Cell phone
3. What you will need:
   - Blow-up mattress and blanket (don't expect to sleep much!)
   - Any toiletries you might want and a pillow
   - A sleep mask if you are sleeping by an exit light
   - An alarm clock
   - Extra flashlights

Room Setup

It is best to use your largest programming room for this event. Two rooms could be used, one for sleeping and one for activities. Whatever room you use, most of it should be empty of clutter. You will need some tables for the craft and building activities. Line the sleeping bags along the outside walls until needed. You will need a projector and movie screen set up. Have all the food items you will need in a nearby kitchen. I suggest you pump up your air mattress before the students get there. Have a table set up close to the programming room entrance where you can meet and greet students and parents as they arrive. This is where the forms will be for parents to sign that give permission for their children to spend the night. Also display movies here that might be shown at the sleepover. Have your volunteers come early to help you greet. Place one volunteer at the front door to let students in. Have a clipboard with each student's name on it to check off as they enter the building. Another volunteer could help escort families and their belongings to the "overnight" area.

Permission Forms

Parents must sign a waiver, a release of liability, and an image form for their child to attend. Have your legal department write content to use. You will be taking pictures to put on your website or use with future publicity. Include a section for any allergies the student might have or any other information that you might need from parents. Also, include on the form wording that indicates no bullying, fighting, or any form of disrespect will be tolerated. Parents will be called to pick up any child who breaks these rules. Be sure to have the parent's cell phone number as well as a home number for emergencies. Make sure the parents know that pickup time the next morning is 8:00 A.M.!

Suggested Overnight Activities

* Toilet paper dodge ball (same rules as dodge ball, just substitute with toilet paper rolls). Use masking tape to make the two back lines and one middle line on the floor. Make two even-numbered teams. Place the toilet paper rolls on the center line (about five or six rolls). If the roll or any part of the roll hits the players, they are out. If it is caught when thrown, the person throwing it is out. Be sure to have sideline judges! Have enough cheap toilet paper to play several games. Remember to buy enough for BOTH nights. This is where you will need plenty of water bottles because this game will make the students very thirsty! Use a marker to write the names of students on the bottles. A volunteer could do this for you ahead of time. Keep the water bottles in the refrigerator until needed.
* Flashlight scavenger hunt. Using the library, have students find 10 items on their list in 10 minutes. The students should work in teams of two. A volunteer escorts each team with a flashlight to "see" the items they find and cross them off the list. This way nothing is moved, and you can do one group after another. Supply a clipboard and pen for the adult to carry. I used the children's area so I could hide things and make a special area display of an "I spy" showcase of odds and ends from things we had. You could use a shelf or a table to do the same

thing. Examples to find: stuffed animals, books on display, pictures on the wall, something you bring in to use from home, or posters. Maybe a glow-in-the-dark item could be hidden! Use books with creepy titles for them to find. This activity can be done at the same time as another activity in the program room. Just send two students out with the volunteer and keep sending them out until both activities are over. This activity does not work well while dodge ball is being played.

• Plastic building blocks such as LEGO. Find someone who will let you borrow these popular red, blue, and yellow blocks. If you need to borrow from different sources, you could set up several building stations so they don't get mixed together. The students love to build space stations, medieval castles, or other creative things. This a great group activity to participate in while others are doing the flashlight scavenger hunt.

• Crafts. Girls like to do these more than boys, so find something cute for the girls like sand art or jewelry making. Boys might like to make paper airplanes and then have a contest flying them. Be sure to have all the supplies ready ahead of time.

• Booktalks. I found that the girls are really interested in seeing new books and listening to my booktalks. Boys were not as interested, but if you get some popular titles and some nonfiction, you might hook them! Pull some "I Spy" and "Search and Find" books for students to sit down and look at if they need a rest.

• Movies. I pre-selected about six movies that I thought would be fun to watch. I had different movies for each night selected. If possible, try to have some new release titles available. I put these out on the registration table for the parents to see as they arrived for the overnight. If there was a movie a parent didn't approve of, I pulled it from the pile. Later, I had the students vote on what they wanted to watch. It would be best to choose movies not longer than 70–90 minutes long. Hopefully, the students will fall asleep before the movie is over. Be sure that everyone takes a bathroom break before the movie begins. The volunteers can help out with getting the popcorn and drinks ready. I bought popcorn to fix in the microwave, though you can get some bags that are already popped. Use brown lunch sacks to put the popcorn in. Drinks do get spilled, so don't fill too full. It might be worth the expense of buying the small bottles of soda pop that can be resealed and not use cups at all. Have plenty of paper towels available to use for spills. After the movie, you and the volunteers can scout around and pick up bags, glasses, and/or bottles. Have students take one last bathroom break before going to sleep. Some may have already gone to sleep during the movie (don't wake them up!). I suggest that you sleep near the main exit and the other two volunteers spread out in the room or by other exits.

Wake Up Time

Rise and shine is at 7:30 A.M.! You and the volunteers might want to get up a few minutes early and hit the bathrooms first. While the students are waking up and going to the bathroom, have the volunteers get the donuts/milk/juice ready. You should have some small paper plates and napkins ready to put donuts on as well as cups for drinks. I found that most students preferred chocolate milk. Have one of the volunteers go to the main door and let in the parents to pick up their children. Make sure everyone gets all of the stuff they brought. Clean up and go home!

Summary/Results

The first year of this program was very successful. I had about ninety students registered out of grades three through five. I found that the third-grade students were the most responsive to the program. The second year I only offered the program to the third-grade students. Since they are new to the Intermediate building when they enter third grade, this is a great way to welcome them to the school and to the library. Students were very excited about our overnight contest. They especially liked the fact that they were the only students in their school who had a chance to stay overnight at the library! A direct result of this program is that we saw more students and families coming into the library, and they continued to come over the next year, as well.

This program was a positive joint endeavor with our school. The teachers did not have to do much except encourage the students to come over to register and visit each month.

After the first year, be sure and show videos or pictures of the previous years' overnights during your initial presentation to the students. Do a few booktalks with some new titles, and maybe mention the word "ghost"!

The greatest cost to the program is your time. The rest can be done for under $75. Remember to take lots of pictures and videos of your event, and be sure to post them on your website or Facebook page.

Decide which grades best fit you and your local school when holding this contest. An overnight stay at the library can seem like a daunting program, but I have found that it is a great experience not to be missed!

Art Outreach
A Library Success Story
Mary Lou Carolan

Walking into the children's room of the Wallkill Public Library on a Wednesday afternoon is often a feast for the eyes and ears. The exchange overheard during the "Masterpiece Art Workshop" sounds like sophisticated dinner party conversation, only it is occurring between one instructor and an animated group of grade schoolers. Recently the group was discussing how the sculptor Louise Nevelson used only "found" wood for her sculptures, and the class wondered together why she chose to paint these sculptures in only one color: black, white, or gold. Interesting anecdotes are shared about how, after every page of homework he completed, Andy Warhol's mother rewarded him with a Hershey's chocolate bar. The class considered if this may have had something to do with the subjects he chose to paint. Then the discussion turns to Wassily Kandinsky, an affluent lawyer when he quit his job and decided to paint instead. He received a lot of criticism for all of the bright colors he chose to use. The kids are asked why people at the time may not have liked how colorful his paintings were.

These lively and thought-provoking conversations ensue with prompting and parameters provided by Christine Adams, aka Ms. Christine, the library's children's programming assistant. Her brainchild, this six-week "Masterpiece Art Workshop" series features student-created projects in the style of famous artists and illustrators, including the artists mentioned above as well as Giuseppe Arcimboldo, Eric Carle, Pablo Picasso, and Laurel Burch. The participants in this after-school art club are introduced to, and explore the background of, the artists, the period in history in which they worked, and the influences in their lives, all while discussing color, form, placement, and materials. Then each participant creates an original work of art in the style of the master. Christine also created a "Mini Masterpieces" series for kids ages three to five years, which explores these same topics but scales down the concepts and perspectives.

In the rushed and scheduled world of today's children, programs like these offered by the library provide an alternative for parents and their children to thoughtfully explore creative projects and learn by doing in a fluid, unstructured environment. But first, before all the great conversation and amazing artwork could take place, we had to get the word out.

149

The Right Way to Milk a Cow

For many years, we have offered a variety of art and cultural programs at the Wallkill Public Library as a response to community requests to offer more creative opportunities for kids. These requests come from information we collect through in-house and online surveys conducted several times a year and through a formal program evaluation that follows our popular summer reading program. While our community does an incredible job of promoting sports and other physical activities, access to quality artistic and cultural programs for kids is at least a 15-minute drive away from our downtown. Often this means art programming is out of the range of possibility for many of the children our library serves. So how do we reach these children? How do we let parents know what we have to offer?

Each week our library uses a variety of techniques to promote and advertise our offerings. There are as many methods to use to reach out and inform people as there are to teach and educate children, and not every method works for everyone. Built into every program plan is a promotional strategy that asks two questions:
1. Who needs to know about this?
2. How will we get the word out?

Years ago, during a fundraising course I was taking, the instructor—who incidentally was a generous donor as well—bluntly stated, "You don't get milk from a cow by writing it a letter. You have to sit down and get close to her." In other words, you must do more than just passively post signs about library programs around town and hope people show up. Libraries invest way too much money and staff time in their programs to take that risk. We need to consider how to draw people in, make them care, see what is in it for them and for their children, and communicate the value and the benefit of library programming. We need to go where the people are and get close to them.

Stepping Out

Visiting the soccer field on Saturdays throughout the fall provides a captive audience of hundreds of parents who will talk with you about programming, and into whose hands you can place information about the library. Getting on the agenda for the Parent Teacher Organization (PTO) meetings gives a monthly opportunity to put a face to the library. This is your chance to offer information and allow attendees to ask questions they may have about the library. It is also a good way to get library news into the school newsletter that gets sent home with all of the kids. Never assume that parents have ever been to a library, or know what programs, collections, or services today's library offers. Don't even assume they know that library cards and programs are free. People understand surprisingly little about libraries, especially those born in the 1980s and beyond with young children who would be perfect participants for our library programs. Make sure they understand that what you are offering will help educate their children and keep them busy and learning after school. Their kids will have access to high-quality art and cultural programs in their own local community that could cost a fortune elsewhere. Offering field trips to the library for elementary school classes not only encourages teachers and children to visit the library, it also introduces parent chaperones to what the modern-day library has to offer.

Getting close to people also gives you the chance to gather contact information to keep them informed and aware of what you are doing on a regular basis. Gathering e-mail addresses provides a quick and easy way to communicate event information for free to hundreds of parents at once. Over a year ago, we created a weekly e-mail blast using the easy-to-learn online tool Constant Contact. This blast reaches over seven hundred people every Friday afternoon. What began as a simple event notice has now turned into a colorful online newsletter featuring book reviews, information on downloadable e-books, online research tools, community information, informational blogs, photographs of families at our events and programs, and our calendar of programming and events. The feedback we receive from this one communication piece has resulted in increased attendance, awareness, and sharing of our programs. Additionally, daily updates to our Facebook page and Twitter feeds enable us to reach an audience of potential participants quickly and easily at no cost to the library. Our weekly outreach on Facebook is around 300 people, primarily for those between the ages of 35 to 44 years—the exact audience we need to connect with. Social media is essential to spreading the word about library programming, and it connects the library to a much broader network than its immediate service area, all at no cost. Save a tree: send a post or a tweet!

The benefits of collaborating with local public and private schools to bring awareness to your educational programming cannot be overstated. Our local school budget cuts just reduced the full-time art teacher to a part-time position in the area elementary schools. This kind of community predicament creates a culturally creative void for our library to fill, and art is a perfect vehicle for changing and enhancing perceptions of the value of the library.

Why Art Works

Art is important in the life of a child. By exposing children to various art forms, they learn more about themselves and become comfortable experimenting with new forms of self-expression and self-awareness. As they conceive, design, and create, they develop a knowledge and strength in their abilities as well as an understanding that there are many ways to communicate. Through the use of art, music, dance, and theater arts, our library has steadily offered programming that provides a forum for children to learn visual, physical, musical, and tactile methods of creation, communication, and expression. Art programming also teaches important life skills. By presenting problems or situations for kids to figure out, they develop skills for testing possibilities as they experiment with different materials, textiles, and formats. Learning to use a variety of handheld tools in all shapes and sizes develops fine motor skills and a confidence for learning to create and build by hand. Because our artistic offerings are almost always group activities, the children also strengthen their social and emotional skills by learning to communicate and collaborate with each other. They learn how to provide constructive feedback as they are encouraged to express their opinions, thoughts, and ideas.

Despite a plethora of competing activities in the area, children's coordinator Carolyn Thorenz and programming assistant Christine Adams painstakingly review school calendars, sports schedules, and other town and organizational lists before planning after-school programs and creating the monthly library calendar. After-school library events compete with soccer, football, cheerleading, scouts programs, religious education, and music lessons. A loyal and consistent group of weekly participants generally comes out for our art programs, but depending on the season, attendance may ebb and flow. Even with registration, the staff is never truly sure how many kids will attend, making it difficult to plan.

Efforts have been made to plan special programs for school holidays in order to gauge interest and see if attendance is affected. A "Black Friday" arts and crafts event that ran for three hours the day after Thanksgiving was attended by over twenty kids, which for us was a great turnout. But it proved to be too ambitious an effort for two staff people to manage, and the number of children, combined with the complexity of activities, proved too chaotic to repeat again without instituting new parameters and scaling back the projects. Trial and error and a willingness to be flexible and try any number of ideas is essential to a good children's library program.

Reaching Further

One of the greatest side benefits of the after-school programming is the influence it has on the parents and grandparents who come into the library to bring children to the program. Waiting for the children enables the adults to peruse the library, picking up flyers and calendars for upcoming events that they may not otherwise have ever known about. Parents are enthusiastically greeted by front desk staff when they arrive with the children for programs, and this welcoming environment encourages them to stay and visit with other parents, creating a comfortable, social atmosphere that enhances the image of the library. Parents observing the art programs and their children's level of engagement will generally check out books on the subjects their children are studying. This boosts circulation numbers and continues the learning process at home. These experiences have encouraged our library to revamp the children's nonfiction collection to reflect our programming, and it provided the impetus to display books on the subject of the programs for that week.

One of our most popular events at the end of the season is our Young Artists Club Art Show. This event showcases the artistic accomplishments of the art club participants and encourages great enthusiasm for the art program. Last year's event was attended by over 75 parents, grandparents, aunts, uncles, and siblings. The show featured the work of the 13 program participants and six of their projects. It was a celebratory event that transformed our children's room into a gallery of original art in mixed media. Projects included chalk drawings on black paper; paintings made using sponges, dowels, paper tubes, bottle caps, and Q-tips; self-portraits; sculpture using random materials; animal faces; two group projects featuring the traced hands of all participants made into a group collage; and a floor-to-ceiling American flag composed of painted paper tubes. The artists stood next to their work and answered questions, explaining their designs and the choice and usage of the materials. It was a memorable event for these young artists as they stood beside their wall-mounted photo and biography and enjoyed their moment of fame with family, friends, and the town newspaper reporter who brought attention to the show with a four-color spread featuring the kids, their stories, and their creations.

Books, Theater, and Music

Using the arts to attract children to the library has proven to be a successful draw for our library year after year. In 2005, we experimented with bringing storybooks alive through drama with our children's theater art project called *Books Alive!* Now in its eighth year, it is clear that we tapped another artistic void in our community. Since theater is not offered until middle school, we decided to try our hand at helping kids experience literacy in a new way using drama, movement, and song. Each year, this program attracts around 25 to 30 participants between the ages of eight and 13. They meet twice a week after school and on Saturdays for 10 weeks. We have found that by offering this program from January to March, the library does not compete with many after-school sports programs, and the parents enjoy having something for the kids to do during cold winter months. The culmination of their hard work is the creation of a full-scale show with two performances that have attracted over 500 people each year. A nice crossover between *Books Alive!* and our art club is that many of the artists contribute their skills in the creation of backdrops and sets for the performance. This is a nice connection between the two successful after-school programs.

Music programs have been popular for our library, as well. A few years ago, with funding from a local community arts foundation, we offered an African dance and drumming workshop series for six weeks that taught aspects of African culture through movement, painting, story-telling, and call-and-response drumming. The final session was a community performance where attendees—parents, grandparents, community leaders, and children—were encouraged to make authentic African dishes to share. As the children drummed, everyone danced and sang and ultimately collapsed into an exhausted heap an hour later. It was exhilarating, refreshing, and such an out-of-the-box experience for our community that it prompted one father, whose young son was in the program, to say to me at the end: "This library is an oasis for the arts in this town." Library directors dream of moments like these!

Curriculum Connection

Our next venture into the world of art and creativity was an in-house program designed to correlate directly to the newly implemented Common Core Standards curriculum in the public schools in New York State. The foundation of this curriculum is a set of inquiry-based methods centered on learning and discovery. Since the school budget cuts in recent years eliminated all library media specialists from the three elementary schools in our district, our library decided to work with the school system and help support this new curriculum. By requesting and then making an appearance before the school board, our library laid the groundwork for supporting the teaching staff, children, and their parents. We educated them about our online research tools, after-school programming, homework help, and print and digital collections. This led to a request from the school district for us to conduct a parent workshop to show parents how library resources can be used to assist their children in meeting the Common Core Standards. We didn't wait for the school district to ask us for help; the library went to the school board and offered help in the form of a free solution for their very real need.

Focusing on inquiry-based methods of learning and discovery, our library has created a hands-on, child-driven program called *Figure it out!* This after-school program series incorporates the help of local professionals as experts in the arts, the environment, agriculture, politics, music, and the culinary arts. The professionals serve as facilitators, bringing an aspect of their work—an invention, a process, an art form, a technique, a machine, an instrument, or a recipe, for example—and the kids will collaborate to explore, investigate, inquire, and ultimately work together to determine what it is the expert does. Once again, responding to the expressed needs of the community, our library strives to provide programs, materials, and services that fill a void, spark an interest, inspire an inquiring young mind, and support the initiatives of the school curriculum.

Conclusion

As libraries navigate this technological age, it has become increasingly important to assess the specific needs in communities and consider repurposing library space to make less room for books on shelves and more room for common learning spaces. Libraries can become a learning commons and social gathering place as well as a place where art and culture form the gateway to learning about creativity, art forms, expression, individuality, risk-taking, and collaboration. There is a need for study areas, meeting rooms, and multi-purpose spaces that can be easily transformed from an art workshop space for programs like the art club, to a computer training classroom, to a gathering place for handcrafters, a meeting location for book clubs, a space for traveling exhibits, conference space, fundraising events, and the like. Not only do we need to create this kind of atmosphere, we have to make sure people know the library offers these kinds of programs and spaces. The best programs in the world won't be attended if no one knows about them.

As local budgets and the competition for funding with other community services place tighter fiscal constraints on libraries, it is more important than ever to step up and promote programming that meets the specific needs of the community. Most importantly, we must be the architects for the future of libraries, or others will create our future for us. There is no more impactful way to do this than to offer quality, creative, and innovative children's programming and to develop tools and methods for reaching those in the community who will benefit most from what we have to offer.

Promoting the Library and Summer Reading Program
Grabbing the Attention of Middle School Students
STEFANIE BLANKENSHIP

The Problem

Do you want to attract more teens to your library? Would you like to start successful teen programs, advisory groups, and volunteering? Perhaps you have tried to recruit teens to your library for the summer reading program. You might have visited a school to talk about upcoming summer programs at your library only to have the students in the assembly stare blankly at you. They might be unresponsive and clearly bored. You want your programs to be well attended. Furthermore, you want teens in your library. So how do you grab the students' attention and make them want to be a part of the library community? The students might think yours will be a boring assembly, especially if they believe that the library is boring. What can you do to really make an impression? How can you sell the library as a fun, exciting place to be during the summer?

An Opportunity

In middle school, assemblies are an escape from class. The escape should be informative, entertaining, and memorable. I used to go to the middle schools and just talk on a microphone to blank faces. After a couple of years, I decided to stir things up. The teens love to get free stuff, and they love to be entered into raffles for prizes like popular new books or movie tickets to films based on popular books. I applied this concept of handing out rewards to my school visits. I believed that if rewarding teens was successful at the library and made the teens return, then giving teens incentives at the middle school would entice them to come to the library. However, the teens at the assembly wouldn't be given a reward or chance to win a grand prize without paying attention to what I had to say first. Once the students understood that they received recognition for listening to me, then I knew I would have the attention of all (or most) of the group.

I also wanted to encourage behaviors at the assembly that might be frowned upon in class. Though the library is still thought of as a quiet place, my neighborhood branch library is the complete opposite. It is a boisterous place, and teens use the space as an after-school hangout, or "third space," as it has come to be known. The encouraged behaviors at these school assemblies are not foreign to my library environment. I wanted the teens to know what kind of librarian I am, that I can tolerate noise, and that participation and enthusiasm is expected. Here is a list of encouraged behaviors at the assembly to get the students involved and excited about library programs:

- Let the students answer questions without raising their hands. Have them call out answers as they come to mind.
- Reward students instantly for their answers.
- Allow applause and noise.

This program plan works because you are not the teacher. You are not setting rules and asking students to abide by them. This makes you fun and memorable. Students will want to visit the library to see if you follow through on the promise of a fun summer. I have received standing ovations from the students, and so can you!

How to Begin

Before you even get into the school, there are important steps to take. Here are a few ways to help get the ball rolling:

- Contact the middle schools in your library's neighborhood. Talk to the secretary and school library media specialist. If you do not hear back from them within a week, call back. Don't give up. Working to build a rapport with these individuals early on will make it easier to return in future years.
- Suggest dates that you are available, but stay flexible. Work around the school's schedule to be accommodating.
- Have a list of programs that your library will be hosting over the summer. Pick out the most exciting programs that you know will have good attendance.
- Prepare copies of the list to distribute at the school.
- Think of questions you can ask the students about programs being offered. Write them down.
- Think of ways you can reward students at the assembly for answering questions.

Ways to Reward the Students

Rewarding the students is important because it makes them want to keep listening to you. There are many ways to reward students. Here are some reward ideas that have worked for me:

- Buy promotional items that are related to popular book-based movies. Party stores and Walmart usually have these in abundance. Don't forget to check clearance aisles.
- Gather surplus items in the library that have been used as rewards in the past. Better to give them some useful purpose than have them take up space.
- Reward volunteers or library users that are in the audience. Pick them out and call them by name. In this way, their friends and peers will see that it is okay to go the library. I

have found that when I call the students I know by name, other students will want me to call them out, as well. I tell them that I do not know their names, and if they come to the library, they will get a "shout out" next year.

• Ask if students have their library cards with them. If they do, instantly reward them with book-themed school supplies.

• Play a slideshow of pictures of the teens engaged in library programs at your location. I started doing this last year, and it works very well. The students who have attended programs get recognition while their friends will want to be in photo slideshows in the future. The other advantage of including the slideshow is that it provides a visual of what I am talking about, presenting students with some concrete evidence that the programs are popular, fun, and that teens enjoy the library. Even if some students are not listening to you, they have a big screen in front of them doing the advertising for you.

How to Execute the Plan Once You Are in the School

Now you've made contact with the school officials, you've got the green light for your program, you've marked the date on your calendar, and you're ready for action. Here are a few tips to keep in mind that will make your presentation pop:

• Use a microphone. A wireless microphone is preferable so you can walk around and be a part of the audience. If you are "one of them," they will respond more positively.

• Introduce yourself to the students. Ask them if they are ready for summer vacation. Be enthusiastic. They will not want to visit you during the summer, or at any time of year, if they think you are not fun.

• Tell the students to pay close attention to what you are about to say. Let them know there will be prizes for students who answer questions.

• Start with smaller-scale programs and work your way up to the bigger programs. If something is popular that year like *Twilight* or *The Hunger Games*, base a program on it and promote it to the students.

• Highlight other aspects about the library besides the summer reading program. Other aspects can include free books for their iPads, Nooks, and other e-readers. Most teens do not know that they can get free e-books and audiobooks on their devices from the library. After last year's assembly, I had three students come to my library so I could show them how to do this. This number isn't staggering, but I know I made an impression on at least a few of them. You can also talk about teen volunteering. I started a teen volunteer group seven years ago, and it has only grown since then. Highlight that they are too young for jobs, but volunteering can help them get a job in the future when they put the library down as work experience.

• After you talk about your programs, start to walk around. This action gives the assembly a sort of game show quality.

• Ask questions based on what you just told the students.

• When students answer correctly, reward them with a prize.

• After the game show portion, reiterate the programs that received the best reaction from the audience.

• Distribute copies of program handouts.

• Thank the students. Tell them you will see them in the summer or sooner.

Benefits of Recruiting Teen Program Participants

Recruiting teen program participants can be essential for their well-being and personal growth, and the library provides teens with a safe space to meet in the community. Successful teen programs at the library can help foster the developmental needs of adolescents. For example, positive peer influences, increased self esteem, and a sense of purpose could be fostered through a teen advisory group, through volunteering, and through attending teen programs. Making a positive impression on the teens at a school visit can not only benefit the library, it can support the healthy development of the teens, as well. And last, but not least, the numbers of program participants and the circulation of teen materials will increase, which is a good way to make the case for more funding.

My Results

I have found that many teens come to the library and say "You came to my school! I remember you!" This recognition shows how well the students take notice when you know how to grab their attention. In addition to the recognition, my teen volunteers have totaled at least 25 in number for the past four summers. These teens have also started a popular Friday afternoon gaming program that has been running since May of 2011. In terms of numbers for the summer reading program, the teen participation rate has been steadily increasing. This past summer I had over 90 teens at my small branch library. I believe this can be attributed to my presence in the middle schools.

Each year I try to revamp my middle school visits. It was only in the past year that I included a photo slideshow of the teens at programs. I felt the slideshow would work because it shows programs coming to life. There is concrete evidence in front of their eyes as I am speaking about it. They can see that I am not making false promises; the proof is staring right at them. Making a slideshow is rather effortless. I simply made a folder of pictures on my computer and then uploaded them to my flash drive. I had to make sure the schools had a laptop for my use. If they did not, I brought one from our mobile lab at the library. Once the flash drive is inserted into the USB port, the computer will ask if you want to see a slideshow of the pictures. It is that easy! There might be the issue of privacy by using photos, but I make it understood that if teens attend my programs then they are fair game to be used in advertising for library programs. I tell them that if they do not wish to be included then they should not be in the picture. I have never had any teen turn down the opportunity to be a photo ham. It is especially great when the pictures are shown at the school and the students erupt into laughter upon seeing themselves or their friends. It is the teens' way of being represented as a vital part of the library. Without them, I would not have a purposeful job.

This model of reaching out to middle school students can be translated and modified for reaching out to elementary school students, as well. Future middle school students are in elementary school, and those students right on the cusp of going to middle school are important to consider. They may have participated in the summer reading program in previous summers as children. At my library, there are two programs: the children's reading program and the teen reading program. Explaining to the students who are entering middle school that they are now considered "teens" in our programs certainly makes them feel special. I talk about how the teen program differs from the children's program, especially making sure to point out that they receive "better" prizes than the children and are entered into weekly raffle contests. The weekly raffle contests grab their attention because the prizes are gift cards to local food spots such as Dunkin' Donuts, Johnny Rockets, Friendly's, McDonald's, and Burger King. Food is a constant guarantee that teens will show up at the library, even if it comes in the form of a gift card for free food that they can get later.

Inviting the new "teens" to the library for programs and letting them know about opportunities available at the library provides them with a rite of passage. They may feel stuck between worlds by being older but still attending an elementary school. The library programs provide these students with a multitude of ways to interact with other students on their specific age and grade levels. These ways include tween/teen-specific programs where no younger children are allowed, volunteer opportunities only open to a certain grade and older, and a special section in the library designated for teen materials separate from the younger children.

Another positive result I have seen from promoting library programs is students from different schools meeting and becoming friends at the library. The students from elementary school will be attending middle schools with students from other elementary schools, and the library provides a way during the summer for the students to meet and become friends before school begins. Making friends prior to the first day of school can be a huge anxiety relief, as they will know some new faces ahead of time. In addition, the younger students can become friends with the high school students and ask questions about the high school experience. The high school students become sort of mentors for the middle school students. At some programs, I have overheard middle school students ask the older students about teachers, classes, and social activities in high school. On the reverse side, I have overheard high school students asking the middle school students if certain teachers were still at the middle school and offer homework help to the students because they have once been in their shoes. The most powerful interaction I have witnessed recently is a high school volunteer becoming a mentor and tutor to a sixth grader still in elementary school. This partnership exemplifies how beneficial the library can be to participants of various ages. In this instance, the high school student gains experience as a volunteer for future endeavors, and the sixth grader gets homework help.

The results of community outreach at my library have improved the library experience for many teens. By attending programs, volunteering, and just visiting the library, the teens have formed friendships, completed community service hours for graduation, and learned responsibility. I have seen friendships form and last for a few years, but sometimes the drama that comes with group formations also surfaces. When there is friction between the teens at the library, I try to resolve it. However, it usually works itself out.

The community service and volunteering aspect of the library has even helped some of my teens get jobs. Because they are young and looking for their first jobs, they do not have any previous work experience. However, library volunteer work can be put down as work experience, showing that the teens have been responsible for tasks and services at a young age. The teens usually ask me if I can be listed as a reference for their job applications, and I always oblige. I have seen these teens get their first jobs, and they are very thankful that I told them to put the library down as previous work experience.

In closing, I would like to reiterate how important reaching out to teens in the community can be for the library. Viewed from a business perspective, our material circulation numbers increase, our number on the door counter increases, and we can justify the need for more materials and money down the road. Without the teen presence, we wouldn't be able to back up our need to improve collections and services for this population because there wouldn't be one to begin with. In order to draw the teens in, we need to have a presence in their lives and be visible in the place where they often spend more time than they do at home: their schools. We need to show them why they should be at the library and reward them for doing so. Once extrinsic motivation wears off, they will need to have enough intrinsic motivation to come back to the library. We can do this by providing them with excellent opportunities to meet new people, allow them to be actively involved in the library, and show them that they are important and needed. This goal can very well be achieved through talking to the teens in large groups at schools.

As this essay has highlighted for you, reaching the teens in schools is relatively easy and straightforward. Do not be afraid to be loud, excited, and enthusiastic when visiting the teens. You want them to like you, and you want them to want to come see you at the library. Don't worry that you're not acting like a teacher when you go to the schools; you do not work in the school, and that's the point. The teachers might actually like a little respite from their daily routines, as well. They could also have teenagers themselves and learn something about the library that they can share with their own children. To conclude, be fun, be interesting, and be there!

Contests and After-School
Activities for Middle School

LEIGH A. WOZNICK

Those of us who love working with students in middle school know that this is a period of enormous change and growth that offers challenges and opportunities for librarians. Middle schoolers are more intellectually advanced, idealistic, self-conscious, socially-focused, and worldly than their younger counterparts, without the sophistication or jaded attitudes they will acquire in high school. We have a crucial opportunity to stoke the fires of the ones who like to read and 'convert' the ones who don't. Unfortunately, it is also the time when we could lose them forever if we don't give them a reason to like reading now. There is stiff competition for their time and attention.

Contests and after-school activities are great ways to reach middle schoolers. However, approach it with the right philosophy. Using contests and activities is not a case of a spoonful of sugar, because what you're offering isn't medicine, and you don't want to give them the impression that it is. Make the media center the teen-friendly hub of the school. Appeal to their inherent love of competition and their powerful need for social connection. Demonstrate for them that the twenty-first century library is a portal to the fast-paced, interactive, multi-media, socially-connected world that Hamilton and Cox call "participatory culture" (2012, 6). Incentive activities can bridge the gap between school and entertainment with experiences, connections, and learning in an informal but meaningful way.

Many of the activities recommended here are tried-and-true staples. To decide which ones will work for you, get to know your audience. Listen to them, as Behen suggests, "using your curiosity approach and not your adult person-in-charge personality" (2006, 19). What are they into? What is going on in their lives? Walk around the cafeteria, attend a school event, read the local newspaper or teen entertainment magazines, do a poll (try Poll Everywhere, Polldaddy, SurveyMonkey, or Google Forms), or form a student advisory group. Remember that activities don't always have to be related to books: it's about knowledge and information, in whatever format that comes. Offer various activities throughout the year to attract different groups, showing that you care enough to do something just for them. My experience is in a school library, but public librarians can follow much of the same advice.

Helpful Hints

No matter which contest or activity you do, taking certain measures will help things run smoothly:
- Get permission from administration.
- Plan ahead. Work out logistics and solicit or purchase prizes well in advance. Prepare and distribute flyers, ballots, forms, instructions, or announcements. Leave enough time for accepting and judging entries (one to three weeks). Start the 'buzz' several days before it begins. Avoid holidays, test days, trips, or assemblies. Thursday is a good deadline day, so you can accept late entries or announce winners on a Friday.
- Advertise. Use the public address system and school radio/TV for announcements. Put up posters in the hall and notices on your website. Distribute flyers or entry forms by placing them at your circulation desk, or hand them out in the hall, classrooms, or cafeteria. Talk it up yourself, and enlist teachers to build hype.
- Put up book displays, decorations, and posters related to your theme.
- Make it relevant. Use a timely reference (fad, holiday, Olympics, election) as a framework. Combine efforts with an existing club. Incorporate pop culture and local or school trivia into themes and questions.
- Invite judges appropriate to the medium from faculty, administration, and/or the student body. This serves a triple purpose: to foster a sense of community, to avoid conflicts of interest, and to get help with the work involved.
- Document it. Take photographs for a display or year-end-report video. Within a day or two, type up what worked and what didn't, and save it for next year.
- Always, always serve snacks!

Tap Creative and Techie Abilities

Middle school students thrive on positive outlets for their talents. Displaying or using their work gives the students ownership and pride in the media center. Their subjects can be books, characters, local history, or landmarks; promoting reading, technology or quirky holidays (Pi Day, International Talk Like a Pirate Day); or demonstrating library skills. Here are some suggestions:
- Art. This can include bookmarks, mouse pads, posters, manga, geography mural or map of authors' hometowns, photography, decorating book carts, coming up with a library mascot, and designing t-shirts for a fundraiser or event.
- Writing. Try far-fetched overdue book excuses, medieval-style book curses, library slogans, six-word novels/memoirs (SMITHTeens is a great resource for this), "Fakebook" pages, and literary mash-ups. Teachers might give extra credit for participation.
- Student-created media. Students can use smart phones or digital cameras to record images or video, then produce videos with Photo Story, Movie Maker, or iMovie. They can also use web tools like Animoto, Xtranormal, Prezi, Blabberize, JibJab, Voki, Audacity, or VoiceThread to create audio/visuals. Some online tools require registration for educational or student accounts. A local cable TV station might be willing to broadcast them.
- Dress as your Favorite Character or Author Day (students and staff).

Stretch Their Brains

Trivia, knowledge, and guessing games are easy and will bring in students who don't otherwise frequent the library. Raffles or drawings give equal chances at winning. Consider pulling names for consolation prizes or a grand prize to increase winners. Prepare the questions ahead of time. Supply a flyer, ballot, or form for students to fill out as their entry and a colorful box to put them in.

• Predict a snow day. Hang a large calendar showing the winter months as a sign-up list. One student per day; one day per student. To win, school must be officially closed.

• Trivia. Use questions from literature, geography, sports, history, television, movies, and music to give everyone a chance. Allow students to look up the answer in your library: that's what it's for! Alternate: a weekly look-it-up challenge. Ask students to list novels that reference other books, books that depict games, bands named after books, national monuments, or sports teams that don't end with "s."

• Guess how many? Fill a container with candy, hair accessories, or other small items. This will also serve as the prize. Alternate: guess how many materials are in the collection.

• What/who is it? Display an image of a historical object or figure and let students guess what or who it is. Partner with a historical society or museum, or simply link to an image page in a database, providing search term clues. Post the answer a few days later. Try using Pinterest to do this.

• Who said that? Students identify the author and source for a quote. Alternate: misquote it, and have students supply the accurate quote and source.

• Nutty news. Students enter a clipping or printout of a strange but real news story. Alternate: stories about happy news, bogus news, technology, or another topic of interest. Provide links to reputable sources or databases.

• Identify initialisms from book titles, common phrases, quotes, adages, or acronyms (e.g., "12 S. of the Z." is "12 signs of the zodiac," and "A.F.I.L.A.W." is "all's fair in love and war").

Encourage Competitive Nature

Individual students, teams, classes, or grades can compete, or an entire school can work toward a goal if teachers and administration are supportive. Throw a pizza or ice cream party for winners or participants.

• Reading challenges. Number of books/pages/words read (keep count via Accelerated Reader, catalog records, or manual logs). Set a realistic but challenging goal (such as a million words or 1,000 books), and put up a chart to track progress. This works best with teacher involvement; otherwise, students will likely just check books out without reading them.

• Student voting. Fantasy sports league of literary characters, character smack-down (Bella vs. Katniss), or election using characters as candidates. Run a simple student poll or a longer project in which students create dream teams or present arguments and vote for winners in an election.

• As seen on TV. Take inspiration from television shows like *Jeopardy!*, *Craft Wars*, *MythBusters*, *Survivor*, or *The Amazing Race*, requiring teams to do tasks or find information. The more hands-on, the better. Watson Adventures' scavenger hunts and Wilderdom's survival skills team-building exercises are also good models.

Seasonal Tie-ins

• Mock Newbery. Students nominate and vote for favorites. Alternate: [Your School's] Best Book of the Year (give six to eight popular choices and allow write-ins).
• Blind date with a book (Valentine's Day). Students check out a book sight unseen and agree to try it. Place books in paper bags and write or paste the barcode number on the outside to ease checkout. Place all the bags in large, decorated baskets (one romance, one non-romance). Students participate on their own and teachers can bring classes. Alternative: I heart reading (fill out a slip for every book read in February, with a drawing for the winner).
• March madness tournament. Brackets pit books against each other, students vote for their favorites, and the winner moves on to the next round the following week. Start with 32, and finish in five weeks.

National Contests and Programs

Consider some of the established regional, state, and national programs sponsored by professional and literacy organizations. For example, the New Jersey Association of School Librarians (NJASL) sponsors an Enthusiastic Reader award every year. I nominate about 40–50 students. Each receives a certificate and free book from me, plus the chance to win the state's prizes. A few years ago, one of my students was a state winner. Even if you don't compete officially, you can follow their example on a smaller scale.
• Battle of the Books
• WrestleMania Reading Challenge (Young Adult Library Services Association)
• Letters About Literature (Center for the Book, Library of Congress)
• School Library Month Video Contest (American Association of School Librarians)
• 90-Second Newbery Film Festival (James Kennedy)
• Great Scavenger Hunt Contest (Kay Cassidy)
• Get Caught Reading (American Association of Publishers)
• Read Across America (National Education Association)
• National Geographic Spelling Bee or Geography Bee
• National History Day (University of Maryland)
• World Book Night

After-School Activities

Middle school students, in a quest to discover themselves and hang out with friends, love after-school activities. They try something new, identify with a group, spend time with teachers and students in an informal setting, and have the place to themselves 'after hours.' Sometimes, there are other perks: one girl came to a book club to see a boy she liked. Activities can be one-shot deals or long-term regular programs, in-person or virtual. You may have to experiment with a few to find the one that takes off and be willing to move on to something else with a new crop of kids.

Book Discussions/Clubs

Be creative with this obvious choice. Let the students pick the books and name the club. Be flexible about attendance, and try alternate days (or lunch or breakfast groups). There are great programming ideas on the AASL website, but here are a few that have worked for me:
  • Invite the teen/tween librarian from the public library to be involved. They can often provide multiple book copies as well as snacks.
  • Specialize for one meeting: guys only, bring a friend/parent/sibling, partner with the high school club, read picture books to younger students.
  • Mix it up by doing an activity, eating food related to the book, hosting an evening party/meeting, adding a community service element (donate canned goods), or doing an individual choice (e.g., award winners in January).
  • Expand discussions onto a wiki, blog, or Edmodo page; arrange a pen-pal program with another school; do a speed book-dating session; post student reviews to a website or in your automation system.
  • Hold a discussion party separate from the book club for a popular book to allow for a different day or new people.

Guest Speakers/How-to Programs

Programs like these highlight the media center as a place to learn information of all kinds and highlight the benefits of an expert source. Hands-on projects are valuable: sometimes students learn best what they teach themselves or each other (using your collection!). Invite a student, teacher, parent, or expert from the community to demonstrate a skill or lead a group activity. Scouting groups and 4-H clubs could also provide programs, usually for free. Other areas to explore include:
  • Science/technology. CSI, cyber-safety, downloading e-books, kitchen chemistry.
  • Everyday skills. Makeup or skin care, changing car oil, banking and investments, outdoor survival skills (orienteering, geocaching).
  • Crafty. Bookbinding, building birdhouses, cake decorating, t-shirt fabric painting.
  • Fitness. Zumba, yoga, meditation, self-defense.
  • History. 'Museum' exhibits; personal memories from a veteran, historical society representative, or town elder.
  • Collectibles. Collector, dealer, or shop owner (autographs, trains, stamps, baseball cards).

Gaming

Games harness middle schoolers' competitive natures, but they also improve critical thinking and problem-solving skills. Video gaming has become popular in public libraries, and there are numerous resources available with ideas and advice:

- Game on! Hold a tournament of board games, games from history or other countries, and retro video games (donated or loaned). Find the rules in your collection or online.
- First lines of novels. Several lists are available online, but tailor it by using books that are popular, funny, or used regularly in your classrooms. Winner guesses the most correctly. This one works nicely with a book group.
- Host a mystery. Buy an inexpensive kit at a toy store or search online for free plans (e.g., Mystery Writers of America's educator page). Students can role-play the characters, play the part of the sleuth, and use scientific detection methods to solve a crime scene you set up.
- The American Go Foundation will send you a starter kit and connect you to a local master to teach about the ancient Asian board game called Go.

Cultural/Arts

Offer outlets to students who love being in the spotlight as well as those with quieter aspirations. Partner with the drama, art, music, or world language departments.

- Open mic night. Singing, poetry slam, rap (original, translated speeches, or book summaries). Borrow a microphone and amplifier from the AV department.
- Reader's theater. Scripts are available online for free, and how-to books can be purchased from professional library publishers. No props, sets, or memorization needed.
- Altered book art. Collect discarded books, inspire students with images from examples online (Brian Dettmer, Cara Borer, Su Blackwell), and provide tools (x-actos, scissors, bone folders, PVC glue).
- Sign language. Invite students or community members who use sign language to come to your library. Translating [clean] pop songs into sign is a fun activity.
- Manga/anime. Sometimes, all you have to do is say "yes," and students will do all the work. In my case, a student created the informational slideshow presentations himself, and the group shared their own books.
- Creative writing. Cumulative stories, fan fiction, and original work can be shared on a wiki, in Google documents, or in person, with members offering constructive criticism. With assistance from a language arts teacher, this could blossom into a literary magazine; apply for a small grant for printing costs, if necessary.
- Author Skypes. Easy to arrange and reasonably priced, they work best with small groups familiar with the author's work (all you need is a webcam; download the free software).
- Armchair travelers. Students film or write a travel blog (places they have been, would like to go, where their ancestors came from). Meetings can be devoted to learning about the culture, landmarks, clothing, and food. This is a great way to foster tolerance and appreciation of others' cultures.
- Mock Oscar. Students nominate and vote for favorite movie adaptations, answer trivia questions, and give casting suggestions for other books. Show the 'winning' movie, with permission and license.

Feeling Ambitious?

- Lock-in. An evening event can combine many previously mentioned activities, such as gaming, crafts, food, dancing, guest speakers, etc. Alternate: do a scavenger hunt with flashlights or use telescopes in an astronomy-themed event. Make sure you get additional teachers and/or administrators to help chaperone.

• Book swap/giveaway. Collect used book donations from teachers, parents, Girl/Boy Scouts, and vendors. Encourage students to bring one to swap, but give them one even if they don't. Do it at the end of the year so students have something fun for summer reading.

• Puzzles and codes. Create stations where students explore word/number/logic puzzles and try to solve secret codes and ciphers. Give them a chance to create their own. There are plenty of online and printed resources to pull from.

• Rube Goldberg machines. Provide the raw materials (discarded books, elements from toy construction sets like Erector, K'NEX, LEGO, Mouse Trap, and Marble Runs). Invite the tech-ed, wood shop, or science teachers to help out. Be sure to record it on video!

A Word About Prizes and Funding

The argument over tangible prizes as reading incentives is an old one. While the research is not definitive, teacher praise, books, and book-related prizes seem to be better motivators in the classroom (Gambrell 2011). But this is not classroom reading motivation, so your rules are different. Of course, recognition, attention, and their name and winning entry displayed or used by other students all have intrinsic appeal. But let's face it: middle schoolers like prizes! Books do make great prizes, as do bookstore or e-book gift cards. Request extra ARCs from book vendors, bookstores, or libraries; you can also pick up free books at conferences and register to win books on Goodreads or Free Book Friday.

Practical items make good prizes. Small denomination gift cards ($5) from Dunkin' Donuts, iTunes, McDonald's, and Starbucks are appreciated. If you have a little petty cash or a decent budget, don't be afraid to spend a little money on gift cards ($10–15) to Barnes & Noble, Amazon, Subway, Love Culture, and for movie tickets, the local laser tag, or an arcade. Search DVD sale bins or marked-down bookshelves to get items for just a few dollars. Make prizes apropos of the contest theme. For the Predict a Snow Day contest, I gave out white mugs filled with hot chocolate mix packets, $5 Dunkin' Donuts cards, winter-themed pencils, and other doodads.

Reach out to local businesses for donations or gift certificates. I get about 200 coupons for a free ice from Rita's Water Ice. Anything that's a national chain typically requires you to contact corporate headquarters: make that an annual task. Professional sports teams will probably donate paraphernalia but not tickets, while semi-pro teams may donate both.

Buy bulk items like pencils personalized with a quote or slogan from dollar stores or Oriental Trading Company. Local garage sales are a gold mine of books to swap and for harder-to-find little gifts; look for things that are still new in their packages. Appeal to the seller's generous spirit and ask for donations (bring your school ID). I also pick up swag at conferences and on sites like www.freecycle.org.

Small grants or gifts may be available from the PTA/PTO, the local teacher's union, or the district fundraising foundation. An active book club, scouting group, or community awareness organization might be willing to do fundraising (e.g., bake sales), especially for an author visit or other special event. Many, many grants are available online.

Where to Get Ideas?

One of the best things about librarians is that they like to share: a quick Google search will result in hundreds of hits full of programming and contest ideas to use or adapt.

• Professional organization websites. ALA Connect; AASL/ALSC/YALSA School/Public Library Cooperative programs. I also get ideas from scouting organizations' badge programs.

• Professional journals. *School Library Journal, School Library Monthly, The MAILBOX, Book Links,* or *Teacher Librarian.*

• Books/anthologies from professional publishers. ALA editions, VOYA Guides from Scarecrow Press, Linworth, and Libraries Unlimited. Your counterparts at other schools or the public library may be willing to lend you their copies.

The absolute best place for ideas is your peers. Talk to colleagues at other schools, at conferences, and on the LM-NET listserv. Many, many librarians have done this before, and they will happily share their experiences with you.

If you try to do everything I've mentioned here, you'll drive yourself crazy. Not every activity or contest is appropriate for every school, and the particulars of your budget, schedule, or district may preclude you from doing some of them. Start small. Pick one. Do it. And go on from there. Have fun!

Works Cited

Behen, Linda D. 2006. *Using Pop Culture to Teach Information Literacy: Methods to Engage a New Generation.* Westport, CT: Libraries Unlimited.

Gambrell, Linda B. 2011. "Seven Rules of Engagement: What's Most Important to Know about Motivation to Read." *The Reading Teacher* 65 (3): 172–178.

Hamilton, Buffy, and Ernie Cox. 2012. "Participatory Culture in the School Library." *Knowledge Quest* 41 (1): 6–7.

Turntables and Tater Tots
Lunchroom Outreach That Works

LEAH DURAND, ABIGAIL HARWOOD
and JOSEPH WILK

As teen services staff at Carnegie Library of Pittsburgh, we noticed that scheduling school visits was becoming increasingly difficult. Educators were simply unable to sacrifice instruction time for our traditional, in-classroom outreach model. Because providing outreach to middle and high schools is an essential part of serving teens, we were motivated to craft an alternative way of reaching students without interfering with the school's tight schedules. Our solution: visits to the lunchroom.

Lunchroom visits have something to offer everyone: a fun lunch environment for students, minimal setup and coordination for administrators, and an efficient method of providing actual library service to an entire student body. Through this, we've been able to advance the mission of Carnegie Library of Pittsburgh—to engage our community in literacy and learning—farther than ever before.

This essay will show you how to implement a successful cafeteria-based outreach program on any scale or budget. You will learn to assess your capacity to perform this outreach, propose a lunchroom outreach program to library and school administrators, strategize remote circulation and card registration, offer a backdrop of cool music, and design lunchroom-friendly craft activities.

Every idea and suggestion offered in this essay has been informed by our experiences in the lunchrooms of middle and high schools all across Pittsburgh, Pennsylvania. Learn from our challenges and successes, and then make this program your own!

Preparing for Outreach

Staffing

The number of staff you can offer determines what your outreach can accomplish. If your department doesn't have enough staff for the program you envision, here are some strategies we've found successful for increasing staffing levels:
- Ask librarians from other departments to offer their expertise.
- Ask clerks to offer remote circulation.

- Establish a partnership with librarians from nearby libraries whose serving population attends the same school. If they serve a different school, you can develop a reciprocal partnership, offering outreach to both schools.
  - Contact local literacy or other nonprofit organizations to coordinate outreach efforts.
  - Invite school staff to work tables and facilitate activities with you.
  - Solicit library volunteers to run different activities.

Technology

With initial planning, you can save yourself time and aggravation when strategizing remote check out and other tech-heavy activities that may be essential to your lunchroom success. Figure out exactly what you want to do in advance and assess whether you have the technology to implement it.

In the time since we began our lunchroom outreach initiative, we've brought integrated library system (ILS)-equipped laptops and aircards for Internet access, used tablets running remote desktop software to control our ILS while receiving Internet from a mobile hub, and have even had to borrow school laptops for wireless Internet access through the schools.

We were fortunate to evolve along with our program's increasing IT needs by testing equipment from different departments before purchasing our own. If you are on a strict budget and don't have this flexibility, try to plan your outreach initiatives at the beginning of the fiscal year so you can make the most future-proof plan possible for your tech needs.

Budgets

While lunchroom outreach may seem like a financial luxury, we were able to make the most of our budget using the following methods:
- Share costs and resources with other departments and libraries in the system.
- Multipurpose equipment and divide the cost among different line items.

If that's still not enough to support your efforts, consider applying for educational or arts grants, as well as grants through professional organizations such as the Young Adult Library Services Association (YALSA).

Proposing Lunchroom Outreach

Internal Proposals

The support of library administration is crucial to justifying your time away from the reference desk. When presenting this model to supervisors, we focused on how lunchroom outreach would reinforce the mission and values of our library, including:
- Raising the library's profile among school students and staff
- Reaching the entire student body in an efficient one- to two-hour visit
- Providing actual library services to the students
- Modeling library services to students and staff who may not already be familiar with the variety of services the library offers
- Strengthening relationships among the library, school, and students, opening the door for future collaborations

School Proposals

Once we obtained approval from administration, we solicited partnerships with local schools. In our experience, the right person to approach varies from school to school. In the past, we've had visits organized through school library media specialists, literature teachers, department heads, and principals, moving up the chain until we found a receptive staff member.

When proposing a lunchroom-based outreach model to educators, it is important to emphasize the positive outcomes to both the school and its students. You will find that school administrators are more receptive when they explicitly understand how the school will benefit from your visits. Try using the following talking points in your communications about the school visits:

- Does not interfere with instruction time
- Requires minimal school staff time and organization
- Contributes to the students' overall enjoyment of the school environment
- Directly connects students with the library and its resources

Ensure your school partners are aware of the flexibility of this model and that you are open to change based on their feedback. At one of our partner schools, administrators felt that music and crafts were disruptive to the learning environment; however, school officials saw value in providing library card registration and material circulation. We were able to modify our visits to address the school's concerns and continue outreach. Additionally, we discovered that the school had an after-school program, allowing us to relocate our entire menu of lunchroom activities to a more appropriate setting.

Remote Circulation and Readers' Advisory

Remote Circulation

Being connected with our ILS, we had the ability to register teens for library cards and circulate materials. However, we found that many students lacked the proper ID required to register for a library card or had forgotten their cards at home. Be sure to discuss these potential barriers with library administration, strategizing new policies and procedures that can offer access. Our staff have had success with the following alternatives:

- Have teachers vouch for students' identities.
- Request school rosters, report cards, or other official school documents from the school for address verification.

If your ILS is unavailable, consider bringing paper application forms, verifying identity through the means above, and following up to deliver students' newly active cards. Be sure that there is a mechanism, whether from the school or library, to inform parents that this process is taking place. Our schools have included information in their parent newsletters so that all parents could be aware of our efforts. Additionally, Carnegie Library of Pittsburgh has a policy of sending parental notification postcards to ensure that no families are surprised by their students' new library accounts.

Furthermore, learn about your circulation policies for when your ILS is offline so that you have an alternate (or primary, depending on your circumstances) method of providing remote circulation. If your library uses paper check out slips, make sure you have them on hand. Despite the technological capabilities our staff has access to, from time to time we find ourselves unable to connect to the Internet or to the ILS. In these situations, we continue to circulate books with pencil and paper, uploading the information to our system upon returning to the library. We also bring due date slips so that all students can have a reminder of when their items must be returned to the library.

Material Selection and Readers' Advisory

When bringing materials to circulate, be sure to prepare a variety to appeal to the largest amount of students at your target school. Consider different genres, topics, time periods, character demographics, and formats. An assortment of fiction, non-fiction, graphic novels, DVDs, and CDs should attract a wide and appreciative audience. For some school visits, our staff will select materials and activities that relate to a predetermined theme. We've chosen the themes by asking teachers for topics that would support curriculum or other school activities, such as musicals or sporting events.

Moreover, be sure to consult professional review sources for age-appropriateness. While we can defend a sixth grader arriving home from the library with a book intended for older teens through our policies and procedures, we cannot do the same for books that we offer through a school setting. As a result, we work hard to inoculate ourselves from potential challenges—and the possibility of having our program pulled from the schools—by carefully ensuring that the intended age ranges of our materials match the age ranges of students we're visiting.

Over time, we have established relationships with students through regularly scheduled visits, soliciting student requests and fulfilling them on return visits. Having a dedicated staff member to discuss reading interests and offer readers' advisory has enabled us to get to know our audience and be better equipped to bring materials that relate to their interests. If you are running the show solo, consider bringing print resources to supplement your knowledge. This will also be helpful if you don't have access to online recommendation sites and databases. Passive readers' advisory techniques, such as attractive displays and print booklists, work just as well as they do inside the library to highlight your collections and begin a conversation.

Music

Why Music?

Whether doing homework or hanging out with friends, popular music tends to follow teenagers everywhere they go—except, for the most part, school. Our staff has found that including a music component has a number of positive results:
- Draws attention to the outreach table
- Makes teens feel more comfortable approaching the desk
- Adds an extra level of excitement and enhances the school experience
- Adds a "cool factor" to the librarians

While music offers enjoyment to the school outreach experience, there are potential drawbacks. We've had issues with sound traveling in unexpected ways, disturbing classrooms and other school activities, such as standardized testing. We've had requests for songs that were inappropriate for the school environment, despite playing the radio version. Now, before the lunch period begins, we test the volume and ask our school contact if there are any activities, just to be safe. We're also sure to look up lyrics to identify inappropriate subject matter.

Amplify Your Outreach

When it comes to audio, you can break through to your audience without breaking the bank. We've successfully used standard, everyday computer speakers, boomboxes, wireless Bluetooth speakers, portable PA systems, and even the school's own speaker system to infuse our outreach with sound and excitement. Do research on all of these options to determine the most cost-effective option for not just your lunchroom outreach, but for your teen and library services as a whole. We've also been able to use our portable PA system for after-hours parties and poetry readings.

Now that you're ready to go, where will you find music? In cases when our staff deejay—who supplies his own music courtesy of a digital record pool—can't make it, we've turned to online radio and digital streaming services such as Radio, Pandora, and Spotify. We've also made use of pre-purchased MP3s from digital music stores and CD compilations of chart hits.

To build our playlists, we've looked at Billboard charts, playlists of local radio stations, blog aggregators such as The Hype Machine, teen culture retailers like Hot Topic, music magazines, and the students themselves. Letting teens contribute to our playlists for upcoming visits has added yet another meaningful element of interaction. We've also had the privilege of showcasing music produced by students, which we solicit in advance so we can examine for content. When teens recognize their own voices on the PA system, alongside nationally renowned artists, they feel valued by the library and their community.

Craft Activities

Why Offer Crafts?

When devising our new outreach model, we asked ourselves: how can we build excitement among students for our in-library programming? We decided to model library programming for students by providing a craft program at each visit; instead of merely informing teens about our programs during outreach, we would engage them with activities.

Choosing the Ideal Craft

Selecting a craft to bring into a school lunchroom requires more thought than you might expect. When planning any lunchtime craft, we always consider the following criteria:

• Lunch periods may be short and in quick succession, leaving the students little time to eat. Choose an activity that the students can complete quickly.

• The project should be easy enough for you to lead entirely by yourself and simple enough for students of all skill levels to complete with minimal instruction.

• Activities should be inexpensive and easy to transport, allowing for enough supplies to satisfy the entire school population.

• Make sure your projects are dynamic and will attract participation.

Our staff has also found the following steps immeasurably useful in ensuring planned activities run smoothly:

• Create an example of the project in advance. To get a sense of what leading the craft in school might be like, ask teens in the library to join you. Did the teens struggle with the project, need a lot of help, enjoy themselves? Adjust your plans based on these preliminary experiences.

• Bring examples of the completed project to attract interest and give teens an idea of what the finished product will look like.

• Make a poster outlining step-by-step instructions. Use simple language and large, easy-to-read fonts, adding visuals whenever possible. Teens can then follow the steps on their own, allowing you to help people where they need it.

Lunchroom Craft Ideas

Duct Tape Bowties

Duct tape bowties are one of the simplest and quickest duct tape crafts to replicate. This project appeals to teens because the bowties are fun and versatile; they can be worn traditionally or used to decorate a barrette, ponytail holder, or headband.

Supplies:
• Duct tape
• Scissors

Instructions:
• Cut a strip of duct tape between 8 to 10 inches long.
• Place the duct tape sticky side up and fold the two ends onto each other so that they meet in the middle but do not overlap.
• Pinch the piece of duct tape in the middle where the two sides meet, and wrap a shorter piece of duct tape around its center.

Collection Connection:
Morgan, Richela Fabian. 2012. *Tape It & Make It: 101 Duct Tape Activities*. Hauppauge, NY: Barron's.

Lollipop Mustaches

Teens will be amused by this mustache craft and will enjoy the added bonus of getting a sweet treat. Be sure to obtain permission from school administrators before you bring any outside food into a school. If the school you're visiting has a healthy food initiative or allergy concerns, glue craft sticks to the mustaches as an alternative.

Supplies:
• Scissors
• Mustache templates
• 8 ½" × 11" card stock (pre-cut into fourths)
• Single-hole punch
• Markers
• Lollipops

Instructions:
• Trace the mustache template onto a piece of pre-cut card stock.

- Cut out the mustache and punch a hole in the middle.
- Place a lollipop in the center and enjoy.

Collection Connection:
Morgan, Richela Fabian. 2012. *Tape It & Make It: 101 Duct Tape Activities*. Hauppauge, NY: Barron's.

Marshmallow Bridges and Buildings

Bring a little engineering into the lunchroom with this fun activity. Try competing to see which teen or team can build the tallest, sturdiest structure fastest. Or you may modify the project to create edible constellations and highlight your collection of astronomy books. Again, be sure to obtain permission from administrators before bringing any food items into the school.

Supplies:
- Marshmallows (gumdrops or grapes for a healthier option)
- Toothpicks, pretzels, or uncooked spaghetti

Instructions:
- Pierce the marshmallows with the connecting pieces.
- Connect the marshmallows to create the structure of choice.

Collection Connection:
Newcomb, Rain, and Bobby Mercer. 2009. *Smash It!, Crash It!, Launch It! 50 Mind-Blowing, Eye-Popping Science Experiments*. New York: Lark Books.

Paper Robots

Paper robots may have special appeal to teens who are interested in science. Print the robot templates onto white or colored cardstock. Let students customize by coloring before cutting and assembling their robots. In addition to robots, there are many free paper toy templates available—both online and in books—that represent a variety of interests.

Supplies:
- Paper robot design (printed or photocopied on cardstock)
- Scissors
- Glue and/or tape
- Markers (optional)

Instructions:
- Cut out robot design.
- Fold cutouts to create the robot's shape.
- Tape or glue the robot together.

Collection Connection:
Bou, Louis. 2010. *We Are Paper Toys: Print-Cut-Fold-Glue-Fun!* New York: Collins Design.
Perdana, Julius, and Josh Buczynski. 2009. *Build Your Own Paper Robots: 100s of Mecha Model Designs on CD to Print Out and Assemble*. New York: St. Martin's Griffin.

Resources for More Lunchroom Crafts

• Use your own teen collection to find easy, age-appropriate craft books that offer an opportunity to highlight materials from your shelves.

• Get ideas and inspiration from experienced professionals who have already done the hard work for you. Use professional literature by librarians and educators including manuals, books, blogs, journal articles, and magazines.

• Pinterest allows you to archive craft and activity ideas. Follow and view the "pins" of others while creating pinboards collaboratively.

Building a Better Outreach

In this essay, we've outlined our experiences in making lunchroom outreach work for staff, students, and teachers in our area. But remember, one of the benefits of this model is its flexibility. If you aren't feeling inspired by the stations outlined earlier, try some of these ideas to spice up the lunchroom outreach model:

• Use technology to showcase the library with dynamic presentations that cycle through book recommendations and photos from library programs.

• Offer gaming, movies, or other audiovisual activities. The Xbox Kinect is a great "hands-free" controller that will minimize the possibility of theft. Also, make sure you have the proper license for showing movies.

• Try audiovisual crafts such as apps for photo manipulation and other fun, creative endeavors. With permission from schools, post these photos on social media to raise anticipation for following visits.

• Reproduce game shows such as *Minute to Win It* or *Silent Library* for an activity that is fun for spectators and participants alike.

Measuring Success

As with all efforts, when we first implemented our lunchroom outreach program, we strategized different ways that the library could measure its success. After some thought, we decided on a combination of quantitative statistics and qualitative stories.

Quantitative Stats

When measuring our gross outreach statistics, the teen department at our main library has seen an astonishing increase in the number of visits and students impacted. In 2009, prior to visiting lunch periods, teen staff made a total of 14 school visits, reaching just 182 students. Since dedicating ourselves to this model in 2011, staff have made 79 school visits reaching just over 6,000 students.

Over the course of our visits, we've also used statistic tracking to determine that we have circulated nearly 1,000 books and answered over 1,000 reference questions. Additionally, distributing slips with our Facebook fan page URL has increased our number of "likes" to over 500. These numbers, when compared against our department's in-house statistics during the same period, have highlighted an extraordinary return on our investment that we are able to share with library administrators and funders.

Qualitative Stories

While administrators and funders have been impressed with the sheer volume of numbers, they have been moved to further support our efforts with stories of how our outreach efforts have impacted library services to teens. We have written down a number of these stories and encourage you to do the same.

• One teen posted a Facebook video of himself participating in library-based cafeteria gaming, bragging about the things the library offers at school. Classmates commented about how fun it was, inspiring another to wish that she could transfer schools.

• One library made its first-ever outreach to the local Yeshiva Girls High School after having proposed a cafeteria-based program. It was so successful that they have since visited all other Yeshiva school branches and collaborated on research instruction.

• One teen made her first visit to the library two months after learning at a cafeteria visit that the *Phantom of the Opera* score was available to borrow. When we showed her where it was, she pretended to faint and told us that the library "made her life."

• One librarian visited a cafeteria, where she saw two teens who hadn't visited their local library since they were small children. After having a chance to reconnect, they both came back to renew their cards and check out books; one even started attending the weekly teen program!

By reaching out to teens in an environment where you can be seen as a mentor rather than an authority figure, one in which they have the choice to engage with you, establishes you and your library as an ally. Hopefully, this essay has shown how to create an effective lunchroom outreach program—one more tool in your toolbox for teen outreach and engagement.

Outreach Outcome
I'm Going to the Library After School!
Joanna Nelson *and* Kaitlin Hoke

Outreach is one of the best ways to connect with teens, that somewhat elusive audience. Joanna Nelson, teen services outreach librarian, and Kaitlin Hoke, teen services coordinator, coordinate Pikes Peak Library District's visits to schools. In middle and high schools, our team presents booktalks, teaches resource classes, coordinates a student library card program, promotes librarianship at career fairs, and much more. Pikes Peak Library District (PPLD) serves a community of over 575,000 residents. With 446 staff members in 14 urban and rural locations, we are a large district serving a diverse population. PPLD supports outreach by providing time and materials for staff to collaborate with community members. Developing a robust outreach program takes time, commitment, and enthusiasm. PPLD's methods have been proven to work in the community.

Since 1997, PPLD has presented booktalks to over 72,000 students, school librarians, and teachers. Additionally, through resource classes, we have created a successful and innovative way to prepare students for college-level research. Over time, relationships have developed with schools, and teachers depend on us each semester for resource classes. Our team often surprises schools with useful, easy, and accessible resources. By working with school libraries, the public library is contributing to "increased student achievement" (Jones 2009, 77).

In this essay, we will share innovative tips and tricks that will help make outreach easy for small and large libraries. These tools are intended to help anyone using them take action quickly and efficiently, and they can be easily tailored to fit the needs and resources of individual libraries.

Reaching Out

Initially, reaching out and connecting with schools may seem daunting. At PPLD, we developed methods that make the process go smoothly. The public library needs a streamlined system when reaching out to balance the demands of everyone involved. Be clear about your resources and expectations by considering the following when developing your outreach program:

• Take time to work with the schools and discover how the public library can support their goals.

178

- Keep communications with the school or library organized for easy reference.
- Remember that you are representing the library to the community. This is embodied by providing good customer service, being friendly, open to suggestions, and flexible.

Tips and Tricks for Reaching Out

Whom to Contact

- Teachers, school librarians, media specialists, district librarians, principals, and school volunteer coordinators

How to Contact

- Collect e-mail addresses or phone numbers (use volunteers, if possible).
- Create a spreadsheet with e-mail addresses and use mail merge.
- Contact schools three times during the semester.
- Make phone calls.
- Send e-mails:
  a. Use bullet points (not long paragraphs).
  b. If you use an image, make it small.
- Visit in person:
  a. Prepare and practice an elevator speech.
  b. Make sure library staff know the services you offer and that they should direct teachers and librarians to you.
- Follow up in a timely manner.

Things to Avoid

- Sending too many e-mails (limit to three or four per semester)
- Presuming that the school library needs the public library's help

Booktalking

A booktalk is a one- to three-minute long spirited "advertisement" for a book with a hook to grab the students' interest. A booktalk presentation enthusiastically promotes library resources and a variety of books. PPLD has booktalked in middle and high schools for over 20 years, and it is a highly successful outreach activity for our district and for teens. Teachers and school librarians count on us to come to their schools to promote the joy of reading and improve literacy. Booktalks provide an opportunity to build positive relationships among the school, teens, and the public library.

Teens can be intimidated by books and libraries, so one of the main goals with booktalking is to break down negative stereotypes associated with reading and the library. We show teens that books are relatable, exciting, and fun. We expand their horizons by sharing the vast variety of genres and formats that exist. Another goal we have is to encourage teens to come to the library; when a teen asks for a book because of a booktalk, we are thrilled!

All of this has taken time to evolve into what it is now. The staff member in the teen outreach position has built-in processes to ensure continued success of the program; for example, saving documents, letters, instructions, and school contact information for future staff members.

Tips and Tricks for Booktalking

Selecting Books

- Like the book or be able to be excited about it
- Include variety:
    a. Books for different grade levels
    b. Books that interest girls, boys, or both
    c. Genres (e.g., nonfiction, fiction, adult books for teens, poetry, steampunk, memoirs, historical fiction, humor, fantasy, and paranormal)
    d. Readalikes for blockbuster books
    e. Diversity in the characters and issues
    f. Format (e.g., audiobooks, e-books, Playaways, and graphic novels)
    g. Books of varying lengths

Writing Booktalks

- Read the book (then write the booktalk immediately after) or find a booktalk from a trusted source. Trusted sources for booktalks include reviews, NoveList, Booktalking Colorado, and a wide range of websites.
- The booktalks should be one to three minutes in length.
- Start the booktalk with a hook: a relatable question, a shocking statement or a "did you like...?"
- Choose a booktalking style, such as excerpt, discussion, or first-person (Cox Clark 2007, 24).
- Know all the formats the book is available in from your library.
- For high-circulating titles, print out the booktalk and a cover image:
    a. Paste on cardstock (the booktalk on one side and the cover image on the other).
    b. Laminate (if possible).

Training Yourself and Others

- Observe booktalks in person or watch videos online.
- Practice makes perfect. Read booktalks out loud to staff, family, friends, or yourself.
- Meet with new booktalkers to share expectations.
- Invite new booktalkers to observe booktalks in the classroom.
- Ask an experienced booktalker to provide feedback for new booktalkers.

Build a Booktalking Kit

- Make one for yourself and/or each of your team members.
- Use a wheeled bag.

- Include:
    a. An announcement checklist (introductions, library locations, library card information, resources from the library and programs)
    b. Method to track statistics
    c. Booktalker booklists for students, teachers, and librarians
    d. Program handouts
    e. Teen library website information
    f. Library resource bookmarks and handouts
    g. Teacher packet (survey link handout, booklists, teen department services for schools, and library resource handouts)
    h. Water (you'll be talking a lot)

Scheduling with Teachers and Librarians

- Be upfront about the times you are available.
- Schedule two weeks out and confirm or cancel one week out.
- Recruit booktalkers from other departments.
- Provide a calendar that all staff members can access.
- Create booktalk appointments with staff members via a scheduling software (e.g., Outlook).
- Encourage teachers to work together to schedule four sessions of booktalks.
- It's okay to say, "we are not available at that time."

At the Booktalk

- Bring different formats to show.
- If you don't have the physical book for a booktalk, bring the laminated cover and booktalk.
- Have some books the students can look at and touch.

Booklists

- Provide for the students, teachers, and librarians.
- Be sure to give to the librarians so they can add titles to their collection and know what their students will be requesting.

Technology

- Use book trailers.
- Show interviews with authors.
- Demonstrate how to use the library catalog or other resources (e.g., NoveList, Literature Resource Center, readalike websites).
- List the booktalks on the library's website to help staff and patrons find titles.
- Add a photo of the booktalker with a link to a list in the catalog.

Statistics

- Record the number of sessions, students, and teachers.
- Set up a tracking system (we use Excel, and it works well).
- Report successes to your supervisor and others in the library.

Things to Avoid

- Too many students in a classroom (keep it to about 60 maximum with two booktalkers)
- Classrooms without a teacher (inform teachers that they must stay in the classroom)
- Too many sessions (four sessions per day is enough)
- Babysitting (avoid scheduling before school breaks)
- Gushing (sell the book, not only your love for it)
- Publication dates (old books are great, but don't tell them when it was published)
- Long booktalks (keep it to one to three minutes; any longer and you might lose them)

Success Stories for Booktalking

- Rob is a great booktalker in middle schools. He understands students' sense of humor and plays into their fascination of gross topics. Rob also happens to shave his head, so when students come into the library, they ask for books that the "bald guy" talked about. In a thank-you letter to Rob, one student wrote, "Thank you for the booktalk, but now I have a risk of checking out too many books!"
- Cara, another booktalker, had a great experience with a student. At the end of a book-talk session, students have about five minutes to look at the books. This brings up some interesting discussions of books. Cara had a student who was very excited about the books they brought. She kept picking up different titles and asking, "What's this one about? And this one?" She was so eager and energized! After the student left, her teacher approached Cara and explained that she was thrilled to see her student, who was a struggling reader, excited about our books.

Resource Classes

The purpose of resource classes is to teach students how to use library resources for homework and to prepare them for college research. We promote public library resources to schools so they can expand the availability of research options for students. Approach schools with the attitude of supporting what they are already doing. This mindset helps open doors and helps develop long-term relationships. Teachers appreciate when we come into their classrooms because we provide an outside voice conveying the importance of good research skills.

PPLD resource classes are available throughout the school year, and we encourage teachers to include them in their curriculum planning. One example is International Baccalaureate (IB) programs that require the students to do an extended essay. The essay involves using advanced research skills and having an understanding of plagiarism (Tilke 2011, 9). This type of program provides a foundation for developing your resource class curriculum. Ultimately, the resource class is more than teaching about research; we build relationships with teens, create lifelong learners, and forge strong relationships with schools in our community.

Tips and Tricks for Resource Classes

Build a Resource Class Plan

- A handout with databases, search tips, library resources, and contact information
- Promotional materials for library resources and services
- Method to track statistics
- Teacher packet (survey link handout, teen department services for schools, and library resource handouts)
- Team of instructors who know library resources (recruit from other departments)

Reciprocity

- Students must have a public library card.
- Students must have a topic and know about the topic before the class begins.
- Assignments must require the use of at least one library resource.

Preparation

- Ask teachers to test the databases to ensure they are accessible.
- Make sure the classroom has a computer, projector, and Internet access (or bring your own equipment).
- Have a backup presentation in PowerPoint or Word.
- Know the resources that are applicable to the assignment.
  a. Do practice searches.
  b. Regularly review library resources to stay up to date.

At the Resource Class

- Instruction time should be 30–45 minutes:
  a. For 90-minute class periods, speak to one class for 45 minutes and visit another class for 45 minutes.
  b. Fill extra time by helping students with their research (via demonstrations or on their individual computers).
- Just before the class, review class structure with teachers.
- Make announcements:
  a. Introductions, library locations, library card information, resources from the library and programs
  b. Tell the class your purpose: "I'm here to make your homework easier."
- Demonstrate how to use library resources and any virtual reference services (e.g., databases, catalog, library-approved websites, chat reference, e-Materials).
- Engage students:

    a. Tell them about your coolest programs and resources (e.g., e-Materials, music, DVDs, and games).
    b. Use students' topics to find fast and reliable information.
    c. After instruction, ask for a student volunteer to demonstrate what s/he has learned.
    d. During the class, involve teachers when making statements about plagiarism and good research.

- Provide instruction to school librarians and teachers:
    a. Present at in-service days or department meetings.
    b. Be ready to present for 15–45 minutes (even a few minutes makes an impact).

Things to Avoid

- Overextending yourself (limit to four classes per day; visit a school more than one day to talk to all of the students; know your limits and your library's constraints)
- Classes without a topic (confirm topics with teacher ahead of time)
- Large groups (teach one class at a time)
- Students following along on their own computers (have them watch you demonstrate the resources)

Success Stories for Resource Classes

- Pikes Peak School of Expeditionary Learning is a middle school that embraces an exploratory learning environment. As part of assignments, the class comes to PPLD for a resource class, a tour, and a full day of research. The teacher said that visiting the library is the highlight of the students' year. They ask when they get to come back!
- An e-mail from Donna, the IB Coordinator at Sand Creek High School: "You were apparently a big hit yesterday. Brett and Joe both tell me they are really impressed with the online offerings from PPLD. They loved the world-at-your-fingertips research opportunities. It was more than either had expected to have available. Some of the kids seem a little over-whelmed (we always have those) and others say the talk was GOOD, and they smile. The smiles are a wonderful sign that they think they can succeed. I'm just sorry I missed it! We all thank you for coming—we really appreciate it."

Student Library Card Program

Outreach is successful when the students can use the resources outside of school and at home. For that to happen, they need a library card. At PPLD, we have created an easy student library card application. We e-mail the application to the teachers and librarians to print out and give to their students. This application removes the barrier of requiring parents to bring their teens to the library to get a library card. When developing a letter and application, work closely with your circulation staff to ensure that you are following library card policies. On the application, include options to update the library card, to replace a lost card, and to issue a new card.

Our Process for the Student Library Card Program

- E-mail the application.
- The teachers or the librarian will print out library card applications for each student.
- Students who are 15 or younger take the application home for the parents to sign; students who are 16 or older fill it out and sign it (per PPLD library card policy).
- The teacher or librarian reviews each application and signs it to make sure that the application is complete and legible (legibility is important!).
- Teachers drop the applications off with teen staff at the library (it is helpful to have the applications sorted in packets by class).
- Circulation staff enters the applications and issues cards.
- The teacher or librarian picks the cards up or we bring them during a school visit.

Encourage teachers to put public library cards on the school supply list to make the process more effective. To motivate students to get public library cards, suggest that teachers give extra credit or make it part of an assignment.

General Outreach

There are many more outreach opportunities available for library participation than the ones we have outlined above. Teen-focused opportunities include career fairs, school open houses, and community resource fairs. It is important to connect with students and parents within a setting that makes the library relevant.

Visibility at community events brings the library to the forefront of people's minds and reaches patrons where they are. Successful outreach is proactive or reactive; both are useful. Invitations are often sent requesting that the library have a presence at an event. These invitations come from schools, community groups, and nonprofit organizations. There are many ways to actively pursue outreach events. Contact schools and ask about career fairs, back-to-school nights, or conferences. Seek out teen support organizations and find out about any events they are doing and ask to join them. Work with your public relations department to find other community events.

Outreach Kit

We have a created a teen outreach kit for each of our library locations. The following list of supplies makes outreach as painless as possible:

- Teen library website information
- Library location information
- Library resource handouts and bookmarks (for teens and adults)
- Teen department services handout
- Program information
- e-Material information
- Laptop and Internet access (if possible)
- Library cards or library card applications
- Table cloth

- Library banner
- Candy/giveaways
- Pen and paper
- Business cards
- Water (you'll be talking a lot)

Conclusion

Outreach as a whole is a big and exciting project. Take time to plan on your end and allow time for the programs to develop in your community. Many opportunities will stem from the people you meet during outreach events. At one school, booktalks led to a collaborative book club between the public and school libraries. Booktalks can also lead to the opportunity to teach resource classes and the promotion of special library programs.

Enthusiasm for outreach is essential for creating a vibrant teen outreach program and for long-term success. Research has found that students want to be taught by people who are passionate about the topic and who treat the students with respect and dignity (Jones 2009, 80). Our team is passionate about serving teens, and it shows when we visit schools. We do this by sharing our excitement about books and resources. We relate to teens by understanding their situations and needs.

Successful outreach programs are achievable. To get started, try just one new type of outreach. If it doesn't work the first time, change your approach and try again. Learn from it and build upon it to reach teens in your community. Start collaborating today!

Works Cited

Cox Clark, Ruth E. 2007. "Become the Character! First-Person Booktalks with Teens." *Library Media Connection* 26 (2): 24–26.

Jones, Jami L. 2009. "Dropout Prevention through the School Library: Dispositions, Relationships, and Instructional Practices." *School Libraries Worldwide* 15 (2): 77–90.

Tilke, Anthony. 2011. "International Baccalaureate Diploma Programme: What It Means to a School Library and Librarian." *School Library Monthly* 27 (5): 8–10.

Teen Volunteers and Children's Programs
Two-for-One Programming
SHARON COLVIN

Inviting teens to help out in the children's room may seem like a crazy idea. After all, teens are unreliable, irresponsible, and require a ton of supervision. They're just taller, sassier children, right? If you give them a chance, you might be surprised. With a bit of training, teen volunteers can help liven up the children's department. A volunteer program is a great way to reach out to teens who would otherwise not use the library. It's also a great way for librarians to interact with teens on a more individual level.

Teen volunteer programs are about more than just cheap labor. Yes, teens can put away books and clean shelves, but they can do much more than that if you're willing to let them. And if they like what they're doing, they'll be more likely to do well and keep coming back. Starting a formal teen volunteer program is a way to get teens involved in the library and ensure continuity of service. Children will have something to aspire to, and parents will see that the library serves children of all ages.

Reaching out to teens benefits the entire library. Teens are often an underserved population in the community. It can be daunting to start a large-scale outreach program, but a volunteer program can be the beginning of a larger goal. Giving them a purpose will make it easier to attract and to keep teens as patrons. Once you know them, they can give advice on programs, collections, and other library services for teens and tweens.

Getting started can be daunting. Talk to the decision-makers and try a small program to start. Go with specific ideas and reasons, and don't forget that you'll be serving children and teens at the same time!

Points to Consider When Approaching the Library Director

- Young children look up to teenagers.
- Teenagers like to be admired.
- Young children like to do creative, crafty projects.
- Teenagers secretly like to do creative, crafty projects.
- Young children need responsible role models.

- With some coaching, teenagers can be great role models.
- Teens will soon be voters. Make the library important to them!
- Teen volunteers may come back as adult volunteers one day.
- Teens need community service hours for high school, the National Honor Society, and their college résumés.
- This is a great project for your teen advisory board, and teen volunteers can serve as a type of teen advisory board if you don't have one already.
- Giving teens schedules and responsibilities will increase attendance, especially among the busy high school students.
- This could be a way to recruit new library users.
- Giving teens a voice in programming will give them a sense of ownership and respect toward the library and its staff.
- Teens are full of new ideas and are endlessly creative. Some are artists, musicians, crafters, and have fun hobbies they could share and/or teach.
- Older children will aspire to be volunteers one day.
- Parents like to see teens helping children.
- Active, helpful teens are a much better library statement than bored and unruly teens.
- The community will appreciate knowing that service doesn't stop once kids outgrow the children's room.
- Teens need to prepare for the real world. Applying to be a volunteer is a good first step to getting a job.
- You'll be serving the teens and the children at the same time.

Trial Run

Begin by looking at your program schedule for the next school vacation week. Try to match the teens with something simple like a craft program or a performer who requires some set-up. What can the teens do to help? Here are some suggestions:
- Gather craft supplies.
- Set up tables or activity stations.
- Make craft samples.
- Explain activities to children and families.
- Set up snacks.
- Clean up.

You will notice that these tasks are not terribly difficult, but they're important. Find some reliable teens by going to your teen advisory board, school librarians, or to your coworkers. Think about how many volunteers you need. Too many volunteers can be a hindrance.

Be flexible when starting out. Ask teens for ideas and input, think about the qualities of a helpful volunteer, and never leave teens alone with children. Give teens small tasks like choosing music, picking out a snack, or helping organize the flow of a program. Create an evaluation period and ask people (including teens) for feedback and suggestions. If the trial goes well, try setting up an official program.

Creating an Official Teen Volunteer Program

Once you've tried working with a teen volunteer or two, you'll be ready to work on your policies and procedures. It may seem like overkill, but policies and procedures will help you with your program. Not only will it help teach teens about the world of job applications, schedules, and policies, it will help teens take the program more seriously. If your program seems more like a job, teens will treat it as such. Remind them that if they do a good job, you're willing to write recommendation letters. Remind them that volunteer experience can help them get a job one day.

Start with what you've learned. What went well last time? What could be improved? Did teens arrive on time, were they dressed appropriately, and were they focused on the kids? Think about the policies you saw at your first job. Write them all down. Teens have never had jobs and will soon be out in the real world. This is a great teaching opportunity. Show them what it's like to apply for something. Make sure to ask all the usual questions, but also add some helpful questions about their interests and hobbies.

Your library will have to decide how many volunteers you need and whether you're willing to turn teens away. One way to avoid having too many volunteers is to have teens sign up for shifts or specific programs in advance. Limit the number of volunteers needed for each event. Think about how you will organize it. Will older teens sign up first? What about teens you already know? See how many applications you receive and go from there. Try splitting up the programming year into terms for ease of scheduling. Train teens when you have a natural break in programming.

Step One: Find Your Volunteers

If your library has never used teen volunteers, a bit of marketing will be necessary. Advertise it like any program. Tell everyone about this awesome new opportunity. Make flyers, put information in newsletters, and post on Facebook.

This is a good time to reach out into the community. The local high school is a good place to start, but there are probably also parochial, vocational, and private schools nearby. Try contacting librarians, teachers, and guidance counselors. Home schooling organizations are also good places to start. Ask around the library. Some of your coworkers might have connections. Post flyers on bulletin boards, hand out applications, and send information to school newsletters. Your local newspaper might even help you out depending on the size of your town.

Spend some time learning about the local high schools. Some high schools have a community service requirement. Capitalize on that! Talk to school principals and find out if they have a community service bulletin board or fair. Talk to National Honor Society advisors to see if they can spread the word. NHS students have to complete their community service by a certain deadline, so it's also a good idea to find out when that deadline is.

The key is to find a few interested students and then let them help you advertise. Word of mouth is a powerful marketing method. They have friends, classmates, siblings, and neighbors who might also be interested. They might be connected to groups you have not yet heard about. Even if they don't want to volunteer, you will be spreading the word that the library cares about teens. Maybe a few new teens will wander into the library.

• Create an application. A basic application is fine, but you need their contact information, parent/guardian information, and a bit about their experience. Have a parent/guardian sign it. Many teens will need transportation, so it's important that their chauffeurs are on board.

   • Stick to a deadline. Make it official.
   • Set an age limit (seventh grade might be a good start).
   • Send applications to school libraries, teachers, and National Honor Society advisors. Hand out copies at your next teen advisory board meeting or other teen event. Put flyers in the teen areas and in the children's room.

Step Two: Train Your Volunteers

Teens may be new to the children's room, the library, or to the town. Make sure they're comfortable in their new work environment. Introduce them to as many people as possible, and show them useful things like the bathrooms, staff areas, and where they can put their backpacks and coats. Make the process as simple and non-threatening as possible. Remember that these kids have never had a job. They need to learn procedures and expectations in order to succeed.

   • Require training for all new volunteers. Have them make nametags and then go over policies and procedures.
   • Policies should include expectations and repercussions for things like tardiness, poor physical appearance, and socializing with friends.
   • Policies should also include who they can go to in case of a problem, and reassurance that they will never be left alone with children.
   • Emphasize that they are unpaid employees and represent the library and the staff.
   • Have teens sign a policy agreement.
   • Give them a copy of the storm closing policy and a list of people they would need to contact in case of emergency.
   • Take them on a tour of the library and introduce them to staff. Make sure to tell them where to check in when they come to work.
   • Show them the staff areas and where you hide your craft supplies. They'll feel important.
   • Talk about the schedule procedure. Schedules could be on paper or online. Make sure they know where to look and who will be responsible for keeping track of their hours.
   • Go over tips on how to work with children and their parents. Think about the things you do automatically, and ask your coworkers for their suggestions.
      a. Kneel down or crouch when talking to small children.
      b. Always greet the child first.
      c. Smile.
      d. Encourage creativity with the children and be complimentary.
      e. Recognize individual creations and discourage competition.
      f. Don't try to figure out what the child is creating (you may be wrong). Instead, compliment a specific element such as color, material, or perspective.
      g. If someone has a meltdown or if a parent disappears, go to the nearest staff member.

h. Be open to suggestions. Kids have great ideas and will think of great new things.

i. Stay calm at all times.

Step 3: Setting Up the Schedule

Teens are busy. They have sports, drama, music, chores, and siblings. They have family obligations, and some teens have more than one family. Many of them do not yet drive. Give them time to go over the calendar with their families. Try including a schedule of programs with the application. Then make the master schedule available to teens who need to double-check or make changes.

• Think about which programs you need help running. Crafts and LEGO programs are great places to start. They're simple and offer great flexibility.

• Consider how many volunteers would be helpful and limit participation.

• Make sure teens know that they are responsible for keeping track of their schedules.

• If you can, include the program list with the application so that teens know what programs are available.

• Make sure teens know that signing up to help with a program is a commitment.

• Reinforce policies for cancelations. One week should be enough for you to find another volunteer.

• Give them several contacts in case something comes up. You may not be there when they need to change their schedule or cancel at the last minute.

• Schedule a party for the volunteers, something simple that recognizes their hard work. Try splitting up the year into sessions like summer, fall, and winter/spring. Then you can schedule parties in August, December, and May.

• If teens miss the training and want to participate, let them know when the next training will be. For example, at the beginning of each session in September, January, and June.

• Make sure to keep track of volunteer hours for state statistics reports. Decide if you will keep track of hours for the teens or if they will be responsible for doing that.

• Compile an e-mail list to contact teens with spontaneous volunteer projects like craft preparation or event set-up. Send out reminders.

Step 4: Following Through

You are now a teen mentor. Remember that teens are still children and need some guidance. They need feedback, encouragement, and structure. Each teen will come with his or her own strengths and weaknesses, and everyone has bad days. Teens often have great ideas about programs for children and for their peers.

• Make sure teens feel like part of the team.

• Be honest with them. If a program doesn't go well, be upfront about it.

• If a volunteer is struggling, pull him or her aside and try to help. Start with the positive and move from there to constructive advice.

• Follow through with policies. Teens won't take you seriously unless you follow through with the repercussions.

- Try to use their suggestions and feedback. They may have ideas on schedules, activities, music, or brand-new programs.
- Ask them about their hobbies. Maybe they can help start a new program for children or even for other teens.
- Give them credit where credit is due. Brag to the director, the Friends of the Library, and the trustees.
- Tell them how much you appreciate them. Clean up time is a great opportunity to do this.

Step 5: Your Established Teen Volunteer Program

Now you have a few good teen volunteers. You need to keep them invested and interested. Together you can create some awesome programs. Programs will be more successful if teens are excited about running it. Sometimes that means improving on old programs, and sometimes that means opening yourself to new ideas. Allowing teens to become part of your team is serving them as well as the library.

- Ask teens about their interests (the application is a good place to start).
- Do you have any teens interested in LEGOs? Have them help you start a LEGO club.
- Are any of them into Harry Potter, Star Wars, or Percy Jackson? They can help you throw a big party for the children. Have them come up with activity ideas, trivia, and decorations. Then assign them stations and have a big event.
- Are any of your volunteers in a band? Maybe they could start a battle of the bands program or have a summer concert.
- Do any of them have skills with paint, duct tape, or percussion instruments? Encourage them start a workshop for children.
- Try soliciting for teens with specific skills. For example: "Looking for teens who do fancy nail art! Apply to volunteer and you could help run a Spa Day!"
- Brainstorm ideas for a holiday party—Halloween, Chinese New Year, and Diwali are all great excuses for a fun party.
- Do you have artistic volunteers? Have them make new signs or art for the library.
- Let teens raid your supply closet and come up with a "leftover craft."
- Teach your very best volunteers to run programs:
    a. Train them to do pajama storytime or a storytelling program.
    b. Have them help younger children with homework.
    c. Invite your most technically savvy teens to help parents with computer problems, train people to use their e-readers, etc.
    d. Start a book buddy program where teens read one-on-one with children.
- Ask them about teen programming. They can help connect you to other teens and create good programs.
- Ask them about volunteer recruiting. What do they think makes a good volunteer? Do they have suggestions for the application process?

Tips and Troubleshooting

Sometimes things go wrong. Some teens don't work well together, some teens are unreliable, and some activities don't work well. Don't lose heart. Try to adjust and improve as you go.

- Try not to take on too many volunteers per event. You don't want bored volunteers.
- Don't allow teens to dictate their own schedule until you know them and their work habits. Instead, give them time slots or events that work for you and have them sign up. Once they've proved themselves, more flexibility can be earned.
- Give yourself a break. If no children show up for an event, have some fun with your volunteers! It's still a program. Pull out a deck of cards or some trivia and make it a teen event.
- Let the teens bond with each other, but remind them why they're there.
- If you feel your teens are immature, try raising the age requirement.
- Too many applicants? Try asking for recommendation letters, do interviews, or implement a probation period.
- Are teens being forced to volunteer? Give them an out. Offer to talk to their parents. Volunteers who would rather be somewhere else are not helpful.
- Be protective of your teens. You are ultimately responsible for them.
- Remind teens of your teen programs when they come in to volunteer.
- Try not to bend over backward for teens who leave their required volunteer hours to the last minute. Remember the hard work that your trained volunteers had to put in.
- Talk to the high school about when community service hours are due and remind volunteers to get those forms to you in a timely fashion.
- Try to identify individual strengths and weaknesses and assign tasks accordingly. Just because a teen is shy doesn't mean he or she isn't good with children.
- Model behavior for them. Show them how you'd like them to interact with children and parents.

Teen volunteers will change the way you run programs. Try to be flexible and adapt to new ideas. Part of running a program like this is creating a chain of role models. You are a role model for the teens, and the teens are role models for the children. Show the teens how to be gracious under pressure, how to go with the flow, how to admit when they're wrong, and how to collaborate with others.

In the end, reaching out to teens and making an effort to serve them will improve your library services overall. You may be able to entice a few more teens into the library while teaching them some valuable life skills; in turn, they can help you provide lively services to the next generation of teen volunteers.

About the Contributors

Gloria **Adams** obtained her MLS from Kent State University in Kent, Ohio. She worked for 17 years in children's services at Cuyahoga Falls Library in Cuyahoga Falls, Ohio, and seven-and-a-half years at Stow–Munroe Falls Public Library in Stow, Ohio, first as outreach librarian and later as assistant head of children's services.

Stefanie **Blankenship**, youth services librarian at the Cranston Public Library Auburn Branch in Cranston, Rhode Island, obtained her MLIS from the University of Rhode Island. She also holds a certificate in information literacy instruction from the University of Rhode Island.

Mary Lou **Carolan**, director of the Wallkill Public Library in Wallkill, New York, has more than 25 years of experience working in community development and marketing. She is also an author, blogger, and speaker; her award-winning programs include the "Find Ike Scavenger Hunt," winner of the Ramapo Catskill Library System's 2008 Children's Program of the Year Award.

Sharon **Colvin** is a youth services librarian at the Chelmsford Public Library in Chelmsford, Massachusetts. She obtained her MLS from Simmons College and her EdM from the Harvard Graduate School of Education.

Stacy **Creel** teaches courses in the School of Library and Information Science at the University of Southern Mississippi. She is the creator of the Graduate Certificate in Youth Services and Literature, has more than 10 years of public library experience and is active in the American Library Association.

Leah **Durand** earned her MLIS from the University of Pittsburgh. She has been working with the Carnegie Library of Pittsburgh since 2005 and became a teen specialist in 2011 at the library's Downtown & Business Branch.

Xelena **González** earned her BS in journalism from Northwestern University and her MLS from Texas Woman's University. She is an early literacy specialist for the Little Read Wagon of the San Antonio Public Library.

Josie B. **Hanneman** is a community librarian with the Deschutes Public Library System in Deschutes County, Oregon, serving the areas of Sunriver and La Pine. She obtained her MA in library and information studies from the University of Wisconsin–Madison.

Susan M. **Hansen**, head of public services at the West Hartford Public Library in West Hartford, Connecticut, obtained her MLS from Southern Connecticut State University. Her memberships include the American Library Association, Public Library Association, and Connecticut Library Association.

Kerol **Harrod** received his MA from the University of North Texas and works at the Denton Public Library in Denton, Texas. He writes and co-produces the television show *Library Larry's Big Day*. It won first-place awards in 2010 and 2012 from TATOA (Texas Association of Telecommunications Officers and Advisors) and received the 2011 NTRLS (North Texas Regional Library System) Margaret Irby Nichols Award.

195

Abigail **Harwood** has been a professional librarian since 2007. Prior to joining the Carnegie Library of Pittsburgh as a librarian in the Main Library's teen department, she worked as a teen services librarian at the San Francisco Public Library.

Kaitlin **Hoke** is the teen services coordinator for the Pikes Peak Library District in Colorado Springs, Colorado, leading a team of 17 teen staff at 13 community libraries. She earned her MLIS from the University of Denver.

Natalie **Houston** is the youth outreach coordinator at the Orange County Library System in Orlando, Florida. She obtained her MLS from the University of South Florida and a bachelor of liberal arts from the University of Miami.

Sarah **Kaufman**, MLS, MPA, has worked in public libraries for more than 14 years. As a youth services librarian at Tempe Public Library in Tempe, Arizona, she presents early literacy workshops to parent groups and educators in the Tempe and Greater Phoenix area. She is also an adjunct instructor for the Library Technician Program at Mesa Community College.

Melanie A. **Lyttle** is the head of public services at Madison Public Library in Madison, Ohio. She received her MLS in 2003 from the University of Illinois at Urbana–Champaign and was an ALSC-sponsored 2010 ALA Emerging Leader.

Amy **Mars** is a substitute librarian for Dakota and Hennepin County libraries in Minnesota. She also teaches information literacy and research skills as an adjunct faculty member at Minneapolis Community and Technical College. She obtained her MLIS from St. Catherine University in St. Paul, Minnesota.

Ann **McDuffie** serves as the youth services librarian at Fauquier County Public Library in Bealeton, Virginia. She earned her MLIS from the University of North Texas in Denton, Texas.

Michelle A. **McIntyre** directs the Roaring Spring Community Library in Roaring Spring, Pennsylvania. She received her MSLS from Clarion University in Clarion, Pennsylvania. Her research interests include marketing, board development, fundraising, and nonprofit management.

Annie **Miller** received her school library media specialist master's degree from the State University of New York at Albany and works at the Greenwich Public Library in Greenwich, New York. She also works as a school library substitute.

Tami **Morehart**, youth services department manager at the Wagnalls Memorial Library, Lithopolis, Ohio, obtained her library media technology degree from Ohio University's Lancaster branch. For 31 years she has worked with preschool storytimes, summer reading programs, and class visitations.

Jamie Campbell **Naidoo** is an associate professor at the University of Alabama School of Library and Information Studies in Tuscaloosa. A former elementary school librarian and youth services librarian, he has written on Latino children's literature, LGBTQ children's literature, and providing library services to diverse populations.

Joanna **Nelson** is the teen services outreach librarian for the Pikes Peak Library District, Colorado Springs, Colorado. She received her MLIS (honors) from the University of Denver.

Brittany **Nethers** is the youth programs coordinator for the Orange County Library System in Orlando, Florida. She received her bachelor of science degree in marketing from the University of Florida and minored in anthropology.

Amanda **Nichols Hess** is an assistant professor and eLearning/instructional technology librarian at Oakland University in Rochester, Michigan. She earned her MSI in library and information services and school media from the University of Michigan.

André R. **Powe** is the coordinator of hospital storytelling at the Child's Place for Children with Special Needs at the Brooklyn Public Library in New York. He received a BA in liberal arts from the

City College of the City University of New York and an MA in communication for development from Malmo University in Malmo, Sweden.

Melanie L. **Ramsey** directs youth and children's services at the Hollidaysburg Area Public Library, Hollidaysburg, Pennsylvania. She received her education degree from Indiana University of Pennsylvania.

Rebecca D. **Richardson** is a research and instruction librarian at Murray State University in Murray, Kentucky, and the former director of the Cresson Public Library in Cresson, Pennsylvania. She obtained her MLIS from Clarion University in Clarion, Pennsylvania, where she was a Laura Bush 21st Century Librarian for the Commonwealth Libraries.

Corinne **Sanchez** is a community services supervisor for the San Antonio Public Library. She received a bachelor of arts in interdisciplinary studies from the University of Texas at San Antonio.

Carol **Smallwood** received her MLS from Western Michigan University and her MA in history from Eastern Michigan University. Her experience includes school, public, academic and special libraries, as well as administration and consulting.

Vikki C. **Terrile** is the coordinator of young adult services for Queens Library in New York City. Vikki earned her MSLS from the Palmer School at Long Island University and her MA in urban affairs from Queens College, City University of New York.

Shawn D. **Walsh** is the emerging services and technologies librarian for Madison Public Library in Madison, Ohio. Working in libraries since 1997, he was most recently a senior technology analyst for the Northeast Ohio Regional Library System.

Carol H. **Waxman** has been the children's services librarian for the town of West Hartford, Connecticut, for 28 years. She has a master's degree in language arts from Central Connecticut University and has been a member of the Nutmeg Children's Book Award Committee.

Krissy **Wick** is a youth services librarian at the Madison Public Library in Madison, Wisconsin. She received her MLIS from the University of Wisconsin–Madison. She is a member of the American Library Association, the Association for Library Service to Children, and the Wisconsin Library Association.

Joseph **Wilk** has served as a teen specialist at the Carnegie Library of Pittsburgh since 2004, where he has overseen numerous music, technology, and outreach programs. In addition, he has served on the YALSA Teen Tech Week Committee and chaired the Music Interest Group.

Leigh A. **Woznick**, media specialist at Bridgewater-Raritan Middle School in Bridgewater, New Jersey, received her MLIS from Rutgers. Leigh is a member of ALA, YALSA, New Jersey Association of School Librarians, Mystery Writers of America, New England Historic and Genealogical Society, and the Joint YALSA/AASL/ALSC Committee on School/Public Library Cooperation.

Sara **Zettervall** is a substitute librarian for Dakota County Library, Minnesota, and project manager at the University of Minnesota Performing Arts Archives. She holds an MLIS from St. Catherine University in St. Paul, Minnesota, and an MFA in creative writing from the University of Michigan.

Index